FINDING A WAY

FINDING
A WAY

LEN JOHNROSE

Matador
9 Priory Business Park,
Wistow Road, Kibworth Beauchamp,
Leicestershire. LE8 0RX
Tel: 0116 279 2299
Email: books@troubador.co.uk
Web: www.troubador.co.uk/matador
Twitter: @matadorbooks

ISBN 978 1800460 959

British Library Cataloguing in Publication Data.
A catalogue record for this book is available from the British Library.

Printed and bound in the UK by TJ Books Limited, Padstow, Cornwall
Typeset in 11pt Adobe Garamond Pro by Troubador Publishing Ltd, Leicester, UK

Matador is an imprint of Troubador Publishing Ltd

To all the families living with motor neurone disease. It's a difficult, and sometimes all too short road. Stay strong and believe that, one day, we will find a cure.

Keep fighting!

CONTENTS

INTRODUCTION

I am not an alcoholic. I don't do drugs. I have never been involved in an orgy. I have never had to sing bollock-naked in front of the senior pros as some sort of initiation rite. And I haven't lost tens of thousands of pounds through gambling. This is not that kind of book. In these pages are the words of someone who had a decent football career and then underwent a life-changing moment during another chapter of his life.

Life throws up an array of obstacles to overcome, and puzzles to solve. How you approach them defines you as a person. Fight or flight? Sink or swim? Some decisions are easy, and some are taken out of your hands. But somehow, you have to find a way!

When I am finally laid to rest, or sent along the cinder path, I will rest knowing that almost all the decisions I have made have been with the best intentions. That, to me, means more than money or materials. Let me have my family, a few close friends, and my dog. That's all I need. And that's me, happy!

Motor neurone disease is brutal. It does not discriminate, nor does it spare. It strips you of your ability to walk, of your ability to move your arms. It strips you of your ability to cough, to swallow and, ultimately, to breathe. You are consigned to live in a body that does not work.

But I have the last laugh, because it cannot strip me of my dignity, my pride, or my spirit.

March 2017. In true Len Johnrose style, I don't remember the exact date, but that was when my life and the lives of those around me were about to change.

About four years earlier I'd felt a strange, but not uncomfortable feeling in my right hand. I remember trying to open a door and struggling to turn the doorknob. I went to see my GP, thinking it might be something like arthritis. I had a number of blood tests and X-rays, and everything came back clear. I didn't really think about it after that.

In May 2015, I was working at St Silas C of E Primary School in Blackburn. I had managed to convince the head teacher to purchase a trampoline, and I used to practise my routines during the dinner break and after school. This progressed into practising front flips, which I mastered after a few days. Anyway, one particular day, I just couldn't land my front flip so I asked one of the teachers to record my attempts so that I could see where I was going wrong. I went into the front flip and everything seemed perfect. I remember tucking my knees to my chest and then expanding as I was about to land. It felt great, but as I landed I fell over and put out my left hand to break the fall. That's when I heard the crack. There was no pain but I knew instantly that

I'd broken my hand. So off I went to the hospital with the head teacher and, after a few hours, it was confirmed – I had shattered one of the bones in my left hand.

Initially, the doctor said I needed to have a pin inserted, but then for some reason decided it would be sufficient for me just to wear a support strap. I was back at work within a week and, as luck would have it, my writing was so bad in the first place nobody could really tell the difference.

I used to do a lot of cycling, but the first time I got back on the bike after the trampoline event was for the annual Preston Bike Binge in July, an event which raises money for local charities. This particular year my brother Fran joined us, which meant a lot of racing would be on the menu, along with copious pints of lager – together, never a good idea. Anyway, during one of our races I came off my bike and landed on my hand. The following day, I went to the hospital. I had cracked my ribs, but my hand was absolutely fine. In fact, they were quite pleased with how well it had healed. I was, however, still a little bit concerned that my full range of movement hadn't returned.

By November, when the weather was getting colder, my lack of movement was becoming more apparent. I began to drop things in the classroom – counters, cubes, things like that. I wasn't too worried, but thought it might be something like carpal tunnel. I was convinced it was a nerve issue. In any case, I went to see my GP who referred me to a local physio. I had a series of sessions which involved massage and manipulation, neither of which seemed to work.

In January 2016 I went back to see my GP. I explained that the physio sessions hadn't worked and I felt that it was a nerve problem. Again I was referred, this time to a nerve specialist whom I saw in March. He explained that the initial break hadn't healed, and that he was going to recommend re-fracturing the hand and resetting it. I was referred (again!) to the neurology department at Royal Preston Hospital. There they conducted a series of tests, which consisted basically of them sticking pins in my hand in order to observe the nerve activity. That was where it all started to go horribly wrong.

While there, I asked them to check my right hand and explained how I'd felt a strange sensation a few years prior to this. At this point, the neurologist looked ashen and dashed out of the room. Never a good sign! He came in with reinforcements, aka a senior consultant. He looked at the images on the screen, and explained that the issues I was experiencing were nothing to do with my break. He then asked me what I thought was the strangest of questions: 'How are your legs?' I explained that they were absolutely fine, but the pensive look on his face did not fill me with much confidence. I was told I would have to come back in at a later date to test the nerve activity in my legs.

I left the hospital a little bit worried, to say the least. I phoned Nade, my wife, but there was no answer. I phoned my friend Paul Turley, and told him what had been said. I think he said something like, 'I'm sure it'll be fine'.

When Nade got home from work I told her what had happened and she assured me that things would be fine. For the next few days, I did a little bit of self-diagnosis on Google (another bad idea). After about a week of searching for neurological problems, I came across MND. I read about how it affects your upper limbs and your lower limbs. At that point I stopped reading and started laughing. My lower limbs were absolutely fine, and while I thought this may be something they were looking towards, I knew it wasn't the issue. I knew about MND – well, I knew about Stephen Hawking – and continued to read.

I read about the awfulness of what it does to you; I read the horror stories of surviving only six months. I knew that I'd experienced symptoms for a few years, so, again, that reassured me it must be something else. Even so, I phoned Nade (my go-to person) and told her that I knew what they were looking for. She went quiet for a while and then said that MND was the first thing she'd thought about. She'd been carrying this around with her for a week but hadn't said anything as she didn't want to worry me. We agreed that when I next went to the hospital, we would ask them outright. And that's exactly what we did.

I knew what the answer would be: 'Of course not, Mr Johnrose, there is absolutely no chance that's what it is!'

When he uttered the words, 'I'm afraid we can't rule it out, Mr Johnrose' – to be honest, I can't even remember what I felt.

And so began the worst year of my life!

Life for me is simple. I am essentially a selfish person. I want to enjoy my life. I want to enjoy my life *for me*. In the past, I have ended relationships because I wasn't happy. I've always believed that life is too short to live your life for somebody else if you are not happy yourself. The caveat is that while I enjoy my life, I do not deliberately trample on people along the way. I would never deliberately insult or offend somebody (unless I *really* didn't like them).

Unlike Morrissey, I do not want the one I can't have, although I don't believe anything is out of my reach.

As a child, I wasn't exactly a loner, but I was very comfortable in my own company. I wasn't a particularly good mixer, and even today I am at my most comfortable when surrounded by my close family and friends. I have always believed that I am an introvert; I do not court attention or fame. I do what I do because I think it's the right thing to do.

In the past, I have been referred to as aloof and arrogant. For aloof, read shy. For arrogant, read confident. Is it possible to be a confident introvert?

I genuinely believe that I am very good at many things. This is where the confidence kicks in (or arrogance, to some). I genuinely believe that I have many good qualities. One of those is the ability to put things in perspective. I truly don't worry about things over which I have no control. I truly don't worry about things that I don't believe are important. I understand that different people place importance on different things, but my take on it is this: when something goes wrong, how important will it seem in an hour, a day, a week?

I understand that people are different, and that people have different perspectives on life. I have genuinely got through life accepting that not everybody thinks like I do. Would I like to be like them? Would they like to be like me? We all think differently; we should all accept those differences, if not embrace them.

I'm not an adrenalin junkie, but I do like an element of risk. If we don't do anything with an element of risk, we won't do anything. What is the worst that can happen?

Being diagnosed with motor neurone disease tested my outlook on life. Why worry about something that I cannot influence? How important will it seem in an hour, a week, a year?

CHAPTER 1

NO MORE HEROES

Born on 29 November 1969, I share the same birthday as a certain Ryan Giggs but, apart from being left-footed, I think that's where the similarity ends. I started watching football when I was around six or seven years old and, like any self-respecting glory hunter, I was a huge Liverpool fan. The game which stands out for me, more than any other around that time was the 1977 FA Cup Final between Liverpool and Manchester United. United won 2–1, and so began my hatred of the Red Devils.

Liverpool dominated football, both at home and abroad, in the late 1970s and throughout the 1980s. During that time, I adored the likes of Kenny Dalglish (who was later to become my manager at Blackburn Rovers), Graeme Souness, Alan Hansen, et al. Another of my heroes at the time was a certain Phil Thompson, a terrific centre half who played over 40 games for England.

When I was 17, I got the chance to see Phil Thompson up close. I was a YTS trainee at Blackburn Rovers at the time, while he was working under Kenny Dalglish at Liverpool. This was a dream come true for me, getting the chance to step out on to the Anfield turf, the place where my heroes plied their trade week in week out. Although I was only a substitute at the time, I didn't mind. Phil Thompson was in the home dugout, which meant that I had a better view of the great man. Life couldn't get any better!

They say that you should never meet your heroes; I was about to find out why. I'd only ever previously been to Anfield once: a 0–2 defeat against Sheffield Wednesday when the Liverpool goalie Bruce Grobbelaar went walkabout to concede one of the goals. A painful memory which paled into insignificance when I was racially abused by some of the Liverpool fans on my way out of the ground. I was 14 or 15 at the time. Along with other members of the Preston Town schools team, I had been invited to the game as part of an initiative set up by Preston schools. Although the name-calling hurt, I just pretended that it hadn't happened and tried not to let it affect me, a tactic that I employed on many other occasions as I got older. One such occasion was when Paul and I attended a Blackburn versus Newcastle match at Ewood Park. We'd arranged at the end of the game for his dad to pick us up about a mile away from the ground. What ensued was absolutely disgusting. Grown men leaning out of the cars calling me every racist name that they could think of. Full marks for being inventive; some of the words I hadn't even heard of. Some of them even started getting out of their cars to hurl abuse at Paul, who should have known better than to be hanging around with 'one of them'. I think it was a relief that it wasn't the

Blackburn fans. The human brain is very complex and I can vividly remember thinking, during this verbal onslaught, how all of these blokes were fat, bearded, balding, angry-looking men. Isn't it funny how certain thoughts can make fear dissipate?

Back to Anfield: although there were only a couple of hundred people watching the game, I remember trying to soak up the atmosphere. I remember looking at the 'This Is Anfield' sign, and wondering whether I should touch it. I chose not to as I didn't want to show our opponents too much respect.

The game started, and suddenly everything changed. The attitude of the coaching staff, and Thompson in particular, was absolutely deplorable. It was as though he felt they had a divine right to every decision, and he berated the referee and linesman whenever a decision went against his team. The abuse that he inflicted on his own players, and the youngsters in particular, was absolutely sickening to hear, and in my opinion was nothing short of bullying. I think they won the game 2–0, but Thompson was ungracious in victory, still finding time to practically accost the officials with his complaints. Right there, right then, I went off Liverpool Football Club!

I did temporarily fall back in love with them during the Fernando Torres era. What a player he was. His partnership with Steven Gerrard used to have me purring, and I *so* wanted them to win the league. I'm still a little bit gutted for Steven Gerrard that he never won the Premiership.

This on–off love affair ended permanently when Liverpool, headed by Kenny Dalglish, publicly backed Luis

Suárez after he racially abused Manchester United's Patrice Evra. This episode left a bitter taste in my mouth and was the second time I was left more than a little disappointed by someone who was once my footballing idol.

CHAPTER 2

NOVEMBER SPAWNED A MONSTER

On 16 August 1974, another monumental date, my family moved into Number 23 Crown Street, Preston. This is where I grew up and spent the next 12 years of my life. I was four years old, and can only remember three incidents prior to moving in. I can't remember living in any other house, but can remember how I once ran out of the house completely naked because I didn't want to have a bath (some things don't change). Being the youngest, I was always the last to have a bath in what was by then fourth-hand water. Bathing in dirty water doesn't seem to make much sense and didn't make much sense to me as a three-year-old – so, naturally, I scarpered!

I can also remember desperately wanting a bike for Christmas, and having seen one in the backyard I mistakenly believed it was for me. Unfortunately, it turned out we were hiding it for a friend to give to their son as a surprise. *Here's what you could have won...* This was a very early lesson in dealing with disappointment.

The third incident had more of an impact (or not) on my life. I have absolutely no recollection of ever living with the person who fathered me, but I remember one evening him coming to pick up two of my brothers (who lived in Preston at the time) and myself for an overnight stay. As we were about to set off, he said that he'd left his wallet in the house and sent myself and Fran, who is just under a year older than me, inside to get it. As soon as we walked through the door, we heard his car starting up and watched as he drove away. Another lesson in dealing with disappointment!

Again, I guess I was about three years old at that time. I've spoken to him since only once. That was over 30 years later; we happened to be at the same function at the Caribbean Club in Preston. For some bizarre reason, he thought it would be okay to put his hand on my shoulder. By this time, in his eyes, I'd made it big and, despite previously publicly disowning me and Fran (and never actually having held a conversation with me since *that day*), he decided he'd show me off to his friends. I think I said something along the lines of, 'Take your hand off me or I'll break your arm!'

It wasn't until recently that I discovered he used to beat my mother so badly that she eventually decided one day to take the children and walk into the night. She's a feisty girl is my mum and, from what I can gather, I don't think she left without giving a bit back. I don't have many regrets in my life, but one of them is the fact that, thanks to my diagnosis in March 2017, I could quite possibly die before *him*, rendering me unable to dance on his grave (metaphorically speaking – anybody who knows me knows I can't dance).

I grew up on a council estate near the centre of Preston. And if you think you've heard this one before, this isn't another one of those misery memoirs. I loved my childhood. I loved falling out with my brothers. I loved playing football inside and accidentally smashing the furniture. I loved staying up till all hours watching *Hammer House of Horror* on a Saturday night. Most of all, I loved the fact that, despite her never actually saying the words, my mum loved me, I knew, and would always look after me.

But we were poor – very poor. I didn't realise it at the time, although as I grew older and went to high school I was more than aware that we didn't have things that others had. When we were younger, Mum had worked as a machinist in a local factory. I remember the day she was made redundant and her not knowing what to do. She wasn't qualified to do anything else so took on a number of cleaning jobs to ensure we had a roof over our heads, food to eat, and clothes to wear. She worked tirelessly, it seemed; morning, noon and night.

Whenever she was working at night-time, she would ask a friend to look after us. Years later, I explained to her that this *friend* used to beat us with a stick whenever he felt we stepped out of line. We were never the best of mates, and it didn't exactly help that when I was about nine years old, I called him a liar straight to his face. He'd accused me of doing something that I hadn't, and although Mum taught us to respect our elders, I felt that you needed to earn respect. That man never did!

My mum came to England in or around 1963. She had been sent for by her husband, but left her sons Stephen and Johnson in Dominica to live with their grandmother. After they (Mum and *him)* had gone their separate ways (remember, I have no recollection of living with *him*), Mum brought us up on her own.

I have spoken to her about this time, and she talks candidly about how she had no concept of Christmas and birthdays – the whole 'buying presents lark'. It was only when I was around four or five years old, when Pete started to buy her presents with money from his paper rounds, that she realised it was the standard thing to do. However, there was no 'Father Christmas has got this for you'. Instead, we were given £5 to go and buy our own presents. I'm not sure why – perhaps due to inflation – but this sum went up by a pound every year. So off we'd go into Preston town centre, looking to see what we could get for our money. The funniest thing was, we'd get home and wrap the presents up and then act surprised when we opened them on Christmas morning. It was the same at Easter. No Easter bunnies for us; just £1 to go and find ourselves an Easter egg. I'm sure I don't need to explain about the tooth fairy…

My mum never learned to drive, so we would walk, or run, or get the bus everywhere. Actually, we rarely got the bus as we couldn't afford the bus fare.

At the start of the school year, we would be issued school grants to enable us to get the school uniform. These came in the form of vouchers which were only accepted by certain shops. The vouchers were suitably large so that everybody else in the store knew that you had no money. The same went for free school meals, where you were issued with a card and had to present this to the dinner lady in order to get your lunchtime meal. Nothing like standing out, is there? It was a bit like the old National Health Service glasses, which were unfashionably brown, large and cumbersome, and may as well have had the words 'I am poor' attached to them.

When I was about 10 I can remember a boy in my class teasing somebody about living in a council house. About six months later, I realised that he could have been teasing me. I didn't know what a council house was; I just knew that we lived where we lived. Anyway, as I said, I loved my childhood. I loved living where I lived. So it came as a massive shock when Mum decided she wanted to move to London, where we had quite a lot of family. Mum had put in for a house exchange with someone from London. There was no way I was going to move there, so my brother Fran and I decided to do something about it. The council were coming to view the house, so we thought it would be a great idea to put holes in the ceilings with a brush – anything to put them off. I remember going to London to visit, and playing football with some of the local lads. My older brother Pete tried to convince us that it would be a great idea to live in London, as there would be more of a chance to succeed if we wanted to be footballers. But we weren't going to have that, so cue Operation Wreck-the-House.

It's fair to say that we were justifiably punished for that one. Corporal punishment was all the rage in those days and, as I mentioned earlier, it wasn't unusual for us to be beaten with a stick to keep us in order. Anyway, the house swap fell through – something on the other party's side (I think she was behind with the rent or something like that). So, it was all for nothing. Another valuable lesson learned.

So we stayed put; my mum would be living there still had the council not sold off the land to a housing association. They knocked down the houses (Mum was rehoused for about a year) and rebuilt these fabulous – by comparison – *ugly* new houses. Tiny living room, even tinier bedrooms, but a bit of a garden at the back and front, and double-glazing throughout. The place that was once home to Mum, Pete, Fran (and, latterly, Ste) and myself was no longer.

Fortunately, we still have the memories. Memories of Pete, who is four years older than me, dragging a comb through my Afro in the mornings (Fran didn't have an Afro as Mum used to hot-comb his hair when he was about three, and it never really grew after that). Memories of Pete sending me downstairs at all hours to find out what the time was (why didn't we just get a clock for the bedroom?) Memories of Pete sending me into the kitchen for 'two b and b' (two slices of bread and butter) while he lorded it in the living room. Memories of Pete re-enacting Saturday afternoon wrestling from the TV show *World of Sport Wrestling*, with me as his 'willing' opponent. Yes, being the youngest in the house really was quite fantastic.

Unlike Fran, I never quite worked out that if I said 'submit' I could have stopped being thrown around the room. Unlike Fran, I never quite worked out that if I messed up with the bread and butter, I might have lived my early years as a brother instead of a slave; and unlike Fran, I never quite worked out that if I pretended I couldn't tell the time, I wouldn't have been sent downstairs at any given hour. Those experiences, however, really shaped me as a person. There were times growing up when I really thought I hated Pete but, in truth, I looked up to him so much that I was never going to let him see me give up on anything. I think it's fair to say that largely I am as determined as I am due to Pete. His influences led to my love of punk rock music (my first single was 'Capital Radio' by The Clash when I was about eight), and my love of Liverpool Football Club.

I wasn't exactly a loner as a child, but I was always quite happy to spend time sitting in with Mum as the others went out and about. On the occasions when I did venture out into the wild (and, believe me, sometimes it was very wild), I would quite often be seen running along the tops of houses or even on the tops of the 15-storey flats that were round the corner. In those days, you would do anything not to be 'on' when playing tig. When we weren't endangering life and limb by pretending to be Spiderman, most of our time was spent in what was a fenced-off area behind the houses. One minute, there would be a couple of us playing football or cricket, and the next there would be about 20 lads playing what can only be described as some sort of 'murderball/ football'.

I was always one of the youngest, with some of the lads maybe 10 years older than I was. Now, these guys lived by the rule, 'If you are old enough to play, you are old enough to get your head shoved into a wall'. It was a hard school but, again, it was something that helped shaped my life. The only thing that brought an end to those wild games was when one of us smashed a window in a nearby house. Within seconds, it would be like the *Marie Celeste*. I'm not quite sure how many footballs or cricket balls we lost every summer, but we were always back the next day for more murderball.

We still regularly talk about our upbringing, and about how there were not enough seats in the house for us all, so when anyone ever knocked on the door, literally nobody would move. You knew that if you were foolish enough to leave your seat, then it would be gone forever. Fortunately, we didn't have a telephone until I was 14 (Mum decided we needed one after I signed the schoolboy forms for Blackburn Rovers), so getting up to answer a call was never an issue.

CHAPTER 3

BORED TEENAGERS

So, the family dynamics! Hilda is the eldest, and came over from the West Indies when I was about one.

Johnson (yes, Johnson Johnrose!) is next on the list. Mum, who is very religious, had a 'visit' while expecting Johnson. She had lost three babies, all before they reached the age of one, and was advised that something had to change in order to break the 'curse'. In the dream, she was told that she had to give the child a girl's name regardless of what sex the child turned out to be. She decided to call her newborn son Marie. Not quite sure when it was, but at some point Marie became Johnson. Incidentally, Johnson named his son Mario, and remained in the West Indies with Stephen when Mum came over to England. Then came Pete, Fran and little old me. There is another one whom I don't consider family. Hilda lived in Preston until I was about seven years old. She is a practising Jehovah's Witness, and after meeting Douglas, whom she later married at the Kingdom Hall, she moved to London. Hilda was diagnosed with ME over 20 years ago, and never once have I heard her complain about it. The things she does while in her wheelchair completely put me to shame. Another feisty girl!

So there was Pete, Fran and myself, who all went to English Martyrs' Catholic Primary School in Preston.

Fran is my absolute best mate. There is less than a year between us, and although we are very different (he's a lot more outgoing than I am, and a lot friendlier), we have always done so much together. He was a very talented footballer and, with a bit of luck, could definitely have made it as a pro.

I actually hated infant school. Even at that age, I couldn't quite understand how it was okay to hit somebody else's child with a slipper or thick strap. I was even more bewildered by the fact that this deed was generally carried out by nuns (who, by the way, were the absolute worst teachers I ever had. This may have gone some way to influence my lack of belief in anything religious). In high school, we 'progressed' to the cane. I lost count of how many times I was given this form of punishment, but I don't think it had the desired effect. I actually remember the fear in teachers' eyes when it was announced that corporal punishment was being abolished. Now they would have to use reason and discussion with these wayward children instead of wafting the cane as if it were some sort of magic wand for good behaviour.

As I moved through school, on to juniors and high school, I began to appreciate school for what it was – a place to have fun, meet my mates, play sports and, more importantly, wind up as many teachers as I could. I began to love school and I still talk very fondly about it whenever I see my old classmates. I'm pretty sure that many teachers, particularly Miss Woods, would have a somewhat different opinion. Paul Turley and I actually made her life hell. It is not something I am particularly proud of, but I am still amused at the fact that two 12-year-olds could run rings round an experienced teacher.

PE and maths were always my favourite subjects at school. This is probably because I was pretty good at both of them and didn't need to work too hard to be good at them. (Does that sound arrogant?) Obviously, football was a big part of this, and we had a very successful school team, but I was also decent at cricket, basketball (don't mock my height; I was this tall when I was 14) and athletics. I was actually the 400m Lancashire champion, and could have possibly made it as an 800m runner (2 minutes 12 seconds when I was just 12 years old). I had no intention of becoming a footballer; it wasn't something that I dreamed of all my life. In fact, I was more interested in doing my paper round (remember, we were skint) than playing for the school team.

When I was 13, myself and a mate (Lee Chester, or Ches as he's known to his mates, and who was equally skint) were approached by Blackburn Rovers. The scout Alan Tordoff had been watching our progress for a while, and made the approach when we were representing Preston Town schools team – the team in which the best players from all the schools in Preston were selected to play. I have to say (well, I don't, but it makes me feel good) that we were probably the most exciting prospects in Lancashire in that age group at that time, but I had absolutely no intention of signing for

Blackburn Rovers or anybody else for that matter (remember the paper round).

Back in those days you were only signed if you genuinely had a chance of making it as an apprentice, or YTS as it later became. So we were given a tour of the ground by Alan, and the chief scout, Fred O'Donoghue, invited us to meet the first team and then took us into the hospitality bars. This signalled the end of Ches's chances of signing for Blackburn Rovers. Remember, we were only 13 and Fred asked us what we'd like to drink. I politely asked for a glass of orange juice, but Ches, who was a bit of a rogue, asked for a pint of lager. Fred nearly choked on his pipe...

I remember getting David Speedie's autograph (I think he was at Chelsea) which may have been the last time I actually asked anyone for an autograph. Fred had encouraged us to do it, but anyone who knows me knows that I don't get particularly star-struck, and I have to admit that I have absolutely no idea what I did with the autograph. (Sorry, Speedo!) So, mixing with the footballing aristocracy didn't really have the desired effect, and I was still intent on playing football for fun and making money from my three paper rounds. But everybody has a price...

In 1985, Liverpool Football Club paid a record £250,000 to sign Wayne Harrison from Oldham Athletic. He was the world's most expensive teenager, and this came at a time when football clubs were rumoured to have been giving parents incentives to persuade them to allow their children to sign contracts. Liverpool were rumoured to have bought Wayne Harrison's parents a new house, and similar things were being bandied around the tabloids. Naturally, being exceedingly greedy, I wanted a part of this. Obviously, Blackburn were not in the same league as Liverpool, but I knew my worth. Even at that age I was a very tough negotiator, and drove a hard bargain. So, armed with a new pair of adidas World Cup football boots, Fred sat me down with Mum and I signed schoolboy forms for Blackburn Rovers, a couple of days after my fourteenth birthday. How times have changed!

Signing schoolboy forms was somewhat different from being an academy player in today's world. For a start, you could continue playing football with your mates in the Sunday leagues. You were also not expected to be driven around three or four times a week for evening training, which was a good job really, as we didn't own a car – in fact the Sunday league attendance when I was playing for Lostock Hall Under 13s and Under 14s was thanks to Malcolm Gray, the father of player Gareth and spectator Warren. Malcolm travelled miles out of his way with his sons and another lad to pick up Ches and me. With there being five of us, it meant every Sunday one of us took turns to sit in the boot! We still keep in touch today.

Training was done during the school holidays and games were played on a Saturday morning. These games were regionalised which, again, made it easier for parents to access them. I think most clubs also used to put on a minibus to travel to away games. Now remember, in those days, clubs only asked you to sign schoolboy forms if they thought you had a good chance of making it as an apprentice (as opposed to the modern way of signing as many children as they can in order to fill their various age-related teams). In those days, you were an asset to the club (or they hoped you would be one day) and they were more than aware that it would be a struggle for some parents to get their children to games and training. Cue travel expenses. Yes, that's right – they actually gave you travel expenses to ensure that you could turn up to training and to the matches, because they really wanted you. They valued you, and they wanted you to *feel* valued. As I said earlier, how times have changed!

With my immediate future apparently sorted out, my last two years at high school were an absolute scream. Every week I used to watch the programme *Scully*, which was set in Liverpool, and I remember Paul and myself speaking in a Scouse accent for weeks afterwards. (We thought it was Scouse anyway.) Imagine that! We got some incredibly strange looks. But after the second week I think just about everybody accepted that we were probably a bit mad. Now, as you've probably guessed, we were extremely intelligent, and were in the top set for every lesson. I remember during one English lesson we had a supply teacher. So there we were, in the last year of high school, having never once volunteered to do anything in our previous four years. The supply teacher asked if anybody would like to read the next passage in a book. Imagine the surprise on everybody's faces when both Paul and I put our hands up. In our best Scouse accents, we uttered the words, 'Miss, miss! I wish I could read!'

She was delighted and said something along the lines of, 'Oh, how unusual it is to have boys offering to read. Of course you can, you can go next!'

'No, miss, you don't understand. We wish we *could* read!'

She looked absolutely mortified. 'Oh, I'm terribly sorry,' she said. 'Please forgive me.'

The class were in absolute hysterics. Set 1 English in the last year of high school, and this teacher didn't think we could read. No wonder the education system is a joke!

In my final year of school, the teachers were on some sort of extracurricular strike, so there were no football teams, cricket teams and so on. Fortunately, I had my GCEs to concentrate my mind, which I took extremely seriously! I remember being thrown out of the English Literature exam (guess who with?) for having a conversation, and we weren't even sitting next to each other. Perhaps if they'd sat us together, we wouldn't have disturbed half the class. Now remember, this is the 1980s when teachers weren't exactly the brains of the outfit. As it was apparently imperative that we took our exams, they decided to put us in a room together with no other teacher to supervise. That was the best session of table rugby that we ever had, and unsurprisingly, neither of us passed English Lit.

I was never particularly creative. In fact, the most creative thing I ever did in five years of high school was to shoulder-barge Paul into Mr Judson, our very camp art teacher. Another teacher who wasn't best pleased with us.

I actually produced my most impressive artwork during that series of GCEs, irrespective of the subject. As I said, my immediate future had been sorted, and I wasn't prepared to waste time and effort revising for exams I knew I would never need. Nowadays, there is always some sort of huge furore when the exam results are released. You can almost hear the frantic footsteps as children race to open the letters that tell them, 'Sorry, son, you're a failure' or 'Congratulations, you can now go to college for the next two years while you decide what to do with the rest of your life'. But, back then, the date came and went without even a whimper – for me anyway. Not the greatest example from a future teacher, I know, but that's just the way it was.

Everything was geared towards that first day of pre-season training as a first-year YTS trainee. Naturally, I did my paper rounds right up until that first day. I couldn't wait to get in and start playing football 24/7. I couldn't wait to see my new 'digs' and who I'd be living with. I had finally found an emotion; I was filled with anticipation and excitement. And I was going to be paid for the privilege: £27.50… Yes, that's right – £27.50. I had made it!

So, day one! The YTS lads were in a couple of weeks before the pros. Two weeks of getting to know one another. Two weeks of learning how to be a footballer. You can imagine how pleased I was when Jim Furnell (who was absolutely brilliant, by the way) introduced us to pots of paint and bags of paintbrushes. The majority of the first two weeks of my footballing career was spent painting the dressing rooms. Character-building, apparently. Soul-destroying was my take on it, but it was something we just had to do, although I'm pretty sure Harry Kane and Dele Alli didn't have to do this at Spurs.

When we actually managed to start pre-season training with the pros, I was really quite taken aback. I had trained during the summer with Franz Carr (a former England youth international, who lived round the corner and went to Nottingham Forest from Blackburn Rovers as a kid) to ensure that I would be in peak condition once training began. I was already a naturally fit lad, but I'd intended to make an impression from the start. Everyone had to be weighed and I remember listening to some of the pros talking about how much weight they'd put on during the summer. 'Pre-season is there to get you fit,' they'd say. Some of them would be easily more than a stone over their playing weight.

Deep down, I was incredulous. I couldn't believe that these guys were where I aspired to be, and they weren't even taking their fitness seriously. I can't even begin to tell you my thoughts when I later saw a couple of them smoking (actually *smoking*) after training or, in some cases, before a game. Smoking was, and still is, my absolute pet hate. I always thought it was the most disgusting thing anyone could ever do. The whole 'fag in mouth' thing just made me feel repulsed. The smell, the yellow teeth, the unmistakable cough followed by the near-inevitable lung cancer, the cost... Oh yes, I can really see the attraction! I was almost equally dumbfounded when I witnessed a couple of the senior players having a shot of whisky before the game. Welcome to 1980s professional football!

Despite this, I believed that my way was the right way, and was going to make an impression once the training started. And that I did! How was I to know that a 16-year-old YTS lad wasn't supposed to burst past all the pros during the running sessions? Apparently, it made them look bad. You'll be unsurprised to learn that I really didn't care. I was doing this for me, not for them.

By this time, there had been another addition to the Johnrose household. Mum had finally been successful in bringing Stephen over from the West Indies. She had been trying for years, but her ex-husband had refused to sign the papers required, claiming that Stephen was not his son. When she finally got the necessary paperwork, the airfares had increased. This meant she had to save for a number of months until, finally, in September 1979 when Stephen was 15, she secured enough to pay for a one-way trip from Dominica to Preston. Mum and I met Stephen at the bus station (he had flown into Heathrow, and spent a few days at Hilda's before getting the coach to Preston bus station) and, save for a few indiscretions on my part, a bond was made.

Until recently, I never realised how difficult it had been for Stephen to suddenly be part of this family that he'd longed to belong to for years. I never realised that he'd felt abandoned by his mother, or how he'd resented the fact that within a year of her coming to England, Mum had given birth to Peter (who he decided must have been some sort of replacement for him). He talks about how, whenever he saw a plane flying overhead, he'd think that it was coming for him to take him to England. It took a few years to realise that this wasn't the case. For the rest of us, we had a new brother with a strange accent. I'm ashamed to say that, in true Jim Davidson style, Fran and I used to mimic him. That was one of those indiscretions! But as I have said, we forged a bond, and Stephen was so proud when I signed for Blackburn Rovers. He saw it as a beacon of hope for all those who had a difficult upbringing. He was the one who ignored all the chants from opposing crowds and continued following my career around the country. He still speaks very fondly about it, and still follows me around the country as I try to raise awareness of MND.

I look back on my time at Blackburn with pride, regret and frustration. There were even times when there were elements of bitterness, though they're passed now.

Leaving senior pros in my wake during pre-season didn't exactly endear me to them, something which became blindingly obvious when I struggled on the training ground. The 'banter' was something I found difficult to handle. Being called 'useless' or worse whenever I made a mistake was even more perplexing. We were all on the same team, right? More character-building, perhaps. I was, as somebody described me, 'all arms and legs', and this probably made my mistakes look worse than they actually were. But there was nobody who put their arm around me, encouraged me, or took me under their wing. It was pretty much every man for himself, and my confidence was taking a battering. I was 16, clumsy, and shy! This wasn't helped by the fact that the owners of the digs where I stayed actually hated me. I was there with David May, who went on to play for Manchester United, Keith Hill (who later went on to be the manager of Rochdale) and a boy named Alex Binnie.

Alex and Keith were second-year YTS lads who'd lived there the previous season, and were absolute golden boys. While they could do no wrong, Dave and I were forced to sit on the floor to accommodate the others. We used to go up to our room and basically slag the owners off. What we didn't know was that Keith and Alex had told them what was going on, so they put a bug in the room to listen to what we were saying. Dave was really going for it, calling them every name under the sun. For some reason, I held back, but didn't hold back my laughter when they burst into the room and chased Dave out the house. It was hilarious and, funnily enough, they never allowed Dave to stay there again. I was gutted that he'd managed to escape, though. I had to put up with crappy meals, whining children, and accusations of my colour washing off on the pillowcases. (It was actually hair gel, which I used to manipulate my wonderful 1980s perm!) Oh, and a failed 'suicide attempt' from the owner. He'd had yet another argument with his wife and had apparently taken a paracetamol overdose. Strange thing was, he immediately came into our room and told Keith and Alex what he'd done. I'm not really sure how serious he was about it. Anyway, Alex could drive, so took him to hospital with Keith. There was no teasing that night.

So, my first year of YTS was a bit of a write-off, but all that changed in Year 2. Again, I put in the hours for my off-season training (I wasn't going to be put off by last year's experience), and came back full of confidence. I was a year older, I had spent the last eight weeks in the gym, and was in no mood to be messed around. I remember Keith saying that I looked like a middleweight boxer, which was exactly what I wanted. This time, I was ready for the banter and approached every training session as though it was a match day. I was strong and aggressive, and felt completely at ease training with the senior pros. Cue another lesson! Not only did senior pros dislike the fact that you left them behind during the running, they also abhorred the fact that this young kid was getting the better of them on the training ground – this same young kid who they had ridiculed the previous season. The treatment they tried to dish out was what I think was called 'putting me in my place'. But remember, I was now a middleweight boxer and gave out much more than I got.

Mark Patterson (Paddy) was one of the worst. He was a tough lad from Darwen in Lancashire, only about 5ft 7in, but really punched more than his weight. He was also an extremely good footballer who wasn't going to give up his place without a fight. He would snarl, kick, elbow, and pretty much do anything to be a winner; just the sort of lad you'd want *in* your team but would hate to play *against*. We had some great battles, and I think I earned his respect by not backing down. The older lads in the team could sense that things were about to change. Keith Hill had been given a professional contract; Dave May was going from strength to strength; I was now beginning to fulfil my potential; and we had Jason Wilcox as a first-year YTS trainee who would go on to represent England.

Back in those days, players were only on a few hundred pounds a week; appearance money and win bonuses were a great incentive to get into the team – unlike today's Premiership players who are earning tens of thousand pounds every week. Some players used to include their appearance money as part of their wage when they applied for mortgages, and I can remember one in particular struggling to pay his mortgage when he was left out of the team for a period of time. One year Panini, who made the football stickers and sticker books, negotiated a deal with all the league clubs, where every club would receive a lump sum of money. At

Blackburn, this money was handed over to the club captain to share out. As you've probably guessed, money was quite tight, so it was no surprise when the senior pros refused to let the first-year pros have any share. Apparently, our time would come.

In those days, there was a reserve team league – I think it was called the Central League. It was regionalised, with the furthest trip for us being to Newcastle United. There were two divisions, and because there was promotion and relegation, it was extremely competitive. For the younger players, playing in the reserves was an opportunity to put your case forward for getting yourself in the first team. It was also seen as a bit of a reward if you had done particularly well playing in the youth team. It wasn't a given that you played in the reserves. If you were still a YTS, in fact, it was pretty rare. Yet myself, Jason, Dave, and a lad called Craig Skinner played regularly that year. I felt completely at ease at this level, playing against hardened pros with hundreds of first-team appearances to their names.

Every Friday during training, the first team would separate from the rest of the pros and work on tactics for the following day (yes, we used to play every Saturday then). One particular Friday, sometime in December, I was called to train with the first team. I knew I was only there as a makeweight, but I really enjoyed the experience. There I was, a second-year YTS lad training with the first team. When we got back to the ground Tony Parkes, who was the first-team coach, put the squad up for the match – away at West Bromwich Albion. And there it was, right at the bottom of the list: Lennie Johnrose. I couldn't believe it. I'd made the first-team squad and was still just a YTS lad. The other lads seemed pretty pleased for me; perhaps it was a bit of an incentive for them. Anyway, I took it in my stride and knew that it was just going to be a great experience: travelling on the first-team coach, listening to the banter (if not being part of it), and then being in the dressing room when the lads were getting changed.

I have to say, the journey to WBA was a bit of an eye-opener. There was no music on the coach, just videos. Not just *any* videos, but actually hard-core porn. Like I said, an eye-opener. I have to say that I found it a little bit strange, a load of lads gathered together on a coach, watching porn. Even now, as I'm writing this, I am scratching my head (metaphorically speaking – MND has ensured that I can't scratch my head properly). Anyway, I think I just read the paper and kept my head down and, as an 18-year-old lad (I'd just had my birthday two weeks prior to this), I wasn't going to embarrass myself by standing up and walking around.

About quarter of an hour before we got to the ground, the video was turned off and it was time for business. I was still pretty relaxed at this point, just soaking up the atmosphere and looking forward to going into the ground. When we finally arrived I helped Tony Parkes and the physio unload the skips, containing the boots and kit, and headed into the dressing room. At about 1.30, Don Mackay, the manager, read the team out. I have to admit that I wasn't paying too much attention … then he read out the substitutes. I think he said Alan Ainscow, and then Lennie Johnrose! There's a story that's gone round saying that one of the lads got injured during the warm-up, and that I got called out of the players' bar to be named on the bench. That actually wasn't the case. Yes, a player did get injured during the warm-up, but I had already been named as a substitute. I think it was Tony Diamond who got called out of the players' bar to be the second sub.

Anyway, the nerves now started kicking in, but I think I was more excited than anything. After about 20 minutes, one of the lads got injured and I was sent on to make my debut. In typical 1980s English football style, I was put on the left wing. Although the game was a bit of a blur, and the pace was frantic, I actually did okay. Or so I thought. It was two years before I made another first-team appearance. No quiet word, no explanation, nothing. So it was back to the reserves, where I flitted between being a centre forward and a centre midfielder, feeling equally at ease in both.

What should have been the start of a fantastic period of my life actually turned out to mark one of the worst decisions I've ever made in my private life. I was only just 18 and had been going out with a girl I'd known from school. One Sunday, I went round to her sister's house on the off chance that she'd be there. She let me in and we started to chat. She began telling me how unhappy she was in her marriage, how badly she was being treated, and how she had no life outside the house. She was a few years older than me, but still, I thought I was Superman and sent to save her from her life of doom. Before I knew it, we were in a relationship and she was ready to leave her husband. To make matters worse, they had a young son who got caught in the crossfire. It's so easy to say now, but what was I thinking? When she left him, her husband actually wished me good luck. I soon found out what he meant! It was a terrible relationship, but I was racked with guilt. I'd taken a young boy away from his father and made him endure awful scenes between the two of them.

The boy and I actually became very close and I tried to bring him up as my own. I was determined to make a go of this relationship, despite the misgivings of my close friends and family. There were quite a few occasions where she was both verbally and physically abusive, but I'd made myself a promise that I would not rip this child's world apart again. I have always wondered why some people stay with their partners, and I look back now and ask myself the same question. But at the time it seemed like the right thing to do. While I don't believe that everything happens for a reason, I can't regret what I did because when I was going through it, as I said, it felt like the best thing to do. The night before we got married, I had a long, deep discussion with my brother. I knew it wasn't the right thing to do. I really didn't want to do it, but things had gone far too far. If I'm being honest with myself, I was a bit of a coward. The wedding day came and went, we went on honeymoon and I remember thinking, 'What the hell have I done?'

Despite the obvious deterioration in our relationship, two and a half years later we had a daughter. This was my last chance to make a go of this relationship. I can honestly say that my daughter is the single good thing I got out of that relationship, either emotionally or physically. Everybody has a limit, and I reached mine on 13 February 1996. After every bout of violence or verbal abuse, there would be no apology. Amazingly, there were only threats to leave. She knew that I couldn't bear to be parted from my daughter, and she seemed to get some sort of perverse satisfaction in me asking her to stay. As I say, on 13 February her oft-used line was repeated once again, but this time I actually said that I would help her pack. I can still remember the relief I felt when the words actually, finally, came out of my mouth. I had done all I could to make the marriage work. But right there and then, I knew that was the end of it.

The following day, I went to work as usual (by now I was at Bury FC) and phoned on the way home to see whether she had gone. She answered the phone and I just hung up, gutted! When I got back, she started ranting on about how I'd been checking up that she'd actually gone. Remember, I can't tell lies, so I simply admitted it. To say that she went mad was an understatement. Putting aside the subject of my daughter, she did the worst thing imaginable. She destroyed my collection of The Smiths videos. She really had crossed the line now!

So there I was on Valentine's Day, having just split up with my wife. What better excuse could there be to get the glad rags on and get myself out to Squires. Paul and I did what we did best. Got dressed, got hammered, jokingly insulted a few people, and got chatted up (well, I did anyway). And for the first time in years I actually had a conversation with a girl, safe in the knowledge that I wasn't going to get slapped or sworn at when I got back home.

A couple of days later, I got home to an empty house – apart from my Simpsons videos smashed up and waiting for me in the garden. No sofa, no TV, no video, no hi-fi, nothing… And I couldn't have felt better. I have to say that

I didn't appreciate the door being kicked in, but, hey, at least it made my entrance easier when I got in from my night out (and there were plenty of those for the next few months). Aside from the nights out, the next couple of years were spent in and out of court trying to get access to see my daughter. I knew this was coming, I had seen it with other men before, but really wasn't prepared for just how difficult it was going to be. Talk about a woman scorned. But it was all worth it: all the sleepless nights; having to turn up and wait at the end of various roads so that I didn't know exactly where she lived (I'm not really sure why she thought I *wanted* to know where she lived); being stopped by the police for 'kidnapping my daughter'; living off a pittance after having to pay off her debts; and pay the CSA … all of it worth it, just to get her out of my life. (Who am I kidding? Her spectre still haunts me!)

At the end of the season, I was awarded a professional two-year contract, along with Dave May. The reserves had won promotion to the top division, so it was a very successful season, which included a trip to Wembley where the first team beat Charlton in the Full Members' Cup. There was even a youth team game before the big event where I was awarded Man of the Match in a 4–3 victory. The celebrations afterwards were as eye-opening as that trip to West Brom. Footballers in the 1980s really knew how to party!

The following season took pretty much the same course as my first year as a YTS trainee. Right at the front in all of the running, but finding it a big step training every day with the seasoned pros, and getting abuse into the bargain.

But things changed massively during my second year. I had been doing well in the reserves and made the subs bench a couple of times for the first team. Finally, I think it was in November, I actually managed to get on the pitch. We were playing at home to Ipswich and were 2–0 down. Don Mackay decided to put me on with about 20 minutes to go. I made an instant impact, scoring within a few minutes, before playing a small hand in a move which led to a penalty, which was dispatched, I think, by Scott Sellars. Fittingly, Paul was there to see my first ever league goal and to help me celebrate it later on. I made the headlines in quite a few of the newspapers. I knew that *this* time I was ready to play football at this level. I was in and out of the team, and was used as more of an impact player from the bench, which I wasn't happy with at all. It was as though the manager didn't have enough faith in me to play me from the start of the game.

The following season, I was given my chance to start and took it by scoring what was the first of a run of five goals in five games. The next two games went goalless, and I was left out with the manager saying that I had 'dried up'. I was absolutely fuming, but took it on the chin and continued to work hard. That run of goals saw me win the Barclays Young Eagle of the Month and there was talk of me being selected for the England Under 21s. I remember Tony Parkes saying that he'd just been to watch one of the England games and I definitely would not have looked out of place. I'm not sure whether that meant the rest of the players were crap...

Anyway, it didn't happen, and as before I was in and out of the team.

The following season began in similar fashion for me, but the team were struggling. I had a lot of time for Don Mackay, but always felt that he wasn't strong enough with some of the senior pros. He is certainly not the only one guilty of this, but he found it easier to leave out some of the younger lads, knowing that it would more than likely avoid confrontation. In the end, this cost him his job, and Tony Parkes was given it on a temporary basis. Now, Parksey didn't take any messing, and immediately dropped some of the older players. In their place he put in me, Jason Wilcox and Craig Skinner.

I was asked to play midfield alongside Mark Atkins (who had a great career) and immediately there was an upturn in results. My last appearance for Blackburn Rovers was away at Millwall. We won 3–1 with me scoring the third goal. The following Tuesday, during training, I went in for a tackle and damaged my medial knee ligaments. The day after, Kenny Dalglish was announced as the new manager at Blackburn Rovers. Talk about dreadful timing. On the Saturday, he watched from the stands as we beat Plymouth convincingly without me on the team. I was absolutely gutted!

By the time I was fit, there'd been a number of new signings and it was clear that I didn't figure in his plans. I had no problem with that, but did have a massive issue with the way I was treated by Ray Harford, Kenny Dalglish's assistant. Ray Harford was, essentially, a bully. He undermined me at every opportunity, and didn't even have the good grace to call me by my name. He would rile me by calling me 'Jenny', and completely shattered my confidence. I was still only 21, and making my way in the game. Had this been a few years later, I would have reacted completely differently, but it really got to me. I know you're not supposed to speak ill of the dead, but surely not everybody who has died has been a good person.

I mentioned earlier my element of bitterness towards Blackburn Rovers – that was it, right there, in a nutshell. I also mentioned how you should never meet your heroes. Kenny Dalglish was one of my heroes, but the way in which he stood and watched Ray Harford rip me to shreds, without saying a word in my favour, in my mind spoke volumes about the man. There was one incident where I was due to be picked up for a reserve game. It had been snowing heavily. I was waiting at the bus stop wondering whether the game would still be on. Forty-five minutes after the arranged arrival time, and still no coach, I decided the game must have been cancelled, so decided to walk home. This was in the days before I had a mobile phone, so there was no way of checking. In the morning, I was summoned to the manager's office, where Dalglish again sat and watched as Ray Harford ripped into me once more. He was all for fining me for missing the game (yes, the coach was about an hour late) but, to his credit (I think!), Dalglish recognised that I wasn't on much money. So, instead, he decided my punishment would be demotion to the B-team. The B-team, where I had played when I was 14. I think I would have preferred the fine. So within three months, I went from scoring a goal in the first team to playing with the kids on a Saturday morning. I was also now training with the kids which, as bad as that was, at least gave me a break from Ray Harford.

CHAPTER 4

NOT QUITE PARADISE

A week later, I was sent on loan to Preston North End, my home-town team. Remember, I had played multiple games in what is now known as the Championship, either upfront as the centre forward or in midfield. I arrived for training, and got the impression that it was some sort of pub team. Les Chapman was the manager, a really nice guy, but one who had been a teammate of some of the players. Again, I felt his relationship was too close and that some of them took advantage of this.

I can't remember who my first game was against, but, cue 1980s football once again, I was put on the left wing (unsurprisingly) and was pretty rubbish. Why, oh why, did managers of that era think that if you were black and quick (and I wasn't even *that* quick) you had to be a winger? Preston already had a perfectly good left-winger in Lee Ashcroft, who I think replaced me after about 60 minutes. That was my last start in the first team for Preston who, by the way, were in the division below Blackburn. I signed off at Preston by scoring a goal at home against Fulham after coming on as a substitute as a centre forward. The next day I went to see Les Chapman, and said that I would not be finishing my month's loan. So I went back to Blackburn, where I played my last reserve game away to Manchester City. Kenny Dalglish attended the game, and told us to play on Colin Hendry. Colin had been at Blackburn a couple of years before, and his terrific performances had seen him make a dream move to City.

At half-time, Dalglish came into the dressing room. We were 2–1 down. He told us that the way back into the game would be to play on Colin Hendry's frailties. He absolutely ripped his game apart during that team talk, but as we came in at the end of the game, having won 4–2, we all thought that Dalglish must have known what he was talking about. Two days later, Colin walked into the Blackburn dressing room as Kenny Dalglish's new signing. Amazing!

Anyway, I knew my time was up at Blackburn and this was pretty much confirmed when I was called into the manager's office one Monday morning. I hadn't been selected to play in any of the first-team squads since Dalglish's arrival, but this particular morning, he wanted to know where I was on the Friday night before the Saturday game. Before I had time to answer, he showed me a clip from the TV show *The Hitman and Her*. This was a roadshow which went around the country to various nightclubs. And there I was, right in front of the camera, dancing away! Rumbled!

At that point I would have gone absolutely anywhere to get away from Blackburn, and with absolutely no disrespect meant, that's exactly what I did. I was sold to Hartlepool

United, who had the unenviable record of having applied for re-election to the league more than any other club. In those days, if you finished bottom of Division Four (League Two) you had to apply to the league to stay in. There was no relegation to the Conference League (now called the National League); just a paper exercise and you were allowed to maintain the status quo. The Conference teams had, for years, complained about how unfair this was, and that they should be given the opportunity to prove that they were as good as the teams in the division above. Naturally, this was always vetoed by the teams in that division above. Surprising that, isn't it?

The success of teams from the (now) National League demonstrates how right they were to keep banging the drum, and the number of league clubs who have since been relegated and not returned is incredible. My very own Hartlepool United, of course, now wish that they were allowed to apply for re-election as they themselves finally dropped out in 2017. Even the famous clubs, such as founder members Notts County, have fallen foul. The knock-on effect has meant that all but Chorley FC, in the National League, are full-time professional clubs.

As I said earlier, how times have changed.

My transfer to Hartlepool was organised by a scout named Glenn Burnell. He lived in Preston and used to work for Hartlepool and Cambridge United. The fee was £40,000, which for Hartlepool was quite a lot of money. I remember driving to a hotel in Darlington to meet the chairman and manager. In those days, I didn't have a mobile phone; in fact, not many people had. The first footballer I ever saw with a mobile phone was a guy called Tony Finnigan. He was one of those 'fly guys' from London plying his trade up north. His phone was about the size of a laptop, but he used to sit in the dressing room with this huge contraption looking ever so cool!

So there I was, driving to Darlington, not really having a clue where I was going. Thank goodness for satnav, or as it was known in those days: the AA route finder. About an hour into the journey, I had to find a phone box and ask for directions about where on earth I was going. (How many times can a person write 'times have changed' in one book?)

When I arrived at the hotel, I was pleasantly surprised. I don't know what I was expecting, but it was really plush. After exchanging pleasantries, we sat down to negotiations. I had been earning around £200 a week at Blackburn and didn't really have a clue how much to ask for. There was no agent, representative, or entourage. Just me: a raw, green 21-year-old, looking to sort my own contract out with these hardened businessmen. I was quite pleased with my hard-bargained £300 a week deal, with a signing-on fee of, I think, about £5,000.

The next day, I drove to Chester to watch my new team play. I walked into the dressing room, and felt all these eyes boring into me. Nobody said anything, but it was glaringly obvious that this was the first time a lot of them had seen a black face in quite some time. To be honest, it didn't really bother me. I was more concerned about the fact that these guys were … how can I put this? … a bit rough around the edges compared to the lads I had left at Blackburn Rovers. They also mainly spoke with an accent similar to those who had abused me as a 14-year-old. It was also the first time I'd seen footballers with tattoos. What I also couldn't fail to recognise was, once they got over the initial shock, how lively and friendly they were. The dressing room was absolutely bouncing. I remember Brian Honour, this old-looking bald guy, taking the piss out of pretty much everyone. He was unrelenting, but it was hilarious, and nobody took offence. They all loved it. I'm not saying that the dressing room in Blackburn wasn't a good one, but it was so, so different.

There were some really funny guys at Blackburn. Andy Kennedy, by his own admission, a tall, dark and handsome guy, was great. He used to have great banter with Ally Dawson as they were from different parts of Glasgow. Andy used to call Ally a 'Fenian bastard' (nice touch; not sure you could get away with that in these times of political correctness) but, again, no offence was taken. Howard Gayle, who was Liverpool FC's first ever black player – and who, in 2016, turned down the offer of an MBE due to his beliefs about the way the British Empire oppressed black people – was a strange character. He was very dry, and used to speak with his mouth barely open. Craig, Jason and I used to slate him behind his back, as whenever we went for a pre-match meal, no matter what it was, whether he had tasted his food or not, he would always ask for Tabasco sauce. In this really droney (is that a word?) Scouse accent, he would say, 'Err, do you have any Tabasco?' We found that hilarious (we were just kids, remember). He used to talk about Liverpool all the time, as though he was still there, and go on about how much money he had.

The YTS lads who looked after him couldn't wait for Christmas, knowing they would be getting a very handsome tip. He used to treat all of us pretty badly. In fact, I remember him squaring up to young goalkeeper David Fantom (who was 17 at the time, while Howard was about 31). But not before he carefully, and very deliberately, took off his gloves, one finger at a time. We all thought, 'what a prick!' and hoped that Dave would spark him out. Fortunately, somebody broke it up before a proper punch was thrown. Dave was quite a big lad and didn't back down, but I didn't really fancy his chances. Anyway, despite his rough treatment of the YTS lads, I think he gave the biggest tip of all the pros. Typical Howard Gayle, had to be the big one.

Most of the banter, though, centred on who had 'pulled' at the weekend. Other than that, it seemed to be pretty much dog-eat-dog at Blackburn, with, as I said, the young lads feeling the brunt of it.

Hartlepool, though, was very different. Everybody seemed to be in it together, whether they were in the first team or not. I can't remember the score of the game, but I looked forward to Monday, when there was a practice match arranged at Billingham Synthonia. I was asked to play upfront and, despite being only 5ft 10in, was very good in the air. So I was taken aback when this young lad who, to be fair to him, was about 6ft 2in, told me that he would go for the headers and I should just go and get the flick-ons. I was also surprised about how upfront this lad was. Although I had only just left Blackburn, I had rediscovered my confidence, and thought, 'who's this young kid to tell me what to do?' This young kid was called Steve Fletcher; I ended up taking his place at Hartlepool and he went on to become a Bournemouth legend, scoring the winner in 2009 to keep them in the league.

My first day's training was, to say the least, a bit of a disappointment. We trained on a field in Billingham, where there was a huge oil plant in view. But the worst thing was the surface. I'm not exaggerating when I say that I had played on better pitches as a junior in the Sunday leagues. It was absolutely horrendous. It was at that point when I wondered what on earth I had done. It was incomparable to the training ground at Pleasington, where Blackburn used to train, which itself is incomparable to the training grounds of modern football clubs. It was a bit like a field for cows, although I gather such fields do undergo some sort of maintenance. I was soon getting the feeling that I would have to learn to adapt to my new surroundings, and that perhaps I'd had it a little bit easy at Blackburn. Worse was to come when I found out that I had to wash my own training kit! Isn't it strange how your experiences change you as a person. Just two and a half years of being a pro at Blackburn Rovers, and I was amazed that I had to wash my own training kit. Get a grip!

My final lesson in adapting to my surroundings came on Tuesday evening, away at West Brom. I was still commuting to and from Hartlepool at the time, so drove to West Brom in a car that had been loaned to me by one of the directors. The car was a brand new Rover 200, taxed, MOT'd and insured. All I had to do was put in fuel and drive. And boy, did I drive. I remember once driving at 115mph on the M6 back home to Preston. It was only when I returned the car that I was told that I hadn't been insured after all. The lessons just kept on coming.

So, I walked into the dressing room at West Bromwich's ground, the Hawthorns, and got a bit of a flashback to the day I made my debut. I had a good feeling about the game. Forget all about the dodgy pitches, forget all about having to wash my own kit – *this* was what it was all about. None of the other stuff mattered; it was about performing on the pitch in front of a crowd. We walked out on to the pitch to have a good look around. The memories of my debut came flooding back. Even though I was asked to play at left wing, it was still a great day. But this time I would be playing at centre forward. I couldn't wait to get back into the changing rooms, get the team talk out of the way and start the game. As we walked back into the dressing room, I had a bit of an uneasy feeling. There was something missing.

'Where's the skip, gaffer?'

'What skip?' Suddenly I felt all eyes on me, again.

'The boot skip!'

Again, I had forgotten my upbringing. Two years prior to this, I would have been helping the physio or kit man carry the skip off the coach. But now, I was a big signing from Blackburn and just walked straight into the dressing room without giving it a thought.

The dressing room went from all eyes on me to everyone laughing at me. Brian Honour (who else?) shouted out, 'You're not at Blackburn now, son,' and then followed this up with something like, 'Slavery has been abolished, man,' in that thick Geordie accent of his. What a start that was for me. I ended up having to borrow one of the squad member's boots which, incidentally, were about a size too small for me. I think the game ended in a draw, and I actually played okay despite my feet absolutely killing. So, that was it. I was officially one of the lads. They completely ripped me to bits at the end of the game, but it was all good-natured, and it felt good to be part of a team.

There was one more big surprise, though, and again it involved an away trip on the team coach. This time there was no pornography. No, these guys were a class above that. Instead, I had to sit through Roy Chubby Brown, recycling his form of wit. Oh, how they laughed! I really wasn't sure which away trip I felt most bewildered by!

The rest of the season was a bit of a washout. Hartlepool had a new chairman, Gary Gibson, who was looking to change the image of the club. We were mid-table, in no danger of being relegated but with no chance of being promoted, but he was starting to build a team to try to get promoted the following season. Paul Cross, a left back, had been signed from hometown club Barnsley, just before me. We also signed Dean Emerson from Coventry, and a young right back called Ryan Cross, who made the unbelievable trip from Plymouth to Hartlepool.

Although they were spending quite a lot of money, most of it came from the sale of Don Hutchinson, a young midfielder who was signed by Kenny Dalglish for Liverpool a few months before he became Blackburn manager. I always found that a strange coincidence. There was even more money spent on John Gallacher who, although he signed on a free transfer from Newcastle, was on considerably better wages than my paltry £300 a week. John had burst on the scene as a wiry 20-year-old winger, making his debut and scoring in a 5–2 win against Leeds United. After being plagued with injuries, he dropped down a division in the hope of relaunching his career. Unfortunately, after only around 20 appearances, injuries put paid to his time at Hartlepool and, ultimately, his career.

Paul Dalton was probably the main player at the football club, and although he too was sold, the new signings meant we approached the following season with optimism.

The new season started really well, with me and Andy Saville (Sav), yet another new signing, forming a terrific partnership up front. With John Gallacher (when he was fit) or Brian Honour on one wing, and a young Nicky Southall on the other, they created lots of chances which Andy and I lapped up. Dean Emerson completely controlled the midfield (he was far too good for that division, having played over 130 games for Coventry in the top division) and our defence was strong, with the two new marauding full backs ably marshalled by John 'Monty' McPhail.

Monty was a great lad. His best friend was the full-length mirror, but on the pitch he was brilliant. He also managed to play in the top division, with Sunderland, and although he was a big lad, and strong in the air, he was good on the ground as well. Alongside him was Mick Tait. Mick was one of the nicest men you could ever meet, but on the pitch he was one of what is now a dying breed of absolute hardmen. At under 6 feet tall, he wasn't exactly a giant, but he more than punched above his weight and was absolutely fearless. I used to marvel at some of his tackles while, at the same time, cringing in fear that the opponent might not get up afterwards. The high point of that season was beating Crystal Palace at home in the third round of the FA Cup.

Palace were in the top division and had made it to the Cup Final a couple of years earlier. It was always cold and windy playing at Victoria Park, but this was especially cold. The pitch was rock-hard and bobbly, and temperatures were falling sub-zero. It wouldn't have been played today, but in those days we thought nothing of it. Back then, whenever a southern team played up north, they would be labelled southern softies. Before the game, they were in the referee's office, claiming that the game should be postponed. And that was pretty much all the inspiration we needed.

We'd already thought that they wouldn't fancy it, a Premiership team playing hundreds of miles away in the freezing cold; we knew we stood a chance. We wired into them straight away, and they couldn't handle our aggression. The ball was bouncing and bobbing all over the place, and that's what they used as an excuse throughout the game. But the truth was, we were right: they didn't fancy it. You could see it in their eyes when they came out to look at the pitch before the game. Their cause was not helped when we noticed that Nigel Martyn, the first £1 million goalkeeper and at that time in the middle of winning over 20 England caps, came out wearing tracksuit bottoms. We had young Steve Jones, making only his third senior appearance, in our goal – wearing shorts! That said it all really about the mentality of the two teams (although I must admit, I did wear long sleeves).

Early on in the first half, goalkeeper Steve Jones (Jonah) was called into action, saving brilliantly from another

England player, Geoff Thomas. Apart from that, though, they barely created any chances. Palace had managed to finish third in the Premiership a couple of years earlier and boasted a host of household names such as Chris Coleman; another £1 million signing in Chris Armstrong (who was later sold for £4.5 million); and, among others, Eddie McGoldrick, who represented the Republic of Ireland and was a member of the 1994 World Cup squad. To us, though, they were only names, and in the second half we absolutely steamrollered them. Phil Gilchrist, another youngster, played at centre half with Monty and kept any threat of attack completely snuffed out. We peppered them with crosses. I remember missing an absolute sitter, a free header from about 8 yards out, and having another effort saved by Martyn. Sav had the ball in the net a few minutes later, which was ruled out for offside.

Palace were holding on and were desperate for the final whistle, but we were being roared on by 7,000 fans, who sounded more like 70,000. I had gone down in the box early on for what I thought was a certain penalty, but the game had already been brought back for an earlier foul. Just under 10 minutes to go and Palace were still complaining about the pitch. Then came the decisive moment, with eight minutes to go. I received a pass just outside the box and played a short pass to Nicky Southall, who had terrorised Richard Shaw all game. He took one touch, and as Shaw turned to try to challenge him, he went sprawling on the floor. Although he was only a youngster, Nick was canny; he knew when to go down and when to stay on his feet. Replays showed that Shaw had pushed Nick, but it was the lightest of touches. Nick didn't need a second invitation, and down he went. That much-acclaimed referee, Dermot Gallagher, pointed instantly to the spot. Sav stepped up and stuck it away. The Palace players hounded Gallagher when the final whistle went, and their season went from bad to worse. Prior to this game they had won six on the bounce in the Premiership, but they went on a terrible run after that game and ended up getting relegated. Like we said, southern softies!

We drew our next game away to Leyton Orient 0–0 before being dumped out of the Autoglass Trophy by Stockport, losing 1–0. Our next game was at home to Preston North End. Again, the conditions were horrendous, with high winds that ruined any chance of a decent football match. That was already unlikely due to the fact that Preston were managed by John Beck, famous for playing the long-ball game. A lot of our lads had their minds firmly on the next game, a fourth-round tie away to Sheffield United. The 0–0 scoreline didn't do justice to just how poor the game was, but we were still doing okay in the league.

I had the next week to look forward to. I met up with my old mate Franz Carr, who had left Nottingham Forest and joined Sheffield United. After a number of hamstring injuries, Franz didn't manage to fulfil his potential and was never quite the same player again. He had lost that explosive sprint but still had a very good career. Who knows what would have happened had he not suffered those injuries.

When he was 15 or 16, he seemed destined to gain a host of full international caps but, like I said, it just wasn't to be. It wasn't to be for us either, as we lost a close game

1–0. Without realising, we'd suddenly gone four games not only without a win, but also without scoring a goal. We also lost Dean Emerson, our midfield maestro, to a fractured cheekbone, and our form dipped alarmingly. Two or three games later, and we'd gone a number of matches without scoring a goal. It was all the local paper wrote about, and the dressing-room banter softened.

We were playing without confidence; sitting ducks, really. Seven games became ten games, and we dropped down the division like a stone. Me and Sav had scored over 20 goals between us up to that game against Crystal Palace, but without the heartbeat of the team, we weren't creating any chances, let alone missing any. We went another three games without scoring before playing Blackpool away. We went a goal behind and you could hear the groans from the few travelling Hartlepool supporters. With about a quarter of an hour to go, we got a penalty and that man Sav stepped up again to score our first goal in nearly two months.

I learned yet another lesson during that game against Blackpool. Playing at centre half for them was Gary Briggs – a seasoned pro, a little bit in the Mickey Tait mould, but with absolutely no culture whatsoever. I knew that senior pros didn't like young lads running past them in pre-season from my days back at Blackburn, but I didn't realise that you weren't allowed to run past them with the ball during a first-team game. I did this a couple of times early on in the game, and was greeted with some obscenity. Me being me, I gave him a bit back and just smirked. Big mistake! In the second half obviously I'd forgotten all about it. We had a corner and, as the ball was cleared, I started running to get back onside. That's when I felt it: the full force of Gary Briggs's elbow, right in my face. He just looked at me and smirked. Touché!

Anyway, we finally scored a goal and really hoped that would kick-start our season, but the chairman had spent big and expected us to get promoted. So, a week later, with the faintest chance of us still being able to make the play-offs, he decided to sack the manager, Alan Murray, and his assistant Eddie Kyle. Former Sunderland coach Viv Busby was appointed, along with his assistant, former Ipswich legend Eric Gates. Despite the new broom, we went another seven games before finally winning. It had been a long 19 games since our last win, and instead of looking to get promoted, we were faced with a realistic prospect of being relegated. We now had no chance of being promoted, and although my goals dried up, Sav continued to score. So the chairman decided to cash in on him and he was sold to Birmingham. We had lost our top goalscorer, and Dean Emerson was still out injured.

We had six games to save our season, and after winning one and losing three of the next four games, we finally secured safety by beating Brighton 2–0 at home. Our last game was played away at Exeter. Both teams were safe but we won the game 2–0 to at least finish the season on a bit of a high note, and look forward to starting the new season with optimism.

We came back in pre-season, raring to go. Viv Busby and Eric Gates had been great during the back end of last season, but Gates was about to show his true colours. Talk about 'little man syndrome'! Here was the angriest little person I'd ever met. Snarly, uncouth, and always trying to discredit some of the lads. I actually got on really well with him (I wonder why). He rubbed a lot of the players up the wrong way. Viv, on the other hand, was mild-mannered, eloquent, and altogether a much nicer person to be around.

Unbeknown to us, there were problems going on at board level that were about to have a lasting effect on the lads. It transpired that Gary Gibson had gambled and lost on us getting promotion the previous season. The expected windfall from the extra revenue had been spent, but some of the players were due signing-on fees. Now this was Hartlepool, so the wages were not astronomical, but we really relied on the money that we were due. So we started the season with a big cloud above us. We had Eric Gates slating half the team, and the other half due money from the chairman. Despite this, we started the season off okay. Three wins, two draws, and two defeats in the first seven league games, but we were knocked out of the League Cup at the first hurdle by Grimsby – another potential revenue stream gone down the pan.

John Gallacher had been the great white hope. But injuries prevented him from playing many games, and his attitude and mentality were questioned by Gates. He was accused of being a bottler and just in it for the money. His crime? To expect the money that he was due when he signed a contract. It wasn't his fault that he was injured, or that the club promised him money they didn't have. But Eric Gates and now the chairman were on his case.

Worse was to come, both on and off the pitch when, firstly, we started a run of 10 games without a win. Pitched in the middle of this was a small matter of the club not paying the players' wages. That's not technically true. The club did pay the wages, by cheque. We would all check our accounts to see if the money was in, and there it was. The only problem was, the club would then stop all the cheques being paid. A couple of the lads cottoned on to this after a week or so, and used to run to the bank and pay £10, I think it was, for express clearance. There were a couple of meetings where we discussed the idea of not playing for the club again until we were paid, but it was explained that if we did that then there'd be absolutely no revenue whatsoever, and absolutely no chance of getting any money. So, despite not being paid, we went out and tried to perform.

I remember a couple of occasions when we got paid out of the turnstile money. Can you believe it? Professional footballers waiting until the end of the game on a Tuesday night and going home with pockets full of change. I felt sorry for the supporters who had been promised so much and, in the end, it was their loyalty that saw us put food on the table. Some of us were really skint, myself included. I was recently married, had just bought a house, and didn't have enough money coming in to pay for a proper meal. To add to the problem, my then wife (I still shudder at the mere mention of her existence) was expecting our first child. I needed to get away, so tried to get my head down and hoped that another club would come in for me. I wasn't the only one thinking this.

The majority of the lads who had been signed by Alan Murray *that* season were on better wages than those who were originally there. And they all pretty much wanted to go. The club, however, had their own novel idea on how to save some money. They decided to ask any of us lads who were due signing-on fees if we were prepared to forfeit them. We couldn't believe it! They were seriously expecting us to give up our money because of their poor management? Like I said, John Gallacher felt the brunt of it. He was due the most money, but played the fewest number of games. The club tried to bully him into leaving, but he wasn't having any of it. They tried to bully him into playing but, again, he stood fast. By the time they tried to actually negotiate with him, they had really and truly pissed him off. He wasn't for accepting a penny less than what he was owed. And who could blame him? If they had tried to reason with him from the start he probably would have played ball. But after they'd tried to humiliate him, there was no way he was going to shift. John was about 6 stone when wet through, and still quite young, but he had a steely determination and he knew his rights. So the club had to think of another way, and this was to try to sell off as many assets as they could.

A couple of players had gone and Deano wanted to be the next one out the door. Although he was a great footballer, his injuries and his age (he was now over 30) meant that he was no longer a saleable asset. Add in the fact that the club were in the middle of a terrible run, and there was no way they were going to let him go for nothing. They essentially priced him out of a move, but he could see others going and he wasn't happy. Now, Dean was one of the funniest men I have ever met. He was a streetwise Mancunian with a wicked sense of humour. He used to have me and Ryan Cross in stitches. And he completely led Crossey astray when they were lodging together at a local B&B. He used to take this 19-year-old lad from Plymouth out drinking almost every night. How they managed to play, at times, amazed me. But he also had an edge to him; once he wanted something, he was going to get it one way or the other.

One night we were out in Sunderland. Viv Busby thought it was a good idea to let the lads let their hair down and take their minds off the goings-on at the club. He was a bit of a name in Sunderland, and we all waltzed into a nightclub without having to pay. He was getting approached by everyone, young or old, male or female. And he loved it. He was in his absolute glory. That's when Deano decided to strike. He started pestering, like he always did when he'd had a drink. He was starting to get lairy and abusive to some of the locals. To their credit, they could have given him a good hiding, but they knew that we were with Viv, so they did the decent thing and asked him to have a word with Deano. Deano just blanked him and turned his back. Like I said, Viv Busby was a nice guy, so he politely asked Deano to turn around so that he could speak to him. Again, Deano ignored him. At that point, Viv Busby put his hand on his shoulder to motion him to turn around. And right there in front of everyone, in a nightclub in Sunderland, Viv Busby's backyard, Deano turned round and punched him right in the face. Viv went sprawling to the ground and, unsurprisingly, Deano was marched out. It was unbelievable, although not so much for me because I knew what he was like.

That was the last we saw of Dean Emerson. It turned out that he knew another club had wanted to sign him, but they weren't prepared to pay any money for him. He had no axe to grind with Viv Busby, he just used him to get a move away. The next day, he signed for my home-town team, Preston North End, on a free transfer.

By now, the chairman was getting trigger-happy. The club was falling to bits and Viv Busby paid the price for it. He walked into a situation where he never stood a chance. He really was a decent guy, a terrific coach, but possibly too nice to be a manager. That should have been Eric Gates's job.

John McPhail was asked to step into the breach! You'd have thought that nobody would have wanted that poisoned chalice, but if you want to be a manager, I suppose you have to start somewhere. Monty had been one of the lads, right up until the day Viv Busby got sacked. The following morning, he called us all in for a quick chat. There was something different about him. Usually he was laughing and joking, or playing with his hair; this time, he had a very serious look about him, and his hands were behind his back.

'Look, lads,' he said, 'I might as well come straight out with it. Viv Busby has been sacked and the chairman has asked me to be the new manager. You don't have to call me gaffer straightaway, but I'll be picking the team from now on.'

I just burst out laughing. You don't have to call me gaffer straightaway? Are you for real, I thought. There was no way I was going to call him gaffer. No offence to John but, in my eyes, we had hit rock bottom.

On a personal level, things weren't much better. Me and the then wife (cue shudder) were practically imprisoned within the home. Billingham was a small town, and they didn't appreciate this black face walking around 'their manor'. The abuse I received was disgusting, but going into train and then play football every day kept things at bay for me. I could handle the abuse, although she found it a problem (understandably). Even without the financial issue, there was no way I would have wanted to bring up a child in that environment. We were desperate to get back to the North West and, fortunately for me, I was one of those saleable assets. I was promptly sold to Bury Football Club in December 1993. It was a dream move for me, a fresh start away from the madness, and I could live in Preston and commute. Thrown into the bargain was Ryan Cross, who originally signed on loan before making the move permanent.

CHAPTER 5

OUT OF THE FRYING PAN?

Crossey and I drove down to Bury to discuss terms. Ryan hated Eric Gates and couldn't wait to get out of the place. But as he was only on loan, there wasn't much for him to negotiate. Bury would be paying Ryan's wages for Hartlepool while getting the chance to take a good look at him. Hartlepool had another player off the wage bill so everyone was happy. My negotiations didn't last much longer. Again, there was no agent, just little old me wanting the best for my family. I had dropped down a division, yet again, but I knew that Hartlepool would probably get relegated in any case – that's if they survived the season. I would be quite a big fish, and would surely get a move back to where I felt I belonged. Wouldn't I?

The manager of Bury was former player Mike Walsh. A big towering centre half in his day, but quite a genial guy now. I quickly put pen to paper, although both he and the chairman, Terry Robinson, couldn't understand why both myself and Ryan were so particular about the money, and why we both wanted assurances that it would be getting paid when it was due. So we shook hands … and then it happened. Now remember, I hadn't phoned Bury Football Club and asked them to sign me. It was *they* who'd contacted Hartlepool and paid money to sign me based, I assumed, on what they had seen of me when I played against them. Another big mistake!

'So, Lennie! Where exactly do you play?'

I just looked at him, puzzled. 'Sorry?'

'Yeah, where do you play? Which position?' he said, as if to clarify. Obviously, I understood the question. I was just bewildered by it.

Okay, so we are obviously not on the same wavelength, I thought. I'd better go along with this, then.

'Well, I've played the majority upfront.' In my head I was thinking: this is weird, this guy has signed a player and doesn't even know where he plays!

It got better!

With a smug look he then said, 'Oh no, no, no! You got no chance of playing up front. Mark Carter plays there, the top scorer for the last three years.'

'Well, my last spell at Blackburn was played in centre midfield, and the last few games for Hartlepool, I played there as well.'

The smug look turned to a snigger.

'You got even less chance of playing in centre midfield. We've got the two best midfielders in the league – Ronnie Mauge and Tony Rigby.'

By now, I must have looked exasperated. 'Where *do* you want me to play, then?' I asked.

'Right! How about we try on you the left wing?' The English disease had struck again. I couldn't believe it! Why, oh why, oh why do we think black players can only play on the wing? To be fair to Walshie, Ronnie Mauge was black, and they also had a black left back.

This had started to have a familiar feel about it. Shades of PNE.

The first game was the following Saturday in front of the home crowd. The dressing room was more like that of Hartlepool than Blackburn. Mike Walsh shared great banter with the lads, and there was this large imposing figure, John King, who was assistant manager. He was great, a really funny guy who knew how to connect with the lads. Throughout all this, one of the most vocal was Mark Carter (Spike). He was one of a few Scousers at the club, who all bounced off one another. When it was time for the team talk, another Scouser, Cliff Roberts, who was chief scout at the time, went through all the set pieces of the opposition. The dressing room was quiet now, almost everybody listening intently. But in the corner, I couldn't help but notice that Spike was sitting, feet up, reading a newspaper. He did this throughout the whole team talk, only looking up when his name was mentioned.

I had always been quite health and fitness-conscious, and loved a good, thorough warm-up. I was given the Number 11 shirt (synonymous with the left wing position) but, despite this, I still couldn't wait to get out and play. I was one of the first on the pitch, and looked into the crowd. It was still early and there were only a few hundred people there, but they gave me a generous cheer, which I acknowledged. The rest of the lads started filtering out, and mainly did their own thing. Back then, there was no whole team warm-up. The players just went through their own routines, sometimes with a mate. Usually, the centre forward would warm the keeper up, but today was different. After about half an hour, we were called back into the dressing room to go through a final few points. Unbelievably, Spike was still in the same position as when I first went out, still reading the same newspaper. I asked him why he hadn't gone out for a warm-up.

'This *is* my warm-up,' he said, and carried on reading. Unbelievable!

And he's the centre forward, I thought to myself. Not only that, but he was also the captain!

Spike looked completely out of shape, was unshaven, and as far removed from a professional footballer as I thought I'd ever seen. When the whistle blew for us to go down the tunnel, he suddenly came to life, shouting all these encouraging words to his teammates. It was surreal. We got out on to the pitch and, without so much as a stretch, he started blasting balls at the keeper. Then he started placing a few; top corner, bottom corner, top right, top left, inside or outside of his foot. They were mainly left-footers, but he could use his right foot as well. Incredible. Absolutely incredible.

In the early part of my Blackburn career, I had a real eye for the goal, and also in *that* season at Hartlepool. I always considered myself to be a decent finisher, but looked up to the likes of Simon Garner. Not in the way that he prepared for the game, or in the way that he trained. But he was a terrific goalscorer, a really instinctive finisher. But this was different; I hadn't seen anything like it. This though, was just the warm-up. Time would tell whether he could put that into practice during the games. For me, at that time, the jury was still out.

The game came and went and, to be honest, I was pretty crap. We still had our house in Hartlepool, so I was driving up and down the motorway, a new baby was imminent, and I was shoved out on the left wing. Crossey had an absolute storm and they couldn't wait to sign him on a permanent deal, but I'm sure they wished it was me who they'd taken on loan.

That PNE déjà vu feeling of unprofessionalism slapped me right in the face when I later found out that some of the players were part-time, so had to train on Thursday evenings after work. Perhaps I hadn't reached rock bottom at Hartlepool, after all. This was another 'what the hell have I done?' moment. The travelling was starting to take its toll and, after a couple of weeks, both myself and Ryan Cross were out of the team. Wednesdays would be the day off and, for a few weeks, me and Crossey would make every excuse in the book to get out of Thursday evening training. How many times can one car breakdown on the way? Mike Walsh must've known what was going on but, if he did, he never said anything about it.

Mike Walsh had decided that I wasn't a left-winger after all – I could have told him that – and that was me out of the team. I would have to bide my time before I got another place in the starting eleven. To be honest, I didn't really mind. My daughter had just been born in Cleveland Hospital, and while I'd found a house to buy in Preston, contracts hadn't been exchanged yet, so I was happy to spend as much time up in Hartlepool as possible. I hated going training knowing that I wouldn't be playing, but having to turn up for the first-team games at home was the worst. At least for the away games I was never in the squad and didn't have to travel with the rest of the team. Credit to Mike Walsh for that, at least.

In those days, as I was more than aware, the dressing rooms could be brutal. While I suffered badly at the hands of first-team coach Ray Harford at Blackburn, it was usually the players who dished the dirt. Anybody with anything slightly different would be picked up on. Ginger hair, spots, a different accent … anything was fair game. And nobody was exempt! So I was puzzled when Ronnie Mauge started to speak with an uncontrollable stammer, and nobody said a word. I sat there and waited for the comments, but nothing came. Not a single word. If the truth be known, I would probably have been one of the first to start, had I been at the club a bit longer. I remember thinking: come on, then. Somebody say something! I couldn't understand how he could get away with it. I was about to find out, two or three weeks later.

I was now living in Preston, and had hooked up with Ian Stevens (Steevo) as a driving partner. I asked what the score was about Ronnie, and why nobody pulled him up about his stammer. He looked almost scared, as if he was being listened to and said, 'Ooooh! You don't mess with Ronnie, he's a psycho!' Now I wasn't exactly big, but Ronnie was shorter than I was – and about a stone lighter. Obviously Steevo was exaggerating, and I didn't give it much thought after that.

I had finally managed to get a game in the first team, away at Wycombe Wanderers. Wycombe were a very strong, physical side and I think Mike Walsh wanted to add a little bit of steel into the midfield, so I came in for Tony Rigby (Tigger) who was more of a flair player. They had a guy called Steve Brown playing directly against Ronnie. He was about 6ft 2in and around 15 stone of sheer muscle. The two of them were going at it, leaving nothing out there, for the whole of the first half. Ronnie, to his credit, never backed down, and never shirked a tackle. But at half-time he was raging. He hated the fact that Brown had actually managed to win a few tackles against him. I soon realised that Ronnie paid no attention to either his or anybody else's stature. Throughout the half-time break he couldn't sit still and, with that stammer of his, kept saying to himself, 'He's gonna get it, man, I'm telling you, he's gonna get it.'

He was still saying this as we ran out for the second half. And after about five minutes, the ball bounced between the two of them. You could see it coming; it was like watching a car crash about to happen. Both players went in two-footed. I think the ball was in there somewhere. Ronnie was the first to his feet and, as Brown lay on the ground, Ronnie just stamped on his chest. Then he bent over him and pointed a finger in his face, shouting, 'You c**t, you f***ing c**t! I'm gonna f***ing kill you!'

The ref couldn't get his red card out quick enough. Ronnie was still screaming when Brown stood up, towering over him. The ref managed to get in between them, but Ronnie refused to go off. I grabbed hold of him and tried to drag him off. He was screaming, 'I'll see you outside, you f***ing w**ker!' I'd never seen anyone lose it like that before. And all because this guy had dared to challenge him. Now I was beginning to realise why no one took the rip out of him. What an absolute lunatic!

I can't remember the score, but as we went into the dressing room after the game, he seemed to have calmed down. Well, compared to what he was like 45 minutes earlier. He was still in his kit, and I was waiting for Mike Walsh to give him an absolute blasting. But nothing was forthcoming. Not a word. The dressing room was deathly quiet until someone asked Ron if he was all right.

'Yeah, yeah, man. I'm fine!' We had a shower and went to get on the coach. I walked out just in front of Ronnie and, as I was about to step on the coach, I saw Steve Brown out of the corner of my eye. We just nodded to each other (a black man thing, apparently). He was on his way to the players' bar and had to pass our coach on the way. That's when Ronnie caught sight of him. He barged past me, uttered some obscenity and punched him square in the face. There was blood everywhere, and Ronnie went into screaming mode again, as though it was Brown's fault. I have known footballers in the past threaten to 'see you outside', but, normally, by the time they've had a shower, common sense has prevailed. But not this time; not Ronnie.

I have to say, I'm not scared of anything (apart from deep water), but I was a little bit wary of him after that. I was even more wary when I saw him laying into one of his teammates after they'd foolishly spoken to his ex-girlfriend. We had our own little dalliance a few weeks later when we were in the gym playing head-tennis. The gym was tiny, and Health and

Safety would have had a field day. There were cracks in the wall, bits of metal and screws coming out of it, and pieces of wood lying around. There were also these two large benches at the back of the court. There was an unwritten rule that if the ball was ever going towards any of these danger zones, you could leave the ball and simply replay the point. But for some reason, on this occasion, those rules didn't apply. Probably due to the fact that both of us were ridiculously competitive and didn't want to give an inch.

The gym was full of players looking on, in the hope there'd be a flare-up. They knew that neither of us would back down, and they loved the fact that someone had come to the club who wasn't scared of Ronnie. Me being me, I would deliberately try to get the ball going into one of those zones. Now, if the roles were reversed, he'd have done exactly the same thing. The difference is, I wouldn't have risked life and limb just to save a point. But Ronnie being Ronnie, he was never going to let the game go without a fight. So when I judged it absolutely perfectly, he dashed over and smashed his leg on the bench. Not for the first time in my life, I started wetting myself with laughter at a very inappropriate moment. Cue Ronnie's blood starting to boil.

The stammer was in full flow as he tried to say, 'What are you laughing at, man?' I was still laughing, and about to ask him why he didn't just leave it, when he turned round and bent over to pick up a bench. He was actually going to throw the bench at me! Only he'd chosen the wrong bench. One of the benches was like the ones that you get in a primary school – nice and light enough for the children to carry. The other one, however, was one of those old-type benches with iron legs, far too heavy for Ronnie to pick up. I could see his face straining as he tried to lift it and, again, that strange brain of mine made me think of Monty Burns from *The Simpsons*.

That was it for me; I was uncontrollable. Tears were streaming down my face as he kept trying to pick this bench up. He managed to get it a few inches off the floor but, realising that it was never going to happen, he dropped it and then flung himself towards me. I swear he was going to kill me. *Fight or flight, fight or flight? Find a way!* I instinctively stuck out my left arm and grabbed him by the throat, holding him at arm's length. I didn't say anything, or throw a punch; I just held him until I felt his resistance drop. I let him go. He muttered his favourite phrase ('you f***ing w**ker') and walked out of the gym.

As at the Wycombe game, the gym had fallen silent by now, most lads too scared to say anything, just in case. He never mentioned it again and, to be honest, for some reason we never really got on, after that. To be fair to him, though, when he heard about my diagnosis, he gave me a call to see if I was okay. He was later sold to Plymouth, and then Bristol Rovers. Our swords crossed only once more, when I was at Burnley. We were fairly pleasant to each other and, amazingly, the game started and finished without any flashpoints.

I played very few games in the early part of my Bury career. Mike Walsh had been true to his word and only ever played me in midfield when he had to. That was fair enough for me, I had no problem with it. I realised that I had no divine right to be in the team, even though I felt that I should have been, but, as footballers, we all think that, don't we? The 1993/94 season was drawing to an end, but I'd been wishing it away since about February.

On the home front, things were getting worse and the arrival of my daughter didn't help the situation. I was caught between the devil and the ditch. I hated being at home but dreaded going into work. I always hated not playing in the first team. There are some players who would quite happily pick up their wages while not turning out on a Saturday. But that was never good enough for me. I would become miserable and irritable. It was the same whenever I was injured. Later, Nadine would always say that I was a nightmare to live with (I think she meant when I was injured).

The worst thing was, and I'm not proud of this, I would be watching the team, hoping that they would lose. I knew that the only way I would get back in was if somebody got injured, or if there was a poor performance and they lost the match. I could never understand it when guys who were not in the team cheered when their team scored. I used to think: there's no way you're going to get a game now, is there? In particular, I would hope that the person in my position would have a nightmare. To my credit, I never once wanted a teammate to get injured (that's big of me, isn't it?) Although they weren't exactly setting the world alight, the team were doing sufficiently well (in Mike Walsh's eyes, anyway) to remain largely unchanged. The saving grace when the season ended was that I could spend more time with my brother Fran, and see my mum more often. She (the ex-wife) would go out regularly in the evenings. This suited me, as it meant that I could spend time with my daughter. But we were drifting further and further apart, to the point where I couldn't wait for pre-season to start. Anything just to have a reasonable excuse to get away from her.

When pre-season did eventually begin it was clear that, once again, I would be feeding off scraps in my quest to be part of the first team. I'd been at the club for over six months, and had made about 10 appearances. Now *I'd* hit rock bottom. The 1994/95 season followed the same pattern as the last. Only *this* time, armed with a few new signings (not great for me), the team performed pretty well. They were in and around the top 10 for most of the season, eventually getting a place in the play-offs. I was gutted! I knew that I wouldn't be involved, and it meant that the season would drag on for at least another two weeks. Just to rub a bit of salt in the wounds, our play-off semi-final was to be against Preston North End. I really wasn't sure who I wanted to win. Not even a disastrous performance would have meant me playing in the second leg, and the green-eyed monster in me played havoc with my sense of loyalty.

My mind was quickly made up when, watching from the stands at Deepdale, a group of Preston fans turned round and started abusing me. Apparently I was a traitor for living in Preston and daring to play for a team other than PNE. How the minds of some supporters work intrigues me. Not content with questioning my parentage (classy), those who were just about sober enough to speak started threatening me with violence. The best thing about it was that they knew which pubs I frequented, so they challenged me to meet them there (if I dared) on the promise that they'd smash my face in. Hmmm, tough decision! Cue laughter at inappropriate time, once again. I managed to keep it together just long enough to ask them if they were serious.

'So,' I said, 'you want me to meet you outside the pub, where you and your twenty mates will be waiting to smash my face in? What a great idea! I tell you what, give me your phone number, and I'll give you a call when I get there. I don't want to be waiting too long.'

It's at times like these that I really find myself amusing, and that was me off again. They were absolutely fuming. I had yet another déjà vu moment of somebody wanting to kill me. And while I had to give them credit for resilience and perseverance, they got absolutely nothing for intelligence. I was in the stand above them, yet they charged towards me and started jumping up as if that would somehow cause me to be miraculously drawn towards them. I then did what any other self-respecting coward would do. Safe in the presence of the stewards, I started chanting as loudly as I could for Bury. The look on their faces, and the anger in their eyes, really cheered me up. Strangely, though, I decided against going out that night.

Bury managed to safely negotiate the tie and were on the way to Wembley for the play-off final against Chesterfield. That meant another week of agony for me. This time, there was absolutely no question of my loyalty. Particularly after Mike Walsh pulled me to one side and said, 'You don't want to go to Wembley, do you?'

This, loosely translated meant, 'I'm not taking you to Wembley.' So, the biggest match in Bury Football Club's recent history, one in which everyone at the club should have been given the opportunity to be part of, and I was being told that I wasn't invited to the party. I was rooting for Chesterfield! Not only had Mike Walsh totally pissed me off, but I knew that if they gained promotion that would be my Bury career over. I had dropped down two divisions in two years, and feared for my footballing future. I'd split up from my then wife, which was a high point of the year, but this almost brought me crashing back down.

I didn't watch the final, but kept checking the score, fingers crossed for a Chesterfield goal. We ended up losing 2–0, and while I was happy with the result, I was gutted for the lads. In my heart of hearts, I knew that I'd have made a difference had I played, but there was no point in focusing on that. Despite the defeat, it was decided that there would be a civic reception.

Jesus! I thought. At what point in our existence did people start to celebrate a defeat? What the hell do they have to celebrate? They lost, for goodness' sake! There was no way I was going to be on that open-topped bus. I hated that sort of stuff anyway; I wouldn't have gone even if they'd won. How embarrassing would that have been for me, to be milking it in front of the fans for a defeat that I wasn't even invited to be part of? So, the reception went ahead without me. There were pictures of the lads drinking champagne and celebrating. What a joke! What an absolute joke!

So, the end of another wasted season. Fortunately, I had the turmoil of my marriage break-up to keep my mind occupied. Every cloud…

As ever, I spent the end of season break ensuring that I was in the best possible shape for pre-season. I'd begun seeing somebody else (as one door closes…) and had managed to get away for a couple of weeks in the sun. When I returned, the presence of a new girlfriend meant that the old wife well and truly lost the plot. She'd hoped that we would get back together, but all her hopes were extinguished now, and boy did she let me know it. And so began months of trying to gain access to see my daughter. The things people do out of love!

CHAPTER 6

PRE-SEASON 1995

There were a couple of new additions to the squad, one of them Shaun Reid, brother of Everton legend Peter Reid. Like his more esteemed brother, Shaun was a midfielder, and very experienced in this division. I'd played against him while he was at Rochdale and, to be honest, didn't really see him as a threat to my first-team chances. I came back, as ever, absolutely flying.

Running was never a problem to me, but I still took my fitness very seriously. I would always have about a week off after the season, and then pound the streets and get myself to the gym. My lack of first-team football meant that I still had plenty of gas left in the tank, so my two-week break didn't really have any adverse effects. In fact, I'd actually lost weight by the time I got back, although that was due to a bout of food poisoning.

I was one of the few pros who actually enjoyed the hard toil of pre-season. I loved the feeling of leaving other players in my wake, whether it was repeated sprints, hill running or longer distance stuff. My attitude was always: *bring it on!* Being at the front of all the running would put me in the manager's eye; it would give me a psychological edge; it would show what a great attitude I had. Bollocks! None of those things ever happened. The truth was, the manager pretty much had his idea of his starting eleven before pre-season training even started. Not just Mike Walsh, but most managers. Injuries or very poor form might force a change but, by and large, the first team was set in stone. But I'd put it in anyway, 100 per cent every time. It was the only way I knew.

In matches, whenever I played up front, I knew that I'd have enough energy to close defenders down for 90 minutes and have plenty left to do the running needed to get myself in the box. In midfield I knew that nobody would ever outrun me. I could keep making runs into the opposition box and still get back to make last-ditch tackles on the edge of my own box. Every time, no problem!

The club was now no longer a 'part-timer's club'. A couple of the players had been offered full-time contracts, one of those being Nick Dawes – another midfielder! The thing I instantly noticed about Nick was that he had great technique. I loved the way that he used to control the ball, shift it, and make a pass. I also loved the way that he very rarely ever passed it backwards. There are so many midfielders nowadays, and I'm talking about top professionals, who take the easy way out and play it back to their back four.

When I was just starting in the game, the coaches would always say, 'Play the way you're facing!' That was about the sum total of coaching back in the day. As time has moved on, midfielders are now coached to be on the half-turn, encouraging that forward pass. But time and time again, for fear of making a mistake, the safe pass is often the chosen option. As with Shaun Reid, despite Nick's obvious ability I still didn't see him blocking my path into the first team. He'd only just gone full-time, and had a bit of work to do to get to my level of fitness.

Once the running was over, it was time for the balls to come out. It was probably about two days before I realised that I would be out in the cold, yet again. Ronnie Mauge had been sold to Plymouth Argyle (apparently he wanted to be closer to London!), but Tony Rigby was still the apple of Mike Walsh's eye, and Ian Hughes – who represented Wales Under 21s as a defender – was putting his case forward to be a midfielder. So five into two didn't go, and I was easily number five. Number five became number four when Hughesy came back from international duty following a game against Moldova. He was playing as a right back and had the ball when their left-winger started closing him down.

Walshie was screaming at him to clear it, but Hughesy, being a ball-playing defender, decided to come inside to play it to a centre half. He played it straight to their centre forward, who took a touch and blasted it straight past our goalkeeper, Gary Kelly. The manager went absolutely mad, screaming and swearing at him. He still hadn't calmed down when the half-time whistle went. We all sat down and he really laid into Hughesy.

'Moldova? F***ing Moldova? Where do you think you are? You're at f***ing Bury now! Not Wales: Bury!'

He dragged him off and that was pretty much it for Hughesy as far as Mike Walsh was concerned.

I always loved it when one of the players was getting a bollocking. Not because they were getting a bollocking; it just amused me whenever a manager really lost it. In fact, it more than amused me, it used to make me piss myself with laughter. You can always guarantee that it would be the first thing the lads spoke about after the game. While it was going on, you'd see the lads putting their hands over their mouths, or turning their faces round. I'd always have my head down, my eyes streaming. It was never quite as funny when it was directed at me. I'd just answer back (the cardinal sin in the dressing room, apparently) or sit and smirk. Now that really wound the manager up. I'd love to say that I used to smirk on purpose, but I really couldn't help it. I remember Stan Ternent, when I was at Burnley, screaming at me to stop smirking after he'd given me a roasting. I protested my innocence, but he just became incandescent. Yet another time when I felt somebody wanted to kill me. About four of the lads came up to me afterwards and asked me why I didn't just stop smirking. I didn't even know I was doing it!

Hughesy's public flogging didn't make a difference to me. Even with him out of the picture, I still wasn't going to make the starting eleven. That had been made abundantly clear to me during the pre-season games, where I was, again, just a fringe player.

Sam Ellis, who I think had been long-time mates with Mike Walsh, had started to appear in the dressing room and at the training ground. He was out of work, I think, after leaving Manchester City, and was just keeping his hand in. I instantly warmed to Sam, who was a big character, loud and brash, but he really knew his football, and was full of good advice. He used to put his arm round me after training, pull me to one side and encourage me to keep doing what I was doing and soon my time would come. I was encouraged, but knew that I would most likely still be up in the stands.

The first game of the season was away to Northampton; I didn't even make the squad. The manager chose to go with Tony Rigby (of course) and Shaun Reid. So it was back to the TV to sporadically check the scores in the hope that we would get beaten. The result couldn't have gone any better as we were battered 4–1. Would this see a change in the team selection for the next game? Did this mean that I would finally be given a chance? I didn't exactly hold out much hope for the next game, away to Chesterfield in the first round of the League Cup, even though I was still training well. I shouldn't have been surprised when I was named in the starting line-up, and ordinarily I would have expected to play, but Walshie was so 'loyal' to *his* players that I wasn't really expecting it.

We managed to win 1–0, and I kept my place for the next game at home to Chester, with Tigger being named as sub. That was the point where I remembered Walsh's first words to me in his office. It may have taken the best part of two years, but I'd finally got a game in midfield, despite there being the best player in that position in the league in our team. (I'm nothing if not resilient.) We drew the game 1–1, which was followed by a 4–3 win away to Hereford United. I scored what I think was my first goal for the club, while Spike scored his first two league goals of the season;

one a penalty, and the other a right-footer after turning the centre half inside and out. He scored many, many more goals like that throughout my time at Bury. He was a top goalscorer who showed that, despite playing for a number of years at non-league level, he was more than capable of succeeding in the higher divisions.

Tigger still had to make do with a place on the bench, and a fitter, leaner Nick Dawes was beginning to push for a starting place. This came in the next game where we were partnered for the first time in a 0–0 draw, at home to Preston. I had now played four games in a row, a run that saw us win two and draw two. Next was a home game against bottom club Plymouth, who had lost four out of four, scoring only two goals and conceding eight. Despite my obvious influence (in my head anyway) in our four-match unbeaten run, Mike Walsh recalled Shaun Reid and Tony Rigby, with Nick being left on the bench and me consigned to the stands. I felt that he had been looking for an excuse to leave me out, and the draw against PNE was obviously enough for him. Furthermore, it was an absolute home banker, which I thought would give him the ammunition to keep me on the sidelines, and keep Shaun and Tigger in the team.

I watched from the stands and did a mini fist pump when Shaun Reid missed an easy chance from about 6 yards. It was to get better (for me, anyway) when, against the odds, Plymouth took the lead. A score of 1–0 soon became 2–0 and the crowd started to become restless. Things weren't made any easier by the fact that Ronnie Mauge, on his return to Gigg Lane, supplied the cross for the goal. Right on the stroke of half-time, Plymouth made it three and we (they) went off to a chorus of boos. I'd never seen the Bury crowd like that – I know that football fans can be very fickle, but this team had come home to a hero's welcome only a few months earlier, and though we hadn't set the world alight this season, it hadn't exactly been a disaster. I was a bit surprised by the reaction, to be honest. I thought it was harsh on the lads, but in the second half, things got even worse. Ian Hughes was sent off, which was soon followed by a fourth and then a fifth goal.

By now, the crowd were in the throes of directing their anger at the manager. Chants of 'Walsh out!' gathered steam remarkably quickly, which seemed, even to me, somewhat unfair. After the previous season, this seemed a tad premature. I'd been at clubs before where the crowd were baying for the manager's blood – twice at Blackburn Rovers under Bobby Saxton and Don Mackay, and at Hartlepool. And although I'd never really seen the point in supporters giving out negativity on the terraces, at least on those occasions they were following particularly bad runs. This time round we had only played five league games, and granted we had only returned five points, but there was plenty of time left to right the wrongs.

We knew there was an expectation of promotion, especially after getting so close last time round, and Mike Walsh looked a worried man in the changing room afterwards. There wasn't much said about the game. I think everybody felt a bit numb. Not even the lads who had been in the stands seemed to get any pleasure out of it, myself included. I still knew, though, that this had to improve my chances of getting back in the team. These chances were enhanced further when I heard the shock news that the chairman had decided to sack Mike Walsh. I liked Mike Walsh, I really did. Clearly, I didn't agree with his team selections, but I never thought that it was personal. I did, though, think that, like Les Chapman at Preston, he was too close to the players and found it difficult to leave out some of his 'boys'.

I've never been a manager of a professional football club, but I guess that you need to have a sense of detachment in your relationship with the players. It's slightly different for the assistant, who can play good cop, but, at the end of it all, the manager lives or dies by his decisions, his team selections and, ultimately, the results. There really isn't any room for sentiment, and *that*, in the end, is what I think got him the sack. The chairman had expected us to gain automatic promotion, and five points from five games wasn't the flying start he'd hoped for, but it still seemed harsh. Perhaps things had gone on behind the scenes, or perhaps he'd seen something in Mike Walsh that nobody else had (except for me, of course). In any case, football is a selfish game, and from a professional perspective I wasn't sad to see him leave. It's funny how some managers see things in a player that others don't, whether that's good or bad, and for some reason Mike Walsh just didn't take to me. Not to worry, I'd have the last laugh.

CHAPTER 7

THE GLORY YEARS

The new brush swept in very swiftly as Stan Ternent and Sam Ellis were installed as the new manager and assistant of Bury Football Club. Michael Jackson (Jacko) couldn't resist having a dig at Sam, who he accused of plotting Walsh's downfall with his recent visits. That was Jacko all over. Always taking the rip out of people, but always with a smile on his face and always good-natured. He was a good footballer to go with it, a tough-tackling centre half who pitched in with more than his fair share of goals over his career. Jacko was sold to Preston the following season, after struggling to get in the team. I always thought we should have kept him, but with Chris Lucketti and Paul Butler (Butts) at the club, it was going to be difficult, and I fully understood his reasons for going. Preston had enquired for me at the same time, but Stan clearly saw something in me that Mike Walsh never did, and refused to let me go.

At the end of the season they made another approach, this time a tad more covert. I received a phone call one

Saturday morning asking if I'd be interested in signing. I'd been there once before when the club was a little bit like The Dog and Duck. But things were different now. They were really growing as a club, had a much bigger fan base than Bury, and were offering a lot more money. Ever since I was very young, I was never motivated by money. I saw, and still see, money as a means to an end. Growing up as we did, I don't think I had much choice, but I never really wanted things that everybody else (it seemed) could afford. I did, however, always feel that I knew my worth, and didn't think I was getting paid what I was worth at Bury. I was, though, very happy at Bury. I loved the atmosphere in the dressing room. I loved the fact that we never knew when we were beaten. I loved the fact that, regardless of the opposition, we always thought we stood a chance of winning the game. And I loved how we all had each other's backs. That was the most important thing: the trust, the bond that we had for one another. This was something that I hadn't experienced at Blackburn Rovers. This was more typical of what I felt at Hartlepool United.

Maybe it's a small-club mentality, although I remember reading how Alex Ferguson (I'm sorry, but I don't subscribe to all this 'Sir' nonsense) and José Mourinho created the same sort of mentality at their esteemed clubs. Despite all this, I was still tempted, very tempted. I felt wanted by a club, a bigger club, that I thought was going places. I would be playing in front of a bigger crowd every week, and the longer term prospects of the club were definitely better. Why couldn't I have experienced the same atmosphere as I did at Bury and Hartlepool? Strangely, the only doubt that I had in my mind was the fact that I actually lived in Preston. I would have to go on a night out somewhere else! I had played at three clubs by this point, but I'd never had the desire to go out socialising in the town or city where I played. I always managed to have a great rapport with the supporters at whichever club I played, but I also managed to separate football from home life, and once the game had ended, I would switch into home-life mode. And after a game, particularly after a victory, that would generally mean me organising a night out with close friends or family. I loved my nights out, and would often bump into football supporters. And I'd be more than happy to spend as long as they wished discussing how crap I was (usually).

There were times when this went on a little bit too long, especially if I was out with Nadine (who has absolutely no interest in football whatsoever), but generally it was okay. But I never, ever courted it. I didn't go into football for attention, or to be in the spotlight. Now, I'm aware that I could, and still can, handle being in the spotlight or getting attention, but I would never willingly look for it, or go somewhere it's likely to be thrust upon me. So signing for Preston would have given me a bit of a dilemma.

Despite its city status, Preston has always been a town to me; a friendly, multicultural place to live. In the end, there was no decision to make. The manager at the time got the sack, and that was that. No formal offer was made. I can honestly say that I haven't regretted it once. I don't believe that things happen for a reason, I just believe that things happen – and you have to deal with it one way or another. And I chose to deal with that situation by just continuing to do what I had always done at Bury Football Club and any other football club. And that was to work hard, give 100 per cent (why do people insist on saying that they are going to give 150 per cent?), and accept that what will be will be. That mantra has stood me well so far in life and, I believe, will continue to do so.

Stan's first game in charge was the return leg against Chesterfield in the League Cup. A 2–1 victory saw us advance to the next round, where we were drawn against Championship side Sheffield United. But before that tie, there were league games against Wigan, Lincoln City and Cambridge United. The game against Lincoln City was the first time I came across a right-winger by the name of Dean West. I have to admit, though, that I didn't really take much notice of him, but he must have done okay as we signed him a few weeks later. That was when our friendship began. We instantly connected, although he was a few years younger than me. The control freak in me meant that I did always look on him as a bit of a younger brother, making sure he washed his hands when he went to the toilet (unlike most footballers I have come across, I have extremely high standards when it comes to hygiene), ensuring that he never got into any trouble when we were on a night out (which was fairly frequent), and generally looking after him.

The truth is, we looked after each other and we became close friends very quickly. We were teammates, roommates, we share the same wedding anniversary, we went on golfing holidays abroad together, we stopped at each other's houses after nights out, we even became landlords together (and discovered just how disgusting students really are). Westy was the first person I told after I was diagnosed with MND. And it was at that point the role reversal started. I was now the younger sibling, and he was going to do anything and everything he could to make sure that I was okay. In truth, he was never *just* a teammate. He was always a mate, a true friend and, although I didn't need reminding or showing, the last two and half years have shown just how important true friends are, and what they are willing to do for the cause.

Time to change the subject, I think. I don't want tears on my laptop!

The three matches before the Sheffield United game yielded one win, one defeat (my first defeat of the season) and a draw, so we were 11 points from 7 games; hardly earth-shattering, but we still fancied our chances. We lost the first leg 2–1. But worse than the defeat, for me anyway, was a hamstring tear that kept me out for about eight weeks. I clearly remember sprinting for a ball before feeling a sharp pain in the back of my leg, which felt as though I'd been shot. I knew what I'd done, and I knew it was serious. I am the world's worst watcher of football matches. Apparently, I would sulk and strop and generally be a nightmare to be around, so I really wasn't looking forward to the next few weeks. To make matters worse, injured players had to be in early, which meant me trawling through peak-time traffic, doing my injured leg no good at all. I always felt that this was some form of punishment. It didn't just happen at Bury, it happened at every club I played at. It was as though the manager was saying, 'That'll teach you to get injured.'

My brother Fran talks about something that he calls 'football logic'. This is where strange or irrational things happen in football and no one bats an eyelid. Things such as berating your own players as a supporter, or shouting at the TV when you're watching. Or the manager chastising his player like a naughty child and then expecting him to go out and perform. Or booing! That's my personal favourite. Grown-ups actually shouting an elongated 'boo'. Really? Just how old are you? I have never understood booing, or chanting, for that matter. The best thing is, some supporters think it's fine to berate a player for 90 minutes, yet at the hint of the slightest retort, they start screaming blue murder and get terribly offended. Apparently, this is okay as 'we've paid our money.' Or, even better, 'we pay your wages!' Football logic! And what about leaving the game with 15 minutes to go? Football logic! Here's another one: not celebrating when you score a goal against one of your former teams. Football logic! Oh, and one more: a player from Team A commits a foul and injures a player from Team B. What does football logic do? It allows us to decide that it's okay to force the injured player to go off for treatment, meaning that the team whose player committed the foul and injured the other player now has a numerical advantage. Football logic? You can keep it!

Football logic deemed that I had to travel in every day at a ridiculous hour, just to sit around for about an hour before getting any treatment. You can imagine how that sat with a man of such principles as mine. By about week three, being injured was driving me insane. By week five, I was so desperate to play that I insisted I was fine. I was held back for another week and then made a comeback in a reserve game at home to Wigan. The plan was for me to play just the first half and then come off. I came through the first half comfortably, and felt good. The manager then decided that, despite it being my first game for over a month, and despite the fact that it was a bitterly cold night, I was to continue in the second half. You know what's coming; about five minutes into the second half I felt my hamstring go again. Football logic had played its part, yet again. This was where, certainly when I played anyway, the manager always had the final say on an injured player. Not the medically trained physio whose job it was to assess, treat, and ultimately decide whether a player would be fit enough to play a game. No, that would make too much sense. And nobody, nobody ever questioned it!

So I was out for another two weeks, only this time, after giving the physio a bollocking for letting me come back too soon (!) the manager said I was not to come back until I was 100 per cent fit. Brilliant!

In the two games that we played after I was injured, we managed a 0–0 draw at Barnet, and got hammered 3–0 away to Gillingham. In the five league games that we'd played since Stan had taken over, we'd managed to get five points from five games. Mike Walsh had been sacked for a similar run, and we had the difficult second leg against Sheffield United to come, where we were already trailing from the first leg. I watched from the stands (this time hoping for a win) as an inspired Tony Rigby starred as we won 4–2 on the night, going through 5–4 on aggregate. Any thoughts that this would signal a resurgence in results were quashed when, after picking up four points from the next two games, we suffered a humiliating 4–0 defeat in the Auto Windscreen

Shield against Scunthorpe United, before a 2–0 home defeat to Scarborough.

I have to admit that being injured for the Auto Windscreen game was a real bonus. I always hated that competition, in whatever guise. This particular year, you were put into groups of three teams, divided into the northern and southern sections. There was very little fan interest in the early rounds, and even less player interest. My take on it was that it was an extra two games that we had to play, which were just a hindrance. I never ever gave less than 100 per cent on the pitch, but I was honestly never concerned if the result went against us. They eventually changed it to a knockout format in the first round, and I remember playing in one such game away at Wigan (again!) where I actually had a conversation with one of the opposition players when we were both hoping that the other team would score.

Seven points from the next three league games saw us climb up the league, and get a bit of confidence before our League Cup trip away to Reading. Although we lost 2–1, we put in a good performance, and there was a bit of a buzz about the place. The next game should have been a relatively easy home tie in the FA Cup first round, against non-league Blyth Spartans. They were three divisions below us, were missing their top goalscorer, and a couple of their key players were said to have worked a night shift before being driven in the manager's car to the game. There's a lot to be said, though, for effort, endeavour, organisation, and a little bit of luck. And on the day, the part-timers of Blyth had all of those in abundance. We lost the game 2–0, and while we went off to a chorus of boos, the Bury fans stayed and applauded the efforts of Blyth Spartans. Again, although I hated being injured, it was a good game to miss.

Likewise, the last round-robin Auto Windscreen game against Wigan. A 0–0 draw meant that we finished bottom of our group, and thankfully didn't progress on to the knockout stages. With that out of the way, I returned for the next league game – a 1–0 win away at Cardiff. Two more victories and two draws saw us end the year on a high note. Taking away the Cup games, we'd gone eight games without defeat and had picked up 18 points during that spell. We were climbing up the table and, for the first time, looked as though we could mount a challenge for promotion. We knew it would be difficult, but we certainly had the play-offs, at least, in our sights.

We lost the first game of the New Year, but went on a run which included more victories and draws than defeats. We continued our assault up the league, and Nick Dawes and I had begun to forge a great partnership in midfield. Nick had become the player that I thought he would be, and we complemented each other perfectly. We also became great mates off the pitch, along with Rob Matthews, who we signed from York. Rob's debut was away at Chester City, a 1–1 draw, where he gave us a glimpse of his ability when he scored a great goal to equalise late in the second half. It was a game that I remember vividly, as I was sent off early in the first half for two yellow cards. The upside was that I had a great view of Rob's goal, sitting up in the stands.

Our great form continued, and a run which included a 7–1 thrashing of Westy's old club, Lincoln City, meant that with three games to go, our fate was in our own hands.

We were in the third automatic promotion place. Our next game was away to Darlington, who we were now four points ahead of after they'd drawn away to Wigan, while we had beaten Scunthorpe United 2–1. Darlington were having a great season, and their team included players such as Robbie Blake and a certain Sean Gregan, both of whom had great careers and played in the top division. It was the first time that I'd played against Gregan, and although he played centre half, he completely bossed the game. He was getting the ball off the keeper, dribbling past forwards, making runs into midfield, and feeding the forwards and wingers.

Robbie Blake was equally impressive, and we got absolutely spanked, 4–0. We were all gutted, but with two games to go we were still one point ahead of Darlington. We were away to Exeter City, who had no chance of being either promoted or relegated. It was an away banker, or would have been had our goalkeeper that day, Lee Bracey (Brace), not dropped a clanger with us leading 1–0. At any other stage of the season, a 1–1 draw away to Exeter might have been acceptable, but in the penultimate game when you needed to win both games to ensure you got promotion, it was never going to be enough.

In the dressing room afterwards we tried to stay positive. I remember somebody saying something like, 'Okay, okay, lads. We don't know how Darlington have done yet, do we?' Stan was always pretty much on the edge, but for some reason he was surprisingly serene. We were all expecting him to blow up, especially Brace who'd always been a bit of a whipping boy. But nothing, absolutely nothing. Just at that point, Sam shuffled past him and whispered, 'Darlington have won, gaffer!' And then it came! He absolutely laid into Brace, really slaughtering him. It brought me back to when Mike Walsh was having a go at Ian Hughes, but that was nothing compared to this. I'd seen him give rollickings before, but this was the master of them all. And Sam's timing … he couldn't have planned it any better. It was perfect! It was almost as though he was waiting for somebody to make the Darlington comment. Once more, football logic meant that nobody spoke a word in defence of Brace. It was just another of those things that were accepted in the game. I was trying not to chuckle (of course). But most of the lads were just sitting there with their heads down, hoping that he wouldn't turn his anger on to them.

We went into the final game of the season knowing that we had to win at home against Cardiff City and hoping that Darlington failed to beat Scunthorpe, otherwise we would be in the play-offs. I remember talking to Gary Kelly on the way into training the following week; neither of us felt that we would get promoted if we ended up in the play-offs. But it was out of our hands; we just had to win and hope for the best.

The week leading up to the game was the longest of my life (if I erase from my memory the time living with the ex-wife). Nothing really prevents me from sleeping, but this particular week, it probably took me an extra 10 minutes to fall asleep! As we got closer and closer to the game, for some reason I became more and more confident that things would turn out okay for us. Stan, who still likes to be referred to as 'gaffer', and Sam ensured that training was light-hearted and fun, and tried to take our minds off the game, but we all just wanted to get to Saturday.

On the morning of the game, I went through my usual routine of up early for a light breakfast, shower, change, beans on toast for a pre-match meal, and then in the car to meet up with Dave Lancaster (Lancs). Gary Kelly used to travel in on his own on match days if we were at home, which was just one of those funny habits he used to have. The dressing room was absolutely buzzing before the game; not a sign of nerves. It was as though we all expected to win; I certainly did, anyway.

As expected, there a great atmosphere inside the ground, almost like a carnival atmosphere. Again, I went through my usual routine. I was always the first out on the pitch, doing my own warm-up. This would start off as a number of slow, long strides across the width of the pitch. Next would be an increase in pace, again across the width of the pitch. My runs would then become shorter and faster until, by the time I'd finished, I'd be almost at full speed. It would then be back into the dressing room, shin pads on, listen to the manager give a quick chat about the opposition, get my instructions on who I was to mark at set pieces, but mainly it was a time for me to get in the zone before going back out again, as part of the team this time, for a final warm-up. Not sure exactly how Stan and Sam were feeling, but on the outside they were very calm and measured. I'm sure deep down they were feeling the pressure, particularly taking into consideration Stan's outburst the previous week, but they definitely kept it together. Great management!

Out on the pitch ready for kick-off, I got the same feeling that I'd got when at Hartlepool; Crystal Palace were beaten before they started in that game, and I felt that Cardiff felt the same. Surprisingly (or perhaps not) I don't remember too much about the game, apart from the fact that my quick throwing to, I think, Nick Dawes led to our opening goal. From then on in, it was easy for us. There were no scares, no threats to our goal, nothing! We won at an absolute canter. We now had to wait for the Darlington result. We hadn't been told the score at half-time, but as our full-time whistle went, there was a bit of a hush on the terraces. Gradually, though, the hush became a buzz which, in turn, progressed to some of the fans singing and chanting. Within a few minutes, there was euphoria. I didn't know the score, but I knew that we'd done it – or, rather, Scunthorpe had helped us to do it. About a minute later, the euphoria died and the ground fell silent again. The Darlington game hadn't finished; the euphoria was because Scunthorpe had scored to make it 3–2 with a couple of minutes to go, but a minute later Darlington equalised. Jesus! It was so tense. After what seemed like an eternity, the crowd started cheering. Actually, the crowd went wild. This time, we knew that we had been promoted. The scenes were incredible. On a personal level, I felt vindicated with the thoughts I'd had about the team being better when I was in it. I also felt vindicated over feeling glad that Mike Walsh had got the sack. Nothing personal, just like I didn't think it was personal when he didn't play me as often as I thought he should.

Obviously, now I was going to celebrate with the lads long into the night, right? Wrong! I did what I always did. I went home, got a taxi into Preston with a couple of close mates, got drunk, staggered around a nightclub, complained about the rubbish music and the price of alcohol, and then staggered again, this time to get a pizza from a very dodgy-looking eatery which had an even more dodgy-looking animal's leg spinning in the window. Then it was queue-up time for a taxi, where I would invariably slate the taxi driver for going too fast/too slow/going over bumps/going the wrong way/not dropping me off where I'd asked him to… Anything really! I really don't know why they do it. Give me credit, though, I always used to tip well. Shades of Howard Gayle, circa 1986.

Darlington, for the record, lost in the play-off final against Plymouth. Plymouth, who had started the season so wretchedly before spanking us 5–0, stuck with their manager and ended the season in fourth place, one place behind us. I'm sure Mike Walsh wonders sometimes whether, if he'd been afforded the same level of patience, he'd have got the same result.

CHAPTER 8

LIGHTNING DOESN'T STRIKE TWICE

Pre-season couldn't start soon enough for me. After a couple of weeks away, I was back to pounding the streets and hitting the weights at the gym. This would be Stan and Sam's first pre-season, so I wasn't exactly sure what to expect. Apart from the usual running for running's sake, which I didn't really mind. I remember Gary Kelly's contract being up, and his certainty that they would offer him a new contract. He was right, but it was far less than he'd expected. He was going to hold out for more, safe in the knowledge that he was the first choice goalkeeper, and that there was no way they would let him leave. Wrong! Stan had secured promotion and, save for a couple of meltdowns, had been pretty chilled throughout. He was now about to show his hand. It later became blindingly obvious that Stan was not the sort of guy who liked to be messed about. It was either *his* way or no way at all, so when Kel walked in on that first day of pre-season and saw another goalkeeper sitting in the dressing room, his face dropped. In Stan's eyes, he'd offered Kel a contract which he'd refused to sign. No problem. He needed a keeper so he just went out and bought one. Not just any keeper, though: Dean Kiely – a very confident Manc who slotted in straightaway. He reminded me a bit of that other Mancunian, Dean Emerson; unbelievably witty, intelligent, but a very sharp tongue. Anybody was fair game, although I always seemed to get away with it (to my face, at least).

Dean Kiely is the best goalkeeper I have ever played with. He was only just 6 feet tall but unbelievably agile. I knew how good he was from his first training session; it came as no surprise to me when Bury sold him a few years later for £1 million, having signed him for about £125,000. Now, that's how you run a football club! Back in those days ('here he goes again,' I hear you saying), some football clubs would be aware of their revenue, and cut their cloth accordingly. Bury were one such club. They even had part-timers, for goodness' sake! The players were not on massive money; some of them were coming towards the twilight of their careers, while others were just starting out. A few of them had been plucked from lower league clubs and were nurtured and improved before being sold on for a healthy profit. That was the business model that kept teams like Bury Football Club afloat. Expectations were high, but not unrealistically so. And you couldn't get away from the fact that, at the end of each season, the books had to balance.

Fast forward 20 years and mismanagement at the highest level has seen Bury Football Club expunged from English football. A lot of mud has been thrown, and I was at an event recently where former employees of Bury really laid into members of the English Football League (EFL). Now, there is absolutely no doubt in my mind that the EFL played their part in Bury's demise, but surely some of the blame must be apportioned to whoever thought it was a great idea to hand players in the third tier three-year contracts, and wages far in excess of anything that had been paid at Bury Football Club before. There is absolutely nothing wrong with having aspirations, but which dream were they chasing? The Premiership? The Championship? There is no way a club such as Bury – surrounded by Manchester United, Manchester City, Oldham Athletic, Rochdale, Bolton Wanderers, and neighbours to many more – would ever be able to afford to pay those wages with a fan base of around 3,500–4,000. As far as I am concerned, that's when and why the downward spiral began.

Dean Kiely was now the undisputed number one, and before too long Gary Kelly had signed for Oldham Athletic. As I said earlier, there is no room for sentiment when you're a manager. Mike Walsh would have pandered to Kel and given him what he wanted, but not Stan. No way! That was not his style. I was about to find that out very early on in the season.

Pre-season had seen a number of new faces appear. As well as Dean Kiely, Paul Butler was signed from Rochdale, Gordon Armstrong (Stretch) from Sunderland, and Ronnie Jepson (Jeppo) from Huddersfield. The manager had added experience and hunger to an already successful squad. For some of the players who were already there, it was a step up in quality. For others, particularly some of the younger players, it was part of their progression towards playing regularly at a higher level. One such player was David Johnson, who Mike Walsh had signed the pre-season before. As he told us on numerous occasions, Jonno had been at Man United as a trainee.

My first thoughts of Jonno were similar to those I had when I saw Spike Carter for the first time: there is no way this guy can play football. He was about 5ft 5in and, in my opinion, very much overweight. He won't be able to run, was my view. And I was right! In all the running sessions he really struggled, and was at the back for every single time. What the hell had we signed? Then the balls came out. Now, I wasn't lightning quick, but I was always quick enough to stick with the forward when chasing back. I used to preserve my energy, and only slipped through the gears when I needed to. So that particular afternoon when Jonno fronted me up to knock the ball past me and run, I did what I always did – started off slowly at first, knowing that I would be able to speed up at will to get the ball. The lesson here was not to judge a book by its cover. He had been absolutely shocking in all the running, but this was different. This time there was a ball involved. He absolutely left me for dead! This short, fat kid with dodgy hair totally embarrassed me. He probably doesn't even remember it, but I'll never forget. He was so sharp over 10 yards it was frightening. The boy could definitely play. And he knew it! In fact, we all knew it because he told us so often. He was about 20 when he signed, maybe a couple of years younger than I was when Ray Harford bullied me out of Blackburn. But this 'kid' had so much front, there was no way he was going to be bullied by anybody. I always remember Jeppo calling him a 'cocky little shit'. To be fair, he wasn't the only one. But, as I say, he really could play and, this season, he was about to come of age.

When the new season was finally upon us I was, as expected, selected to start for the first game. I'd been an integral part of our promotion, I'd played in all the pre-season games, and knew that my place was secure. The first game was at home to Brentford. I played on the left-hand side of three in midfield, not my favourite position (it seemed too much like left wing to me). After about half an hour – I think we were a goal down – I saw my number coming up from the bench. Is that a joke? There's no way he's taking me off in the first half. I couldn't believe it; the first game of the season and I'm being dragged off and it's not even half-time. Not happy doesn't begin to describe it. I was fuming, absolutely fuming. What the hell? We ended up drawing the game 1–1, not a bad start for the newly promoted team, but I was gutted. Not because we managed to get a point, but because I hadn't played a part in it. There I go again: selfish! I also thought about the likelihood of me playing in the next game. Selfish!

David Pugh, who we'd signed from Chester the previous season, had replaced me in that first game. I had a lot of time for him, and the truth was that he was better suited to playing in that position than me. He was naturally a winger, and was so fit that he could get back and help in defence one minute, before putting crosses in the opposition box the next.

The next game was away to Notts County in the League Cup. As expected, I wasn't in the starting eleven. The manager, quite rightly, played the team that had done so well to get back into the game against Brentford, and that did not include me. As ever, I overthought my situation. It would be weeks, months before I got back in the team. I didn't have to wait that long. In the first half, Pughie went up for a header and landed awkwardly on his arm. He was writhing in agony. He'd dislocated his elbow, a really nasty injury which ultimately cost him his Bury career. I was on in his place, but I really didn't want to get back into the team like this. We drew the game, but all thoughts were with David Pugh.

Our second league game was away to Chesterfield, a game which we won 2–1. We were still just dipping our toes in the water, not sure what to expect from this division. Yes, we'd strengthened the team in the summer, but had no real expectations. Winning the next four games changed all that. We knew that we could more than compete in this division, a point that was made to us by the manager. I remember him telling us that we'd nothing to fear, and that we were a match for anyone on our day.

The players who were signed in the summer didn't just improve the team – they improved the dressing room. There were some great characters in that dressing room, and they came to the fore every Friday morning during the weekly 'court case'. Throughout the week, we (the players and coaching staff) would spy on each other and make a mental note of any misdemeanours that occurred. For example, you had to wear flip-flops (or *sliders*, as I believe they're now called) in the shower. Anyone caught not wearing them would be fined £2. There were other things fines were issued for, such as turning up late for training, using your mobile phone in the dressing room, wearing the wrong training kit, and wearing dirty boots.

Throughout the season, this list was added to by such things as having a stupid haircut or wearing crap clothes (thanks, Stretch). And it became a mission to stitch up as many people as possible. We'd get the women from the office to call somebody's phone during the meeting, or we'd hide somebody's flip-flops. I'd try to take it as far as possible by going into the manager's office to steal his towel, or to plant something incriminating. It was all really juvenile stuff, but it was brilliant. Everybody loved it, and it really helped us bond. As our team progressed, other teams and some pundits criticised Sam and Stan for our playing style. We were 'long-ball' or 'bullyboys'. What they should have been doing was heaping praise on them for building a cohesiveness, a group of men who looked after each other, both on the field and off it. As a group, we had a 'never say die' attitude and, yes, we could definitely all look after ourselves, but there were also some very good footballers at the club. Dean Kiely went on to represent his country, Dave Johnson and Chris Lucketti were sold for a lot of money, and Paul Butler played in the Premiership. And while Stan didn't necessarily sign all of the lads in that team, he put us all together and created an atmosphere that I hadn't experienced before, and haven't since.

Our five-game winning run ended with the 2–0 defeat away at Crewe. That was the first in a six-match winless streak, which included being dumped out of the League Cup and picking up only two points from a possible twelve. We were still sitting very pretty in the league, although we'd lost a bit of momentum. Six wins and three draws from the next ten league games soon cleared away any doubts that may have been appearing. We were absolutely flying, and by the turn of the year we were within touching distance of automatic promotion. The run had seen us beat Preston 3–0 at home, and once again I braved the friendly locals on the night out that followed. I always got great satisfaction from beating Preston, and this one was made even sweeter after I scored the first goal against Bobby Mimms, an old teammate from my Blackburn days. Gigg Lane was dubbed 'Fortress Gigg' after we lost only three games at home throughout the whole of 1996, none of which came that season.

Five defeats in the next ten games hampered our progress, and one of those games allowed Preston fans to get their own back after we were hammered 3–1. At least we had the consolation of being knocked out of the Auto Windscreen Shield during that run.

On 25 March, just before we were getting on the coach for the game away at Notts County, the manager pulled me to one side and said he needed to have a quick word with me. Preston had tabled bids for both myself and Michael Jackson.

'We're letting Jacko go, but you're going nowhere. Okay, get on the coach. We've got a game to win!'

And that was it… It was never mentioned again. I'm really not sure what the thinking was behind telling me a couple of hours before a game; perhaps it was just Stan playing his weird mind games, but I can honestly say that it didn't affect me at all. And that was taking into consideration the fact that I was sent off that evening, soon followed by Gordon Armstrong. But the determination and the character of the team that I spoke of earlier saw us win the game 1–0.

We won the next five games, which meant that with eight games to go we were in prime position to make it two promotions in two seasons. Despite losing games away at Bristol City and Blackpool, our amazing home form continued as three more victories made it nine wins from the last nine games.

Nick and I were practically inseparable in the middle of the park. The previous season Gary Brabin (Brabbs), a midfielder from Doncaster, had been signed 'to keep us on our toes'. I'd played against him a couple of times before, and he was a really tough competitor. A former bouncer, he looked more like a bodybuilder than a footballer. Brabbs introduced himself to the squad by doing single-armed press-ups during the warm-up prior to a training session. I think as much as anything else, it was a bit of a calling card. He had a reputation for being a loose cannon, and I think that was his way of living up to it. But he was great around the dressing room, and generally a really nice lad. After struggling to get on the side (we had two of the best midfielders in the league playing in midfield) and after making only five appearances, he was sold to Blackpool. That was where his reputation was enhanced after he was arrested following an altercation in a match against Brentford City. Further controversy followed him throughout his playing and subsequent coaching career, including being found guilty of a public order offence while at Luton Town. I can honestly say, though, he was one of the nicest and funniest lads that I'd ever met in football.

This time around, the manager bought Adrian Randall, a truly talented footballer. He too found it difficult to break the Johnrose–Dawes combination, and although he scored a few important goals, he made only about 30 appearances in three years. He was a very good footballer, though his personality was what one can only describe as atypical. He didn't particularly like football, training or playing. In fact, he didn't particularly like footballers. In all the time we shared a dressing room, I don't think I ever saw him in the shower (not that I look out for people in the shower). Let me rephrase that: I don't think I ever saw him *take* a shower. I didn't see him in the dressing room very often, for that matter. He'd train and then be off home. I was as surprised as anybody when he turned up for the end of season week away in Magaluf. Nobody was surprised, though, when on day three he decided he'd socialised enough, booked a flight and went home. I was even less surprised when I found out, a few years later, that he'd given up playing football to become a lorry driver.

Nick and I were different characters off the pitch. I did what I did because I thought it was the right thing to do, and I never needed thanks or praise from anybody. I was self-critical enough to know when I had played well or whether I'd had a stinker. And that was enough for me, really. I was a very strong character and, sometimes, Sam and Stan would have a go at me in front of the others. Most of the time it was unjust, and I knew they were only doing it to set down a marker for the rest of the lads. They knew I could take it, but sometimes some of the others thought it was personal. They couldn't have been more wrong. It was actually a massive compliment; using me to get a message over to the others. It was their way of saying 'This guy has done this or that, and plays every week. So if we can give *him* a bollocking...'

I genuinely couldn't have cared less whether they liked me or not. I was there to play matches, not be mates with the coaching staff. It certainly helped that we *were* mates, but that wasn't important to me. I think back to my time under Mike Walsh. I really liked him, he was one of the lads. But that did me no favours whatsoever; for me, it was all about playing. Nick was different. He was a huge part of our success, yet he was very rarely given a compliment by Stan. Join the club, Nick! Others, such as Chris Lucketti and Dean Kiely had praise lavished upon them regularly. But not us. Not the dream team, the engine room. Nick could not understand it. He'd been a part-timer only two or three years prior to this. If anybody deserved praise, it was him. One day after training he had a quiet word with Sam. He didn't make a big deal out of it, he just wondered why he never got so much as a 'well done!'

Sam just looked at him and said, 'He picks you every week!' That was it – that was all he said. Great management!

Three games to go! We were on the cusp of something great. Not since 1969 had Bury ventured into the realms of the second tier. Three games to get two points, and that would be it! We'd have achieved successive promotions, and would be sitting at the table with some of the big boys. Bury Football Club, with an average attendance of around 4,500! Earlier that season, Preston North End, with an average crowd of over 9,500, tried to buy me. With them languishing below mid-table, and us possibly just one game away from being promoted…

First off was Luton away. Third in the league and also with a chance of gaining automatic promotion, Luton had only lost three games at home. It was always going to be a tough game and, after a 0–0 draw, we were quite happy knowing that another point away at Watford would see us achieve our goal. Watford's season was all but over, no chance of being promoted and in no danger of being relegated. We still wouldn't take them lightly, but we had a great chance and we knew it. In the dressing room before the game, as expected, the lads were absolutely on fire. Then things took a bit of a downward turn with the kick-off about half an hour away. Before every game, without fail, Westy would empty his bowels. Today was going to be no different, except for the fact that he was particularly nervous. Stan was doing his team talk, and Westy was jigging about. As soon as Stan had finished, Westy sprang up and burst through the toilet door – or he would have done had I not been standing behind it. It smacked me right in the face. Talk about panic! He thought he'd knocked me out and absolutely bricked it.

Out on the field we didn't fare much better. It was one of the few games during the run-in where we were very much second best. We had a brilliant defence that season, and they were called upon time after time during that game. We created a few chances ourselves but, on the day, I think nerves got the better of us. As full-time approached, the 2,000-strong travelling Bury fans were in a party mood. With five minutes to go, the noise was incredible. Then, just as in the season before during the Chesterfield game, our supporters fell very quiet. Watford were having yet another attack, and Stretch, usually so calm and reliable, stuck out a leg and gave away a penalty. We were absolutely gutted and most of our fury was vented at the referee's assistant who had signalled to the referee that an infringement had been made. No amount of protestation was going to change the referee's mind. That didn't stop most of the team, though. Once we had all been ushered away, it was their striker, Richard Johnson, I think, versus Dean Kiely. Deano had already proved what a fantastic keeper he was during his first season. What happened next saw him written into Bury folklore. In truth, it wasn't the best-struck penalty in the world, but a full-stretch dive which saw the ball crash into his legs meant that we had done it.

Obviously, Stretch was the most relieved person on the pitch, and although Dean Kiely received all the adulation, the truth was, it was a real team effort. Everyone had played their part, and with one home game to go, we had gained promotion.

In the dressing room the celebrations came to an abrupt end when Stan and Sam reminded us that we had unfinished business. Results had gone our way, and if we ended the season with a victory, we would go up as champions! We were given a few days off, so obviously we all went out into Bury to receive the adulation and get blind drunk. Once more, though, I didn't read the script and went straight home. Quick change, quick phone call to Paul, and then off out in Preston.

That last week, training was a doddle. We had a fantastic home record, only conceding eight goals. Only Millwall, who were mid-table, stood in our way of lifting the title. We won the game at a canter, 2–0, with me scoring the second goal from a Ronnie Jepson knock-back. It was celebration time again, before yet another night out in Preston. Some things just don't change!

A few days later we were off on the big bird to Magaluf (again). This was another absolute drink-fest. For all the money that modern footballers get, I wouldn't swap places with them at all (well, maybe). The amount that we drank in the days before social media… You really wouldn't get away with it now.

A few years prior to this, I was diagnosed with a stomach ulcer, probably caused by all the anti-inflammatories I used to take as painkillers. I used to get a terrible sharp pain which would only dissipate by eating food. A course of tablets seemed to rectify the problem, but the pain always seemed to come back after a heavy bout of drinking. That year in Magaluf, after seven days of 18-hour drinking sessions, I flew back to England in excruciating pain. So it was back to the doctors for more tablets, and three weeks without a drink. Lesson learned … until the next time!

CHAPTER 9
THE ENGLISH DISEASE

It had been five years since I left Blackburn Rovers. A lot had happened in that time – married, divorced, fathered a child, moved to a part of the country that was so cold it was unbelievable, left open-mouthed by the ineptitude of one manager, tapped up by another manager, had my home ransacked, questioned by the police for kidnapping my own daughter, had surgery on a damaged Achilles tendon... All worth it! I was now back where I felt I belonged. I couldn't wait to be back playing in this division. I wasn't fazed, I wasn't even excited; I was just eager to pit my wits against some big-name players and football clubs. We knew that season would be about survival, but we were more than ready for it.

Another thing that had happened was my transition as a footballer. I had gone from being a young, quick forward with an eye for the goal to a 'hard-working, box-to-box midfielder'. My role in the team had been completely transformed. The perception of me as a footballer had also completely changed. Those two promotion seasons saw me tagged as a 'battling midfielder'. Supporters marvelled at my work rate, effort, will to win, blah, blah, blah! All the things that should be a prerequisite for any footballer, I was suddenly lauded for. I'm not sure what that said about the rest of the team, or other teams for that matter, but apparently that was one of my biggest strengths. No one spoke about my ability to go past people with the ball; no one spoke about my ability to score goals. I was a good tackler, and good in the air, so I should 'play to my strengths'. Even the coaching staff said I should win the ball and give it to those who could play. Don't get me wrong, I was a good tackler, and I was very good in the air. I firmly believe that in all my years of playing football, there wasn't a better tackler in the league. I genuinely don't think I ever lost a 50–50 challenge in all my career. There were maybe a handful of times when these tackles were mistimed (the recipient never thanked me for this), but generally I was right on the button. But being good at one thing doesn't necessarily mean that you're not good at something else. Cue football logic once more. Football logic in this country anyway.

I always felt that the coaching in this country lacked something. I played under some good managers, some of them good tacticians, others good at man-management. But the one thing that they all, and I mean *all* of them lacked was the ability to improve a player technically.

The very first day that I trained with the other YTS lads at Blackburn Rovers, it was abundantly clear to me that I was not the most technically gifted. Their ball control was instant, whereas with me the ball would sometimes go away from me. At the end of every week we would have an assessment, discussing progress, attitude, areas for improvement… Every week was the same for me: 'Needs to work on the first touch'. This followed me throughout my career. 'If he had a first touch he would be some player.' Or, my personal favourite, 'His first touch means that his second touch is a tackle'. Classic!

But at no time was I ever told or shown *how* to improve my first touch. What should my body position be? What should my movement be as the ball comes towards me? What do I do with my foot as the ball approaches me? Do I relax it, hold it firm, try to balance on my big toe? Just throw me a line, please? Something, anything! Just help me improve the one thing that you said I need to improve! But no, nothing. Not a single coach in all my career ever, *ever* showed me how to improve my 'touch'. No, actually, there was Blackburn legend Tony Parkes. He used to set time aside, just me and him, to help me improve my game. But he was the exception!

Surely the fundamental skill that football coaches should possess, particularly when coaching young people, is the ability to improve their technique. Anybody can *tell* you what needs improving; the skill is being able to *show* what needs doing, and then putting in the time with that young player to enable him or her to improve. Fast forward over 30 years, and still nothing has changed. My son Patrick is currently part of the Academy at Preston North End. At his first coach–parent meeting, we were told that he had some great attributes but that he needed to work on his touch. Obviously, I asked for their advice on how he should do this. I wasn't surprised when, disappointingly, the advice given was for him to get a football and play 'keepy-ups'. That was it! That was all he needed to do in order to become a complete footballer! And people wonder why we haven't won the World Cup in over 50 years. I can tell you why: it's because our coaching is crap!

When I was coaching the Under 14s and 15s at PNE, every session would involve improving technique. We would progress to small games where the group of players could put into practice what I'd tried to teach them. I would put on sessions where they would be encouraged to accept the ball in tight areas. There would be restrictions on the opposition; they wouldn't be allowed to tackle but could intercept a bad pass. This meant that the passing team could improve their technique in a realistic situation but without the pressure of being tackled. Obviously, the progression would be to put things into a game situation. But this had to be done step by step; practise the skill, learn the skill, demonstrate your learning in a small-sided game situation. The real test would come on a Sunday morning when they would have a match against the other academies.

It was during these games that the deficiencies within our coaching system really came to the fore. Remember, we are talking about academy football with children aged 9–16; learning the game, trying to improve week by week, and then demonstrating that improvement on a Sunday; demonstrating what they had learned, demonstrating that when you were coaching, they were listening, showing that when you were demonstrating, they were watching. Surely, that was all that mattered, right? Had the children who you had worked with for a week shown any improvement? Had they demonstrated progression? Each weekend, it became blindingly obvious that wasn't all that mattered. I had done all my coaching during the week. They had heard me going on about tactics, technique, whatever, for two, maybe three sessions. It was now their chance to shine. During those 80 minutes on the Sunday, I never once gave any instruction, I never once tried to coach, and never once told my players where to run, who to pass to, what to say. The only thing that they got out of me was a 'well done' or perhaps 'unlucky, good try!' But never coaching. This was not the case with the opposition coaches, or indeed coaches from different age groups. They would be talking to, or rather shouting at their players from the first minute to the last. Where to run, who to pass to. 'Head it!' 'Clear it.' 'Shoot!' 'Pass it to him!' 'Get a foot in!'

The list was almost endless. They may as well have been on the pitch themselves. Those poor kids did not know where to turn. There were terrified of making a mistake and would take the option of an easy pass for fear of getting a rollicking. My heart would sink every week. It got worse, though!

One of the things I always used to emphasise to my players was that the result did not matter. All I was interested in was whether they could demonstrate progression, show improvement. They could play with freedom to express themselves, take risks. The bigger the risk, the bigger the prize. I say that my heart sank, but what really saddened me was the coaches' *advice* if their team was losing with just a few minutes to spare. 'Get the ball forward!' Or worse than that, 'whack it up!' How demoralising is that? Imagine being a young footballer, learning your trade, trying to become better, and because the result isn't going your way, you have to abandon your principles and everything that you've been taught and whack the ball forward. Depressing!

Has it got any better? I don't think so, but I do know of one club where the head of the academy questioned the coaches, wanting to know why, on any given weekend, they hadn't had a clean sweep of victories.

If the most important thing in children's football is the result of a match, then is it surprising that, as a nation, we don't appear to have progressed in my lifetime? About 15 years ago I said to my brother Fran that we/England wouldn't win a major trophy during my lifetime. Obviously, I didn't realise that at 50 I would be so close to being proved correct (thanks, MND), but I'm not going to turn down the opportunity to be right.

I guess the question is, why didn't I stay in coaching? Simple answer, really. Excuse my repetition, but I am essentially a selfish person. Coaching impinged on my personal time; my family time, my golfing time, my lesson-planning time, my sitting at home and drinking red wine time. Coaching meant that I would spend hours out of the house every Sunday. Time that could have been spent with *my* children was spent with somebody else's. It was a very easy decision to make.

Once more, selfishness personified!

CHAPTER 10

THE BIG LEAGUE

The 1997/98 season was always going to be a big year. We were absolute minnows in a league that contained teams such as Nottingham Forest, Manchester City, Sheffield United, West Bromwich Albion, Sunderland, Ipswich Town, et al. The star of the show, though, was probably Middlesbrough Football Club, who paraded an esteemed line-up – Paul Gascoigne, Paul Merson, Andy Townsend, the Brazilian footballer Emerson, and Italian international Fabrizio Ravanelli to name but a few.

There were a couple of new additions to our squad, to bolster our chances of survival. In my opinion, the most significant was a certain Andy Gray. Andy was another one of those 'southern blacks' who, along with Tony Finnigan and Ian Wright, made his name at Crystal Palace. Stan had worked with them all while coaching at Palace and had obviously kept in touch with Andy over the years. Andy had played in the Premiership with Tottenham, and criminally gained only one England cap. This guy had so much ability it was frightening. He was far and away the best I had played with, and probably the best player that Bury Football Club had ever had. In my opinion, he should have had a hundred caps for England, he was that good. I remember at the end of the season (in Magaluf, once again), Stan pulling us both to one side and saying, 'If you had what he has, and he had what you have, you'd both have played for England, a hundred times.' Not sure either of us took it as a compliment!

We made a steady start in the big league during our first three games, and beat Crewe in the first round of the League Cup. Our first real test, though, was against Wolverhampton Wanderers at Molineux, where three weeks earlier, on 9 August, a young lad called Robbie Keane made his debut. This kid was not bad! He absolutely ripped us to bits. We actually gave a really good account of ourselves, but he was just too good. A 4–2 defeat meant we'd lost our first game of the season. Was I disappointed? Yes, for about two minutes. This was always the case after a game. I would try not to dwell on the result, irrespective of what it was. I would also think back to something Dave May said when we were young lads at Blackburn: 'Win or lose, hit the booze!' And that is pretty much what I did after every game. I'd sometimes get stinking drunk; luckily I'm not an angry drunk, I just used to get very tired and fall asleep, either in the club or in the taxi. That night was one such night. There I was, dribbling in the taxi (I suppose that was better than slating the taxi driver) when something came over the radio that not only woke me up, but completely sobered me up as well: Princess Diana had been killed in a car crash! I couldn't believe it. If I were one of those footballers who would get down after a defeat, that would certainly have put things in perspective. Now, I'm not a royalist. In fact, I'm not even sure of their purpose in life, but the public reaction over the next few weeks showed that this was quite a big deal. The fact that I remember, so vividly, the moment I heard it, again marked it out as something quite significant.

Victories in our next two games preceded a run of seven games without a win, a draw against Man City (which would have been better had I finished off a late chance instead of hitting the goalkeeper) and narrow defeats to Sunderland in the League Cup being the highlights. Three league defeats in a row came and went, but four points from the next two games saw us going to Ipswich Town full of confidence.

Despite my tag as a battling midfielder, I was still encouraged to get in the opposition box as much as possible. Not for this game, though. I was assigned to man-mark a young lad who would come up through the ranks named Kieron Dyer. I was told to 'follow him wherever he goes'. Never before had I been asked to sacrifice my whole game for one player, and this kid was a complete unknown. I remember Sam Ellis saying that although he was playing at right back, he would keep bombing forward and then go into midfield at will. 'Oh, and he's quick, lightning quick!' Wow! High praise indeed!

As at Wolves, despite a good performance we lost the game, but my abiding memory was one of chasing Kieron Dyer around for the best part of 90 minutes. Sam was right: he was lightning quick and never stopped making forward runs. Ipswich were a good team, better than us, and he completely nullified my game. They had the ball for the majority of the game. Whenever we managed to win it back, we gave it away almost straightaway. We were set up that day to play for a draw, but at 2–0 down we threw a bit of caution to the winds. This, at last, allowed me to release the shackles and enabled me to try to get forward. At the end of the game, I remember walking off thinking about what could have been. To my mind, there was no point in trying to contain a team like Ipswich for 90 minutes. I understood the need to not get gung-ho, but we should definitely have had more of a go at them. It was the first time that Stan had set us up so defensively, and it completely backfired. We were like sitting ducks, waiting to be picked off.

The following week we were back in East Anglia, where my last-minute goal salvaged a point away at Norwich City. Next up was Nottingham Forest, who'd been relegated from the Premiership the season before. They, along with Middlesbrough and Sunderland, were heavy favourites to get promoted. Forest had, so far, more than justified that tag with the start they'd had, and everybody outside Gigg Lane was expecting an easy away win. We had done okay for a promoted team, but those games against Ipswich and Wolves showed that there was a big gap between the haves and the have-nots. And this was an even bigger step forward for us. But we were absolutely brilliant that night. Forest couldn't cope with our high-intensity game; we got the ball forward early into the channels for Jonno – David Johnson – to run on to. He was brilliant, he terrorised their defence all night. They had former England international Steve Stone in their team, but he barely caused a ripple. We were good value for our 2–0 victory and went into the next game at home to Portsmouth full of confidence.

Portsmouth had only just missed out on the play-offs the season before, but were really struggling this time around. They'd managed an away draw at Middlesbrough in the previous game, but after only two victories so far that season, although we didn't take them lightly, we knew that another performance like the one against Forest would almost guarantee us another three points. Football, though, has a habit of biting you on the backside when you least expect it, and we were well and truly savaged. A truly dismal performance saw us beaten 2–0; we'd gone from the sublime to the ridiculous in a matter of days.

The following week Jonno, who had proved to be an excellent signing by Mike Walsh, was sold to Ipswich for about £1 million. He couldn't get out of the door quick enough, and the club snatched Ipswich's hands off with the offer. Part of the deal saw us sign Chris Swailes, a tough-tackling centre half. He made his mark at the club with a debut goal in a 1–1 draw against Oxford United before treating us to one of his party tricks. We were on the coach taking us on our annual Christmas outing, when he stuck his hand down his pants, shoved his finger up his backside, and produced a small piece of poo. Classy! I never quite understood pranks like that. They were neither clever nor amusing. Needless to say, we let him know what we thought about it, and that was the end of that. He was actually a great lad to have in the dressing room; perhaps he was just playing up for the crowd. But it fell flat, and we moved on.

After the Oxford game, we played host to another of the big boys; this time Sunderland. By their expectations, they'd had an indifferent start to the season but were unbeaten in seven. We'd played them twice already in the League Cup, and knew what to expect. Despite them fielding a host of names with Premiership experience, we got and deserved a 1–1 draw. Four points from two of the big three was a great return, and Middlesbrough were due in a couple of weeks' time. They were absolutely flying, and with a team littered with household names we knew it was always going to be our toughest game at home. Their manager, Bryan Robson, was a bit of a hero of mine as a player. I loved the way he would go through players three times the size of him. I loved the way he would start attacks with a tackle and end them with a header or a shot at goal. He was the ultimate midfielder as far as I was concerned. So his words to Sam Ellis after the game were music to my ears. We lost the game 1–0, but put in another good performance. I had a chance to equalise in last few minutes, but my chest-and-volley sailed over the bar.

I always knew when I'd played well. Never needed anyone to tell me, and with Sam and Stan, no one ever did. I also always knew when I'd had a stinker and, somehow, they were never shy in letting me know it. This time, they went against the grain. Bryan Robson had wanted to know who I was. What was my name, where had Bury bought me from, how much had I cost? I'd had a good game, a very good game, against the best team in the division. Emerson, their Brazilian midfielder, never got a kick. I was all over him, all game. Whatever he tried, he couldn't shake me off. I don't think he had ever been tackled as much or as hard in one game in all his career. Stan hadn't made the same mistake that he'd made against Ipswich. He told us to go out and play, show them what we were all about. I had my man to mark when we were out of possession, but when we had the ball, I had license to go forward and get in the box. I did this at every opportunity, and Emerson couldn't keep up with me. I'm not sure he enjoyed tracking back, and probably wasn't used to it in that division. There was no doubting that they were better than us, and Paul Merson in particular was outstanding, but we had our fair share of chances and could easily have come out with a draw. On Monday morning Sam pulled me to one side. Apparently, had I been a few years younger, Bryan Robson would have put in a bid to buy me. Thanks, Mum, for having me too soon!

After an away defeat at Bradford, which ended with a mass brawl, we hosted Sheffield United, another of the big boys. We drew the game 1–1, with me scoring a header from a well-rehearsed set piece. The goal was shown on TV and looked absolutely brilliant. We had worked on the set piece throughout the week; if we had a free kick around the halfway line on the left-hand side, I was to stand almost out on the left wing, looking disinterested. Andy Woodward (Woody) who, years later, bravely spoke out about being abused as a young footballer, was to play the ball towards the side of the box. I would then run in from the wing and head the ball across the area towards the middle of the goal. The idea was that it would create a better angle for our forwards in the box. When the ball was played in the box, it was about 10 yards further in than it should have been. I had to make up a lot of ground, but did so, and, as rehearsed, tried to head the ball into the middle of the box. The truth is, though, that I mistimed it, and connected perfectly for the ball to sail over Preston-born goalkeeper, Alan Kelly. A fluke! A complete and utter fluke, but I took the credit and wheeled away as though I meant it. For some reason, we never used that free kick again.

With David Johnson sold, we brought in Tony Ellis to score the goals. He made his debut in the game, and could have had a hat-trick. We absolutely battered them, with Nick Dawes getting forward more in this game than in any other I'd seen him play. By the time they equalised with about 10 minutes remaining, we could and should have been about 5–0 up. As good as our performance was, a lot of the credit had to go to Andy Gray. Pre- and post-Andy, Stan would always play me and Nick in the middle as a pairing. But when Andy played, he sat behind us, which allowed us to get forward a lot more. He also never gave the ball away. This meant that we retained possession much more efficiently.

Without realising, we had gone six games without a victory since the Nottingham Forest game. Interestingly, Andy Gray had missed all these games through suspension. The difference his presence made in that Sheffield United game spoke volumes for how good he was. When he left a few weeks later to go to Millwall, I was gutted. We were definitely a better team with him in it, but he chose to leave and we had to move on. I met up with him recently at a charity match for the now, sadly, defunct Bury FC. He had travelled all the way up from London on a Sunday morning for a cause that he believed in. He also regularly keeps in touch following my diagnosis. Actions like these just go to prove what a good guy he is.

Draws in the next three league games were followed by two defeats, and by the time we played Manchester City at Maine Road, we had gone from the heights of beating one of the pre-season favourites to get promoted to the low of going 15 games without a victory. We had dropped like a stone and were staring relegation in the face. We were never the most free-scoring of teams, but losing Jonno and, later, Andy Gray really hit us hard. We were now odds-on to go down. It was safe to say that our confidence was not as high as it could have been, but the game against City proved to be a real turning point.

City were arguably the biggest club in the division, if not the best, but expectations were high and, under Frank Clark, they were not delivering. You could sense that their team felt under pressure; they'd been on a poor run and their fans were restless. From the very first whistle the supporters were slating the board and the manager. I've never really understood it; how was that going to help the team? They were a bag of nerves, and thanks to a Paul Butler goal we claimed a well-earned and much-needed 1–0 victory. The scenes at the end of the game were incredible. This was talked about as the worst defeat in City's history and 3,000 fans staged a demonstration at the end of the game, baying for Frank Clark's blood. He was sacked a few days later!

Actually, the real turning point of our season was probably a battling draw away to high-flying Charlton Athletic, two games before we played City. They had Mark Bright, Ian Wright's former Crystal Palace teammate, upfront. Talk about big time. He must have thought that because we were 'little Bury' we would just lie down for them. I remember him asking me, 'How many houses have you got?' What a prick! I never take pleasure in anyone's misfortunes, but the day they got promoted in the play-offs, I shed a little tear. Well, I might have done had I known how to cry.

Off the field, the catalyst that was about to change my life at that point had been launched. Being such an intellect, I had signed up at Preston College to do a human physiology course (a dumbed-down A level). I'd known for quite some time that football was never going to provide me with a life of leisure and lazing, so had begun planning for the future a few years earlier. I'd previously had absolutely no interest in finding out what results I'd got from school, and until the year before I'd had absolutely no idea. I had decided to enrol on the sports science course, and needed to write down my school results as part of the application process. So, in 1996, I found out that, despite drawing pictures in nearly every one of my GCEs, I actually passed English and maths.

After passing my sports science A level equivalent (!), I was on a roll. Next was human physiology, but when I turned up for the first lecture, there were only about eight people in the classroom. For some reason, Preston College had decided to put on human physiology and human biology at the same time, but both classes had equally low numbers. They decided to merge the two and that's when it happened. This strikingly gorgeous girl walked in. I can picture her now – tall, slim, with dark hair and beautiful blue eyes. She wore this dark jumper with an orange stripe strategically placed across it (that was my excuse anyway). I just remember thinking, *she is absolutely beautiful!*

We didn't speak at all that first night, but she was all I could think about for the next few days. The next week I turned up early, but she wasn't there. I can't believe I did this, but I sat next to the window that overlooked the car park, just waiting for her to turn up. About 10 minutes into the session she burst through the door looking really flustered. That made her even more appealing to me. Being antisocial, as I am, I used to sit on my own, and she seemed to be late every week. Each week, the same thing – through the door, flustered, and then looking for the empty seat – which invariably was next to me.

We got talking, mainly about the course at first, but as we became more familiar with each other, we dared to talk about our personal lives. She made the big mistake of telling me where she worked, and I would find excuses to nip in and see her. I must have seemed like a stalker. During one of the lectures a few weeks later, she told me that she had to dash off early as she was going to meet up with her boyfriend for her birthday meal. Even though I was still with my not-so-new-any-more girlfriend, I felt sick. I tried to tell myself that I didn't have any feelings for her. I even spoke about her to not-so-new girlfriend, as if to somehow say to myself that if there was anything in it, I wouldn't be openly talking about her.

One Saturday night, we bumped into her and her boyfriend in a nightclub. There was a definite spark between us (well, I thought so, anyway), and it seemed that both of our partners had picked up on it. He appeared reluctant to shake my hand when we were introduced, while my partner had a look of 'you didn't tell me she was gorgeous when you mentioned her'.

Any cracks that may have been present in our relationship were widened by the emergence of this gorgeous girl, Nadine Richardson. Nadine and I got on very well and became good friends, but we were both in relationships, so that's how it stayed. But, for me, that was really difficult.

If off the field my head was spinning a bit, on the field I remained fully focused on the task in hand. The victory at Man City was the third in the nine-game unbeaten run. Stan had brought in my old teammate Mark Patterson, and fellow Preston-born lad, Nigel Jemson (Jemmo).

Jemmo had played against us a few weeks earlier for Oxford United. As a kid, he had a bit of a reputation for being a bit 'large'. There was a story that went around Preston, about how he apparently walked to the front of a very long nightclub queue, giving it the line, 'Don't you know who I am?' Now, I don't know how true that was, but it was a very strong rumour. He also had the reputation for being a touch unpopular. His teammates at Oxford more than gave credence to that rumour. I have never known anyone take as much stick from his own teammates. The best thing was, though, he didn't bat an eyelid. He genuinely didn't care, at all. When he signed for us, although he struggled on the pitch, he was great in the dressing room. I thought he was hilarious, the way he would mercilessly rip into people, anyone, absolutely anyone. He could take it as well; any stick he got was water off a duck's back. Talk about thick-skinned.

That unbeaten run meant we had a real chance of survival and, despite only two victories in eight games, we went into the last game away at QPR needing just a point to stay up. QPR were all but safe and the game was played like a testimonial. Vinnie Jones played for them and, after about five minutes, the ball was bouncing between the two of us. I was all ready for a full-blooded tackle, and was just about to launch myself when I heard the manager shout, 'Steady!'

I swear, it was as though a conversation had taken place before the game where the two managers had agreed that we would take it easy on each other. That was the closest thing to a tackle in the whole 90 minutes. Gordon Armstrong scored after about 10 minutes, and that was the end of the action. Those three points hoisted us to the lofty position of seventeenth, not bad considering only Crewe Alexandra had a lower average attendance. It was a great achievement, which probably surpassed the two promotions.

Those last three seasons would go down in Bury folklore as the Glory Years. But in true Stan Ternent style, there wasn't a victory parade in sight (which suited me down to the ground).

I'm sure I don't need to tell you how I celebrated that night.

Not-so-new girlfriend had become ex-girlfriend. My feelings for Nadine were getting stronger and, as I've said many times, I am a selfish person. I just couldn't be with somebody when I was yearning for somebody else. That, though, wasn't the only thing that changed. We celebrated our victory by going away for a week to Magaluf, where Stan spent an extraordinarily long time attached to his mobile phone. We didn't think too much of it then, but it all became very obvious when, a week after we returned, he resigned from Bury to become the manager of Burnley Football Club. Burnley were in the division below but, like Preston, were probably a bigger club than Bury with a bigger fan base and more potential to survive in the higher divisions. Stan took Sam with him for the ride, and left without so much as a goodbye.

So Stan had gone, and shortly afterwards Neil Warnock was appointed…

CHAPTER 11

DRAWN TO THE DEEP END

From the minute we are born, we are being drawn to the end of our days. Some get drawn very quickly, for others it can take over a hundred years. But eventually, we are all overpowered by this gravitation-like pull.

At a very early age, I was aware of death, or more precisely, dying. I hadn't experienced anybody close to me dying, but it was something I knew would happen. I wasn't scared and it wasn't something that played on my mind. It was something that I was not exactly intrigued by, but I just knew that it was part of our existence, part of our evolution. At about the age of 10 I discussed with Fran how it wasn't something I was scared of.

Over the years, I have had a recurring dream of falling into the darkness. Again, I never woke up afraid; more fascinated by the journey down. And it's that journey down that has always kept me going. When I was diagnosed with MND, for a while, the darkness was all I thought about. I guess it's all that most people would think about. I know that, for the people around me, that is still what they think about. But, as in my dream, I am more interested in the journey down. And what things I can experience along the way!

And what of when I arrive, finally? In my dream, I never arrive, but why assume that it is going to be a crash landing? Who knows how it is going to end? For the time being, I make up my own ending – a quiet, peaceful conclusion, an eternal sleep; restful, untroubled sleep.

until he turned up. So we had the longest warm-ups in the world. Quite often, when he did turn up late, he would have his dog with him. He used to pull people out of training and get them to walk the dog. I remember Andy Preece doing it; he used to car-share with Nigel Jemson and me and Jemmo absolutely hammered Preece for it, totally ripped him to bits. What a mug! Warnock asked Jemmo to walk the dog once and got a 'f**k off!' for his troubles. Strangely, he never asked him again.

Another unusual tactic that he adopted: whenever we had a practice match he would make sure the lads wore shin pads, and encourage us to kick lumps out of each other.

With the first game of the season approaching, I was beginning to become a little bit wary of the manager. This progressed to being totally perplexed when, the day before the first game, we were all called into the boardroom. Another Warnock special! Apparently, it was one of his 'traditions' to get all the lads to down a raw egg in a glass of sherry. We had signed a couple of his former players from other clubs, and they duly obliged, along with a couple of those who were already there. And then he came to me! Not a chance! There was no way that I was going to drink that. I wasn't being clever, I just didn't see the point. What was it, character-building? Show how tough you are? Team-bonding? Sorry, but there was no way. Dean Kiely then chipped in; another one who refused. Then Chris Lucketti, then Nick Dawes. See the pattern? That was it for that little ritual, quashed before it got off the ground. Who said player power doesn't exist?

Once the season started, we came flying out the traps. There were two or three new signings but the majority of the team were Stan's boys. After beating Huddersfield 1–0 in the first game, we had Stan's new team, Burnley, in the first round of the League Cup. We absolutely battered them in the first leg but somehow they managed to get a 1–1 draw. The second leg was to be played a week later, and after negotiating a 0–0 draw away at Ipswich we were off to Turf Moor. Again, it was completely one-sided, only this time we got the goals that our performance deserved. A 4–1 victory against our old manager had Neil Warnock absolutely purring. But for Stan it was a different story. His new team got to see a side of him that was to be a regular procedure for the next few months. He absolutely roasted them, pulled their performances apart. We could hear every word, telling them that he'd left 'that team for you lot!'

After the game a couple of us spoke to him and Sam and they were equally scathing; in fact, more so. It was safe to say that Stan intended to make some changes.

Two wins and a draw for the next three games meant that we had 11 points from a possible 15 – promotion form. We lost our first game of the season away at Birmingham City. Bruce Grobbelaar, who Neil Warnock had managed at Plymouth, played in goal after Dean Kiely was called up to play for Ireland. For possibly the first time in my life, I bottled out of saying something that I was desperate to get off my chest: 'How did you feel when you thought you'd been caught for fixing those games?'

Grobbelaar only played the one game, and my chance had gone. Gutted! To be honest, I didn't really bottle it. He'd been a bit of a hero of mine back in the day, and I just thought that it may have been a tad disrespectful (not like that had ever stopped me before).

Despite our great start, the cracks in my relationship with Neil Warnock were beginning to appear. I was beginning to tire of what I thought was a lack of respect for his players. He continued to be late for training. He'd sometimes keep us waiting for about an hour and then expect us to be right at it during the sessions. The atmosphere in the dressing room was changing as well. As with any new manager, he brought in players who he knew and trusted. But I felt that they didn't mix, or try to mix as well as they could have. In truth, we were possibly a little bit resentful, although it didn't feel like that at the time. I also didn't think that the new signings added anything to the team. Those four players who he said he was going to build the team around survived the cull, as did Andy Woodward, who played every week. The rest, though, were in and out of the team, as the manager began to leave his imprint on the club.

I went to see the manager to voice my concerns. I said that I didn't enjoy training, playing, or even being around the place. I wasn't happy and I wanted to leave. The club that I had given my all for over the last few years was changing, and I didn't like what it was becoming. What the manager said next took me right back to what Swanee had shared a few months earlier. Warnock told me that he saw Bury as a stepping stone. His real dream was to manage Sheffield United and he was going to use Bury to help him achieve that goal. His sweetener was that he would take the core of the team with him. Far from being impressed, I saw it as an absolute betrayal. I wasn't being naive, and a few years later I actually looked back and admired his honesty. But at the time, all I could see was Warnock tearing the team apart and filling it with his boys. His boys who would do anything to keep on his good side. His boys who would accept their manager turning up late for training. His boys who would walk his dog during training. His boys who would drink a raw-egg-and-sherry cocktail. But that wasn't for me. If he thought his sweetener was going to make me change my mind, it had the absolute opposite effect. I was more desperate to leave than ever.

The next four games saw two wins and two draws with one of the victories being a 3–0 win over Crystal Palace in the League Cup. Although we lost the second leg 2–1, we progressed to the next round away to Manchester United. The chairman was delighted; we'd get our share of the gates from a near-certain full house, which for a club like Bury was so important. It could make the difference between having to sell one of your better players or being able to buy a new one.

After the loss away to Crystal Palace, we lost the next four league games. Warnock had changed half the team, but the results were getting worse. On the training ground, neither he nor Ron Reid seemed to have any idea of how to get us out of this rut. Eight defeats in twelve games, including losing 2–0 against Man United, saw us spiralling down the league table. There was some good news, though, when the chairman told us that he was whisking us off to St Lucia. League rules wouldn't allow the club to give us a bonus for playing Manchester United, even though they were going to be quids in, so instead they decided to treat us to a trip away.

During that run there was also a 3–1 defeat at home to Sheffield United, which was filmed live on Sky Sports. That was the day Warnock showed his true colours to the world. As I've already mentioned, Sheffield United was his team, the team he supported as a boy, and the team that he wanted to manage. We lost the game, and afterwards, as normal, he went to the post-match interviews. And there, in the full glare of the world's media was Neil Warnock doing the interview wearing a Sheffield United tie. Appalling, absolutely appalling! Maybe he was begged to do it, maybe he was paid, maybe he was threatened. But I can't think of a single reason that would justify that action. The season had started so well for him, but things started to go wrong and that decision, right there, meant he was never going to have the fans on his side. In fact, it was going to be difficult to keep some of the *players* onside.

A win against Grimsby town gave us an all-too-brief respite. Our next game, the day before flying to Saint Lucia, would be away against Bolton Wanderers. The events of the next few days would provide me with all that I needed to convince me that my time at Bury was coming to an end.

CHAPTER 13

THE ONE I LOVE

Away from football, my time was being occupied by Nadine. A whole year after we met, we finally started going out. I was absolutely swept away by her (but obviously played it cool!) Now this is where the perceived arrogance comes in. With other partners, I always felt that I was almost doing them a favour, but with Nadine, I knew that I was punching above my weight. I knew very early on that I wanted to spend the rest of my life with her and we were married less than three years after we got together.

For the most part, it's been fun all the way. Nade (can I call you that?) used to say that things can't be this good forever. 'Something is bound to happen!'

Those words came back to haunt us when nearly 20 years later I was diagnosed. I don't believe in fate! I don't believe that you can be *too* happy! Sorry to repeat, but I've always said that I don't believe things happen for a reason, they just happen. I don't believe that there is some all-powerful godlike being who knows or dictates what is going to happen. I stopped being religious at an early age when I started to question God's rationale behind allowing babies to die. If you are all-conquering, all-seeing, all-knowing and the creator of all, why let bad things happen? Why decide that some good people will die young, yet others will live much longer? Why decide that some bad people can continue to do bad things for years and years? And if it is all written in the stars, is it their fault anyway? Perhaps I did get ill for a reason, but whatever that reason was, I don't believe for one second that it was mapped out from the minute I was born. Circumstance? Genes? Sliding doors? Serendipity (depending on your perspective)? Science? All of these more plausible than fate. So sorry, Nade. I love you dearly, but I have to disagree with you on this one. Bad things happen to lots of people; learning to deal with them and adapt is surely better than searching for answers that we cannot find.

Sermon over!

CHAPTER 14

THE TRIP OF A LIFETIME

The day before my twenty-ninth birthday we played Bolton Wanderers at the Reebok Stadium, as it was known then. A crowd of over 21,000 witnessed an absolute mauling. Bolton had been relegated from the Premier League and were fancied to go straight back up. And they absolutely gave us the footballing lesson. At 4–0 we got off lightly. In my opinion, they were the best team we'd played so far. At the end of the game, Neil Warnock's post-match team talk went along the lines of, 'Not to worry, get home, get your bags packed and I'll see you tomorrow morning.' Tomorrow we were off to St Lucia, and I don't think I could have put it better myself. What could you say? No amount of ranting and raving was going to change it. We knew we'd had a hammering, so why go on about it? It was a case of dust yourselves down, put it to bed and let's enjoy the trip we'd earned.

As I was about to walk out of the dressing room, I was pulled to one side by the manager. Burnley had been on the phone and wanted to know how much Bury were prepared to sell me for. Then he laughed at the suggestion of me going there. I think he and Stan had a bit of history, and there was no way he was going to let Stan get one over on him. So he just laughed! He knew I wasn't happy, he knew I wanted to leave, but still he thought it appropriate to stand there and laugh. I didn't say anything, I simply turned round, got in my car and drove home. I was not going to let it ruin what were going to be a fantastic few days in the sun. Apart from the fact that I was leaving Nadine behind, it was the perfect birthday present.

The following morning, Nade dropped me off at the airport. When we got on the plane, we couldn't believe it. We were in business class: business class, Bury Football Club. The club had really pushed the boat out! The cabin crew found out that it was my birthday and provided champagne on tap. It was sheer luxury. Remember, this was 1998 at Bury Football Club. Obviously today, probably all of the Premiership clubs and some of the Championship clubs will fly business class to games. But this surely was a first for a club like Bury. Taking us to St Lucia would have been enough, but they really went that extra mile with the business class thing.

When we were about to land, the mood changed, for me in any case. I tried to get over what had happened the previous day with the manager, but what he said next brought it all back. I'd just grabbed my bags out of the overhead when he said, 'Hey, carry my bags, will you?'

I looked around at this as if to say, 'Is he talking to me?'

He repeated, 'Here, carry this.' This time, it was less of a request.

I looked at him, square in the face. 'Who do you think I am? Carry your own f***ing bags!'

He started spluttering. 'What's the matter with you? I'm only asking you to carry my bags.'

'And I'm only telling you to carry your own f***ing bags! Who do you think you are? Get them off yourself, or get some mug to do it.' And I carried on with my business. To be fair to him, he managed to get Tony Rigby to take them off. And then we began the arduous journey to the hotel. We were on a stuffy little coach, it was roasting hot, the driver was driving like a lunatic on roads which were, at best, not fit for purpose. A sign of things to come.

We finally arrived at the hotel. There was a large group of children waiting. As we got off the coach, they started cheering. Warnock had a box, which, true to form, he asked somebody to carry off (surprisingly, he did not ask me). He told us that it was some kind of welcoming party, and as a goodwill gesture he'd got together some Bury memorabilia to hand out. So we opened the box! Inside were about a hundred photographs of…Neil Warnock! Seriously? Flashbacks of that meeting in the manager's office. Is this guy for real?

That first night, we arranged to be taken to a local nightclub, a few miles from the hotel. We were dropped off and were to be picked up a few hours later. When we walked in, it was like a scene from an old Western movie. All the glasses went down and everyone stared. Not quite the greeting that we'd received earlier. It was the most uncomfortable few hours of my life. We all just sat in a corner, quietly, too scared to make a scene. Some of the locals looked like they were desperate for a bit of action, but we were on our best behaviour. Our return lift couldn't come quickly enough, and we shot out of there, sharpish.

The next morning we were taken to the training ground. A game had been arranged for the following evening against a local team. I say training ground, but what I really mean to say is, we were taken to some shithole. It was a joke! This field, with broken glass, bricks, pieces of wood, divots, holes… You name it, it was there. I flatly refused to train on it. There was no way I was going to injure myself for the sake of some poxy game. As with most things in my life, if I didn't see a point, then I would question it. And there was no way he was going to force me to train on that, not a chance!

The cracks were widening.

The following morning, it was clear that this trip wasn't going to be all it was hyped up to be. On the way to the game that evening we were greeted by people throwing stones at the bus and verbally abusing us. Great laugh! We got to the ground; it was more of the same. I think the phrase they use these days is 'a hostile atmosphere'. And, like the training ground, the pitch was a disgrace. So once again, I refused to take part. Life for me is simple. If there is no benefit to doing something, then I won't do it, or at the very least, I will protest. It always comes down to, 'what's the point?' Fran always used to say that he thought I had autism. I would take things literally, not find things funny which other people did, or focus on small details that other people didn't seem to think mattered.

He may have had a point, but I just didn't and still don't understand why people do things that they don't want to, if there is no point to it.

We'd been in St Lucia for three nights, but it wasn't the dream holiday we thought it would be. But at least today was going to be a chilled day. No training, no game, just do as you please and enjoy the sun. A few of us were sitting around the pool when the chairman introduced us to a member of the St Lucia aristocracy. After exchanging civilities, we carried on with our sun-seeking. After a few minutes, my ears pricked up. This guy was saying to the chairman how pleased he was that Bury Football Club had accepted the invitation to come to St Lucia and play a match against a local team. It became apparent that, not only had Bury not paid for the holiday to St Lucia, they'd actually been paid for the trip. Unbelievable! Why lie? What was there to gain? What were they scared of? It just summed up the last few months for me. And we still had the worst journey in the world to come, the following day.

I arrived home on Thursday evening, absolutely knackered. It had been a terrible break, and physically I felt worse than before we left. We would have been better having a few days off to spend with the family. We should have known!

Amazingly, we won our next game 2–0 at home to West Brom, my last ever victory in a Bury shirt during that spell. A draw in the next game was the start of yet another dreadful winless run. After defeat against Port Vale, we entered the Christmas period in poor form.

Every year, when I was younger, around Christmas time I would get flu. It used to knock me out for about a week, and I couldn't get out of bed until it had passed. Then I discovered flu jabs. So for the next few years, I was absolutely fine. This particular year, though, for some reason, I hadn't had my jab. I remember training on Christmas Eve, feeling rough. Warnock had given us the following day off, which was the first Christmas Day that I'd had off since I was at school. True to form, I woke up the following morning in a sweat. I spent the whole day in bed, while Christmas Day came and went. The following day, I felt worse. There was no way I could play in the Boxing Day match, I couldn't even shift myself to open my presents. Nade phoned Ron Reid to tell him the situation after she tried, unsuccessfully, to phone Warnock. I missed the 3–1 defeat to Crewe, and also the next game, a 4–2 loss at home to Birmingham. I was back for the FA Cup tie on 2 January, but I still felt like shit, and was absolutely rubbish as we were knocked out 3–0 by Stockport. Footballers are strange people, and during training the following Monday some of the lads couldn't wait to tell me how Warnock had said that I had 'thrown one in' by making out that I was ill over the Christmas period. They also couldn't wait to tell me how he'd accused me of not trying during that defeat to Stockport. I'd dragged myself off my sickbed to play in that game, and that was the thanks I got. Our relationship was pretty much at breaking point by this time. I didn't want to be there, and he didn't trust me. It was only a matter of time!

The 2–2 draw away to Huddersfield in the next game saw me score my last goal for Bury, an equaliser which halted a run of four defeats. But that was about as good as it got. We drew the next game, but there was no game the following week as it was FA Cup second round. Warnock decided to treat us by taking us to his favourite place, Scarborough, for a few days. You know what's coming… There was no way! So, the day we were due to leave, I travelled in as normal. Well, I say as normal. There was one difference. For the duration of the journey, from Preston to Bury, I kept my windows open. Driving along the M61, I kept sticking my head out of the window. By the time I got to the football ground, I was freezing, my nose was pouring and my eyes were streaming. I looked like death! I barely walked through the dressing room door when I was sent home. Apparently, he couldn't take the chance of me passing on my illness to the rest of the squad. I was all, 'Really, are you sure? If you insist!' I had a great weekend off.

The break clearly did us a power of good as we were soundly thrashed 3–0 in the next game against Ipswich. I genuinely can't remember anything about the game, so clearly I had a massive impact on it! The following Wednesday, I got home from college (you are never too old to learn) and picked up a message on my answer machine from Stan Ternent. Apparently, he'd phoned up to enquire about me going to Burnley, but was getting nowhere. We had a chat and decided that the best thing for me to do was to go in and speak to the manager and tell him that I wanted to leave. So, the next morning that's exactly what I did! Warnock must have known what had gone on, but couldn't do anything about it. To be honest, he was probably glad to see the back of me. Twenty-four hours later, I was a Burnley player.

The 2–0 victory against West Brom on 5 December was Bury's last win until 10 April, when a run of three wins in the last six games couldn't prevent them from being relegated. Neil Warnock's record as a manager is absolutely phenomenal. He had the knack of taking over clubs in trouble, and either getting them safe from relegation or getting them promoted. He was never given pots of money to spend, yet always managed to work minor miracles. I genuinely believed that if he'd been foreign, he'd have managed a top club; his record deserved it. But for some reason, it just never worked out for him at Bury. Whether that was partly due to the players, particularly those who were there when he arrived, or whether the job was just too difficult for him, I don't know. But he failed badly at Bury. I'm sure he would admit that it was not his finest moment in football, but he went on to bigger and better things, and got his dream job at Sheffield United.

I met him recently when he was manager of Cardiff City. Cardiff was the next stop on a project that I'm doing; visiting as many football clubs as I can to raise awareness of MND. He couldn't have been more welcoming. He was polite, charming and genuinely interested in what I had to say. Furthermore, he was really concerned for my welfare. A lot of time had passed, but some people would still bear a grudge. You have to take people as you find them, and people change. That day completely transformed the way I viewed him.

It just goes to show that you never really know somebody until you know them.

CHAPTER 15

YOU GOING ON T' TURF?

From the minute I walked in at Burnley Football Club, I felt at home. It helped that Ronnie Jepson, Gordon Armstrong and of course Stan and Sam were there, but the place had a good feel to it. I trained on the Friday and was selected to play against Reading at home the following day. I had started my career at Blackburn Rovers, Burnley's biggest rivals, but I didn't give that a second thought. In an interview, I was asked whether I was worried about how the Burnley fans would react to me. I can honestly say that I wasn't worried at all. As always, I would give my all; if that wasn't good enough, then so be it.

After a 1–1 draw, the next game was away at Wycombe Wanderers. It didn't exactly go to plan as after about 10 minutes I lunged into a two-footed tackle. It was a bit of a trademark tackle of mine which usually resulted in me winning the ball. This time, however, I slightly mistimed it, missed the ball completely and caught the lad smack on the shins. I didn't even wait for the referee to brandish

Blackburn Rovers versus Sunderland at Roker Park, c.1990

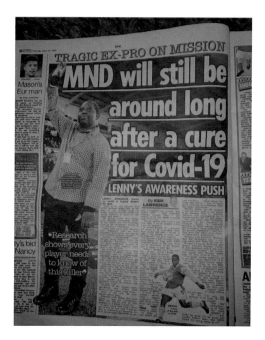

Interview with *The Sun* highlighting MND during lockdown, March 2020

A guest at the Liberty Stadium, Swansea City
with Leon Britton and Kris O'Leary, 2019

Reunited with my shirt from that game versus Hull City in 2003

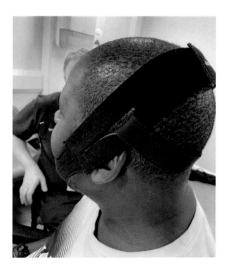

Being fitted for a ventilation mask at Preston Hospital, 2020

In the coach's office at Tranmere Rovers. Former teammates Michael Jackson, Micky Mellon and physio Ian Liversedge

Westy and me celebrating my 50th, November 2019

Always by my side. Elizabeth, Nade and PJ

So lucky to have such a beautiful family. Nade, PJ and Elizabeth

With my brother and best mate, Fran, at his house

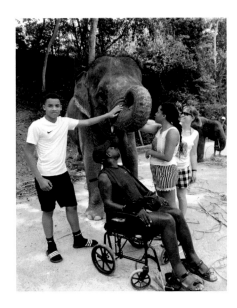

Visiting an elephant
sanctuary in Thailand

It looked worse than it
was. Luckily, Stockport
County player Tom
Bennett escaped
unscathed

● Ord Hargreaves Cup winners — Thomas More U-15 team.

1985 with Ches on my left, and Paul,
three along on the top row

THERE IS NO CURE

Discussing MND at Cardiff City Football Club, 2019

A guest at Burnley FC with Stevie J, Paul and Westy, May 2019

Dermot and I meet again, this time at an
MND Association charity event in London 2019

I met up with some old faces at a charity event at the Victoria ground, Hartlepool United, with Nick Peverell, Andy Saville, Alan Murray, John MacPhail, Paul Olsson, Tony Skedd, Ryan Cross and Stevie Jones

Aged 21, modelling the home kit

Showing off my skills as a teacher at St Silas Primary School, Blackburn

Me and my firstborn, Chanel, age 8, 2002

Guests at Swansea City Football Club, 2019

Ches and me aged 19. He was never a good influence

The YTS lads at Wembley before the Full Members' Cup Final, 1987. Former Rochdale manager Keith Hill is second from the left, with Dave May two along

A hugely successful Leyland Saint Mary's Under 15 team, with Malcolm Gray in the centre and Ches on his left

Me with the Bros Grimm at my wedding vow renewal in 2018.
Stephen, Johnson, Fran and Pete

Me and Paul at a charity function

A programme cover of me celebrating a rare Burnley goal

Westy and I receive our medals following promotion

I didn't score many goals for Swansea City but I believe this one against Hull City on the last day of the season was quite important

Me and Elizabeth following my MND Association charity swim in London Docklands, 2018

Being helped off the pitch following yet another calf injury

Celebrating Ches's 50th and still looking young, 2019

the red card. I knew I was off. Not the greatest start to my Burnley career, which was made worse by the fact that we went on to lose the game 2–0. Strangely, Stan never gave me the rollicking I was expecting. In fact, he used it as a stick to beat some of the players in the dressing room. The team that he'd taken over were not great and they were really struggling in the league. Apparently, if half of them had shown the commitment that I had shown with that tackle, they wouldn't be where they were.

My start to life at Turf Moor didn't get any better when a few days later I pulled my hamstring in training. I was already suspended for three games, but being injured was an absolute nightmare. I missed a 5–0 thrashing against Gillingham, and the 6–0 hiding at home to Man City.

Against Gillingham, we were 4–0 down at half-time. The team had been in the dressing room for about two minutes before they were back outside on the pitch. Stan obviously felt there was nothing he could say, so sent the lads back outside. It was freezing, and the lads spent the half-time break just trying to keep warm. Stan was criticised by certain sections of the media, and I was interviewed by the local radio station to give my thoughts. I'm not sure what they expected me to say, but I backed him all the way. The absolute prerequisite in any football match is to give 100 per cent. Players have good games and players have bad games, but there is never an excuse for not giving your all. There is no way that team should have been 4–0 down at half-time to Gillingham. Yes, there was a lack of confidence in the team but there was also a lack of backbone in some quarters. At times, when the chips were down, some members of the squad found it difficult to pick themselves up, grit their teeth and make things happen. Sam and Stan had made this abundantly clear when we played them earlier on in the season, while I was still at Bury.

After those two crushing defeats, I sat through another home defeat, this time against Preston North End. By the time I was fit again to play, at home to Macclesfield on 28 March, we had won only three games out of the last twenty-one, and were in a real relegation scrap. I'd left a club in the Championship for bigger and better things, but found myself in a fight to stay out of the bottom division of the league.

We had drawn 0–0 against Wrexham to end a run of four straight defeats, but the real turning point of the whole season was the two goals in the last minute which turned defeat into victory against Macclesfield. Four victories and four draws following the defeat to Preston meant that by the time we played Fulham, who with Mohamed Al-Fayed's millions had already been promoted, we only needed a draw to ensure survival. We gave them a guard of honour before the game, and then totally bullied them off the park. Ronnie Jepson scored the only goal of the game, and two successive draws meant that we had gone eleven games unbeaten, and ended the season fifteenth.

Stan Ternent had not left Bury to finish fifteenth, and I believe that he was already planning for the following season. But first, it was on the big bird, this time to Portugal. And then, after another week off, for me it was back to the gym and pounding the streets before returning for pre-season.

CHAPTER 16

SEASON 1999-2000

There was a different look about Burnley Football in preseason. Over ten players had been released, with five added to the squad. One of those was my old mate Dean West who jumped ship from relegated Bury to join the rest of the evacuees; Jepson, Armstrong, Swan, Ternent, Ellis and myself. As with Bury the season before, the dressing room was changing and I certainly felt a level of resentment from some of the lads who were already there. Unsurprisingly, it didn't affect me at all. The lads from Bury were made of strong stuff, and not there to make friends. I felt that it took quite a while to be accepted, despite the exploits of the previous season. But once we were accepted, the dressing room became one of the best that I'd ever been in.

We met up recently at a charity match, and it was as though we'd never been apart. The dressing room was absolutely bouncing, with Glen Little holding court, as usual. Glen was probably the loudest player with whom I've ever had the pleasure of sharing a dressing room. Loud, uncouth and a real pain in the backside – but he had a heart of gold, and was a really good footballer. He looked so ungainly, but he had great feet, balance, and was quicker than he looked. He later got a big money deal to Reading, a move that his talents fully deserved.

The season started really well for us. Armed with a new squad, we picked up fourteen points for the first seven games with only an away defeat to Bristol Rovers blotting our start. Coincidentally, perhaps, I missed that game. I'd always suffered from Achilles problems, and it cropped up again this season. I'd managed to play through the pain for a couple of games but had to sit this one out.

Andy Payton (Payts) was absolutely flying, and scored three goals in the six games we scored in. Payts was an interesting character, to say the least. He was always the last pick in training, and absolutely hated that. In retaliation he used to quote how many goals he had scored; he remembered every single one. Every training session, the same thing. And he never realised that the lads were doing it on purpose just to wind him up. That, and the fact that he wouldn't try a leg. But he could score a goal out of nothing, something he did with amazing regularity that season.

Game 8 was at home to Colchester. We absolutely battered them. Payts (who else?) scored a hat-trick in a 3–0 win, but it could have been 7 or 8, we were that good. We got in the dressing room after the game; the lads were bouncing. But that did not last long. Those in the dressing room who didn't really know Stan up until that point got to see a side of him that became all too familiar over the next few seasons. We were all enjoying the victory, with Payts lapping it up. Then out of nowhere, Stan said something like 'What the f**k was that?' We weren't sure where this was going at first, and then it was 'Happy with that, are you?' And then he exploded. 'Three-nil? F***ing three-nil!! Are you having a f***ing laugh?' At this point, the room went quiet!

You could see the lads thinking, 'What the hell is this guy on?' But I had seen this before. As usual, in moments like this, I just sat there trying not to laugh.

'Three-nil against that shit, and you lot think you've made it.' And then he came up with a classic. 'This result could cost you. If this goes down to goal difference and we miss out, it would be down to you lot only beating this shit three-nil!' We had played eight games, eight games out of forty-six and he was going on about the possibility of losing out on promotion down to goal difference. When the hell has that ever happened? He had lost it, totally! The lads couldn't believe it. Talk about bursting the bubble. As always, I found it hilarious. I couldn't wait to get out of the dressing room so I could openly laugh about it, but most of the other lads thought he was crazy. They had a point! Underneath all that shouting and screaming, there was a hidden message that he didn't quite manage to translate for us. I spoke to him afterwards.

'We need to get the killer instinct. We should be beating teams like that six- or seven-nil. If they'd got a goal back, it could have changed the whole complexion of the game.'

Why didn't he just say that? He was absolutely right, but come on! You've been a manager for like, a million years. Take a breath, take five minutes, whatever it takes. And then get your message across, at the right time, in the right way. Like I said, this was just one of many such occurrences. Fun all the way!

A recurrence of my Achilles injury ruled me out of the next few games, and by the time I was fit again Micky Mellon was having a stormer in the middle of the park. I had to make do with a place on the bench. Cue massive sulk time. It was the same every time, I couldn't help it. I just hated not playing. So I would go into training, train hard, but not engage with the coaching staff. What a baby! I can see it now, but then hindsight is a wonderful thing. To make things worse, Sam and Stan, knowing that I was sulking, would keep prodding and poking, trying to get a reaction out of me. They rarely did, but it really used to hack me off.

Once, during my spell in exile, we had finished training, and were doing a few sprints. There was a reserve game the next day, and Sam started goading me about having to play in it. I started whingeing about having to do these extra sprints before such an 'important' game.

'You too good to play the reserves, are you?'

'Yeah! I am actually!'

At that point, Stan piped up, 'Too good? Too f***ing good? Well f**k off, then! Go on! F**k off and go home!'

I didn't need a second invitation, I hated playing in the reserves and the game was away at Coventry or somewhere like that. So that was me, off. I did the long, lonely walk back to the changing rooms, got my gear and drove home. When I got back, I turned my phone off. There was no way I was going to risk getting a phone call to play, so I had the next day off. I turned up on Thursday and was sent to train with the youth team. I kind of deserved it really, so I just took my punishment, trained, helped the youth team lads clear up all the gear and went back to the changing room. When I got back, Sam was waiting for me, looking at me as though I was a naughty schoolboy. 'The manager wants to see you,' he said, smiling. So off I went to see the manager. He sat me down, and sat there and said nothing. So there we were, both of us sitting down, saying nothing. Then he started going on about wanting an apology. I just thought, are you serious?

'Apology, for what?' I said. There was no way I was going to apologise. Sam had asked me a question, and I had answered it. Was it my fault they didn't like the answer? I was told that if I thought I was too good to play, then I should go home, which I duly did. So where was the problem? We agreed to disagree (after a fashion), and the following day I was back with the youth team.

As usual, the squad was put up on the board for the game the following day. My name was on it, hanging off the end after the names of all the lads who'd never had a sniff of playing that season. Do you think he was trying to tell me something? Fast forward a few days, and I was back doing sprints the day before a reserve game. And as in the previous week, Sam started goading again. This time, though, there was no reaction. I just did my sprints and engaged with the staff as though it was the most normal thing in the world. The reserve game was away at Rotherham; I played and was taken off after about an hour. My attitude, as always, was spot on; I even got a 'well done!' from Sam. On Friday, when the squad went up, I was on it, sitting pretty about 10 names down. Micky had got injured, or was suspended, and I was back in. I barely missed another game until the end of the season, but the season had a lot of life left in it.

We were still bubbling along nicely, keeping in touch with the likes of Preston, Gillingham and Wigan who were all vying for the automatic promotion spots. But we had become over-reliant on Andy Payton's goals. Apart from a 3–0 hiding off Oldham, we were only winning games by the odd goal. Stan decided that we needed freshening up, and so, on Valentine's Day 2000, he made what, at that time, was one of the most sensational signings in Burnley's history. Ian Wright, former England and Arsenal player, was coming to Turf Moor. Stan had known him since their days at Crystal Palace, and he had signed Mitchell Thomas, another old mate of Ian Wright's, earlier in the season. So, between the two of them and the chairman, they managed to persuade Wrighty to leave Celtic and come to Burnley. It was perfect timing. Three of our next four games were at home, with the games against Wigan and Preston instantly selling out. And Stan was right, we did need a boost. On Saturday 19 February, Ian Wright made his debut for Burnley at home to Wigan Athletic. Payts was suspended, and we really missed him in a 0–0 draw. In the next game, away to Colchester, we were grateful for a Steve Davis double which secured a 2–1 win. Then it was back to Turf Moor for the second sell-out game. Preston were seven points ahead of us at the time, and we desperately needed the win to claw them back. We were so confident that day; a full house; Wrighty had played a couple of games and was beginning to settle in; it was all there for us.

I loved playing against Preston. They had Sean Gregan, their talisman, in midfield, who would bully players; he really made their team tick. He was a good footballer who gave everything. But he used to strut around the pitch as though it was his. And he loved a tackle, which suited me down to the ground. He wasn't particularly mobile, but his footballing brain more than compensated. I went into that game with the mindset that I was just going to keep on making forward runs, knowing that he wouldn't be able to keep up with me. And the physical side of it? Well, that was right up my street!

The game started at a frantic pace, and after about five minutes or so there was a loose ball between me and Gregan. There was no way either of us was going to pull out. My mate Paul, who is a big Preston fan, was in the stands watching. He said that he knew what was coming, and that time almost stood still. We both went in for the tackle, without so much as a thought that one of us might get hurt. And in a split second, I heard a scream. He had got to the ball just before me, and I caught him, full on the shin. I was surrounded by the whole of the Preston team, even though the referee didn't even give a free kick. Their physio came on and Gregan tried to carry on, but there was no chance. He was crying as he came off, I think more because he thought he might have broken his leg than because he was in pain. I got singled out for a bit of treatment after that, but it was one of those things. That moment seemed to give them an extra incentive, and they hammered us 3–0. By the time I got to the players' bar after the game, a rumour had started that Stan had told me to put Gregan out of the game. Not a chance!

There isn't a player in the world who I thought was that good that I'd need to put him out of the game. I had only ever deliberately tried to injure one player in my whole career. And that was when I was at Blackburn Rovers, and Gary Flitcroft was kicking me all over the park. This was in the youth team game, and I was a couple of years older than him. But he genuinely didn't care. Every time I got the ball, whack! After about the tenth time, I'd had enough and forearmed him in the face. I got sent off, and he just carried on as if nothing had happened. Brilliant!

There was another surprise waiting for me in the players' bar after that game. Mark Rankin, Gregan's midfield partner, was lording it up. He was telling everyone how that result had 'put them to bed'. I was fuming, but to be fair to him, he was right. We were now 10 points behind; realistically, there was no way we were ever going to catch them. There was a cluster of teams trailing behind Preston, which included Wigan, Millwall, Stoke City and Gillingham. A 2–0 defeat in our next game against Luton town meant that Ian Wright had now played four and was yet to score. In fact, he'd barely had a chance. Andy Payton scored an early goal in the next game to give us a 1–0 victory, but it was now nil in five for Wrighty. And next up, it was Gillingham away.

On the morning of the Gillingham game, we trained as usual. It was just a light session, with a little game to finish. Wrighty was unbelievable that morning. He had a real spring in his step, a massive difference to previous training sessions where, to be honest, he struggled to find the net. But that morning, he was really at it. It augured well for the evening.

In the dressing room before the game, Stan pinned the team sheet up. Ian Wright's name was not on it! I couldn't believe it. Apparently, he had spoken to Stan and asked to be left out. He didn't feel that he was adding enough to the team, and clearly he was not scoring the goals that he and all of us thought he would. But to go and ask to be left out: what a gesture! His reputation was never going to be tarnished. He was an Arsenal legend and had represented England. He'd made his name, and a few games at Burnley were neither going to enhance nor damage what he'd built up over the last 15 years. But, for the good of the team, he stepped down. So that training session was, for me, the result of the release of all the stress he must have been feeling.

We went behind early in the Gillingham game before – yes, you've guessed it – Payts scored an equaliser. Again, they took the lead, but it just had to happen, didn't it? With time running out, Stan threw Wrighty on. It was all set up for him, and with about five minutes to go, he scored a second equaliser, his first goal for the club. He celebrated as though it was the first goal he'd ever scored. He ran over to Stan and threw his arms round him, before being mobbed by the rest of the team.

The league table was really tight. Wigan had 62 points, with 12 games remaining, while Gillingham had 58 with 13 games left. The point against Gillingham put us on 62 points, but we only had 11 games to play. Preston were still way out in front, but other teams such as Millwall and Stoke were also making a fist of it. Millwall, with 66 points from 36 games, and Stoke with 58 with 11 remaining meant that any team who put a run together would have a great chance of going straight up.

Fourteen points from the next six games meant that we'd now gone eight games without defeat. Wrighty was starting to chip in with goals as well, including a last-minute winner at home to Notts County. There were five games left to decide our fate, with the next two against promotion rivals Gillingham at home, and Millwall away. The 3–0 defeat against Gillingham should have been a game that I remembered, but after being knocked out cold early in the second half, it was all a blur. I ended up in hospital overnight with the real possibility of not featuring in the next game against Millwall. But football being what football is, I underwent the most stringent of medicals to assess whether I could play or not. The conversation went something like this.

'How do you feel?'

'Yes, I feel okay!'

'Great, that's it. You're playing!' And that was it!

The defeat left us on 76 points, one point ahead of Gillingham, who, with five games to go, had a game in hand over all the teams around them. Wigan were the team in pole position, with 78 points, the same as Millwall, but they had a nightmare run-in. Not only did they have to play us and Gillingham, they also had to play the runaway leaders, Preston. Stoke had gone on a bit of a charge, but with four games to play, were still six points behind us.

The next round of games saw victories for both Wigan and Gillingham, so a victory for us against Millwall would really make it interesting. Despite the outcome of my thorough medical exam, it was finally decided that it was possibly not safe for me to play. I wasn't the best watcher of games, but this time I was fully behind the team. It was a shocker of a day, heavy rain and howling wind. We had the wind in the first half and practically killed the game with three goals. In the second half, we carried on where we'd left off, and a Steve Davis goal soon after half-time made it 4–0. But Millwall hadn't got to where they were without being a decent team, and scored shortly after our fourth. A second goal came with just over ten minutes to go, and a third with five minutes to go made it a frantic finish. We managed to hold on, and quite honestly didn't care how we got the win, as long as we got it. That blew everything wide open. Preston were out in front with 89 points. This chasing pack was led by Wigan, who had 81 points. We were on 79, with Millwall and Gillingham both on 78, although Gillingham still had that one game in hand. So, three games to go and it was anybody's guess who was going to get that second automatic place.

Our next game was away at Brentford, who were below mid-table. Wigan had a tricky game away at Luton, but the game of the day was at Priestfield where Gillingham hosted Millwall. On the day, we couldn't have asked for much more in terms of the results. Gillingham and Millwall drew, as did Wigan. For our part, Paul Cook missed the game through illness. He was joined by Ronnie Jepson who had picked up an injury, but I was back from my head injury, recovered and fully ready to go. We played really well in the first half, but found ourselves a goal down. Stan took Payts off and threw on Wrighty. John Mullin (Mullers), who had come into the team in place of Paul Cook, had a great game, and after about an hour scored an equaliser. A few minutes later, Wrighty went through, one-on-one, and slotted it past the keeper. Mullers capped off a great performance with his second goal of the day to practically kill the game off. Although Brentford scored a late goal, we fully deserved those 3 points and were now on 82, along with Wigan, although they had a far superior goal difference.

A comfortable 2–0 win against Cambridge in our penultimate game, with two goals from Andy Payton, put us on 85 points. Preston, who a few weeks earlier had 'put us to bed', did us a huge favour by beating Millwall 3–2. They'd crashed and burned as far as we were concerned, and after only picking one point from a possible nine, were on 79 points with one game to go. Wigan were also having a bit of a stumble, and they slipped up to a home defeat against Wrexham. Gillingham, though, kept the pressure on by beating Brentford 2–0. Three days later, they battered Cardiff 4–1 at home to move into second place on 85 points, above us on goal difference. We went into the last week of the season knowing that Wigan, Gillingham and ourselves all had a chance of gaining automatic promotion the following Saturday. We had an away game at Scunthorpe, who had already been relegated. Wigan were away to mid-table Bournemouth. Gillingham, who had won six and drawn two of the last eight games, were away to Wrexham.

It was Monday morning, five days away from the game that could change the fortunes of Burnley Football Club. I had been in this situation before, with Bury, and was totally relaxed about the whole situation. I don't believe in fate, or any external being having an impact or influence on what goes on, but I just felt very confident about things. Stan had also been here before, but as we know he did have a tendency to be slightly more unpredictable than me. Even so, I didn't expect what happened that morning at training. It had been a long, hard season. As with every club in the country, most of the players were out on their feet, but ready to give it one last push. I couldn't believe it when Stan told us to get changed and get into our cars. In the past, particularly during bad runs at Bury, he would adopt this tactic and take us all off for a breakfast pizza. Fair enough, I thought. Some of the lads were quite tense, so it seemed a good ploy. I should have known never to be surprised by anything that Stan did, but I really didn't expect us to be going hill-running. He decided for some bizarre reason to throw in a mini pre-season day. It was incredible. We were probably the only club in the whole country who would be doing a running session. And right on cue, after about the tenth run, I felt my calf ping. Great! One of the most important days in the club's recent history, and I'd pulled my calf because of some stupid, idiotic idea by the coaching and management staff. He gave the rest of the squad the next two days off, but I was in early getting extensive treatment, hoping for the best.

Using the same tried and trusted formula to determine my fitness, I was selected to start the game. We went into it knowing that we probably had to win to have any chance of getting promoted. Matching Gillingham's result would not have been enough with their big advantage in goal difference. We started the game pretty nervously, but the travelling army of Burnley fans were in full voice. After about 10 minutes, Wrexham had gone 1–0 up against Gillingham. We really weren't playing very well, and went a goal down after about 20 minutes. Scunthorpe had other chances to score, but just before half-time, Micky Mellon scored an equaliser, which meant that at that time we were going straight up. The second half followed pretty much the same pattern as the first, with Gillingham creating chances, and us just showing grit and determination to stay in the game. I was playing on pure adrenalin; my calf was knackered, to be honest, but it was the final game of the season so there was nothing to lose.

Stan put Glen Little on in the hope of ensuring we kept the ball, and with around 20 minutes to go, following a Paul Cook corner, Glen lashed one in from the edge of the box. That sparked a premature pitch invasion which was quickly quelled by the stewards. Twenty minutes or so later, though, with Wrexham holding on for a 1–0 victory, the Burnley fans stormed the pitch again. It was my third promotion in five years, a far cry from the day I was left at home while Chesterfield were beating Bury at Wembley.

Scunthorpe had only allowed the Burnley fans 2,000 tickets, so 7,000 supporters who'd watched the game on a big screen at Turf Moor were there to greet us when we got back. I believe it was party time in Burnley that night. Me? I was straight off home to be with my nearest and dearest. We had succeeded in what we had set out to do, so for me, it was a case of job done. I always demanded a lot from myself, and was well aware of the capabilities of this team. So while it was a great day for the football club, anything less and I'd have seen it as a failure. Remember, I had left a team in the Championship and fully expected to get promoted that year.

Things were gathering pace in my private life. Nade and I had bought a house together, and set a date for the wedding. We had even bought a dog. There were still issues though with Ex-wife, who decided that the best way to deal with my 'misdemeanour' of allowing her to leave me was to criticise me to my daughter at every opportunity. It was a constant theme, but now she had another target. Nade was next in line, and Ex-wife was determined that there would be no relationship between my daughter and my wife-to-be. I had played the role of step-parent myself, and it's a difficult job at the best of times, but this was insane. Ex-wife didn't care who got hurt as long as I was in the firing line. She created an image in my daughter's mind of Nade and myself, which, 20 years later, is still lingering and still having an effect. The amazing thing is, that having been divorced for over two decades, Ex-wife still calls herself Johnrose. Make of that what you will.

CHAPTER 17

SEASON 2000–2001

I'd spent most of the close season trying to recover from my calf injury. I'd put myself out for the club on that final game of the season, but I knew it would mean nothing once pre-season started. Once it did start, I knew that I was behind where I normally was at this stage. I still looked fairly fit, but I could feel the difference. I felt half a yard slow, both in my movement and in my thinking. On the days that I was close to my optimum fitness, I felt unbeatable, but when there was something missing, the sharpness I needed just wasn't there. And that is how I felt that pre-season. The manager had brought in Kevin Ball (Ballie), a Sunderland legend who, although his best days were behind him, was still a good acquisition. Stan had said that he had planned to play myself and Ballie in the middle of the field. 'No one will get a kick,' he said, during one of the training sessions.

Ballie was a shoe-in to play every week. He was on big money, and despite what Stan had said, I always felt that myself, Micky and Mullers would be battling for a place.

Paul Cook was also pretty much guaranteed a place in the starting eleven, where he tended to play a deeper role in front of the back four. I had the shirt for the first pre-season game, but I was still searching for fitness, and consequently, form. In the next few games, Stan tried the three of us alongside Ballie, seemingly not sure what his best line was. It didn't even occur to him that his best line-up might not have included Ballie or Paul Cook. Anyway, the decision, as far as I was concerned, was taken out of his hands when, a week before the season started, I landed awkwardly during one of the games and damaged my knee ligaments. By coincidence, Westy did something similar a few minutes later. So two of Stan's 'boys' would miss the start of the season; two of his boys who had helped him gain three promotions in five years. Obviously, he was going to wrap us up in cotton wool and gently nurture us back to health. Not a chance! For some inexplicable reason he decided he would use this as an opportunity to make us whipping boys. Most of the time when we were injured he would act as if we weren't there. On the few occasions that he acknowledged us it was just to tell us how pathetic we were, or in his words, 'soft as shit'. Westy got it worse than I did; Stan really treated him like a dog.

From a personal perspective, it was a terrible season. It was a season that was hampered by injuries; calf, back, and my old favourite, the Achilles tendon. After a fractured season, and only 20 or so appearances, more damage to the Achilles and a subsequent operation ended it for me. The saving grace, I suppose, was that at least I was in and around the squad whenever I was fit and available. But with Westy, he really had it hard. Mitchell Thomas was Stan's preferred right back, and although he was nearing the end of his career, he was superbly fit. He very rarely got injured, and that was all the encouragement the management seemed to need to rip into Westy at every opportunity. Westy trained harder than anyone else at the club for absolutely no reward. I can't emphasise enough just how badly he was treated. He travelled all over the country knowing he was never going to get in the squad, but Stan made him travel anyway. Towards the back end of the season, Mitchell Thomas *did* get injured, and Stan turned to Westy as though it was the most natural thing in the world. I'd have been tempted to tell him what to do, but Westy just got on with it and in the end I think he made about six appearances.

This was typical of Stan's erratic behaviour. Throughout that season, he fell out with his own players and his own staff on a regular basis. He treated them like shit as well; in fact, they probably got it worse than the players. I genuinely believe that living in the town heaped too much pressure on Stan. He was certainly never predictable at Bury, but this was different. He became unlikeable, to me anyway. There was one game, away at West Brom I think it was, where something had wound him up in the morning, so he decided not to attend the game. Incredible! Sam spouted some rubbish about him not feeling very well, and that he possibly wouldn't make it, but the truth was he was in one.

We got a flavour of his unpredictability in pre-season. One of Stan's mates, an agent, would often turn up at training with a player. This player would usually be foreign, and would just join in training. One morning it was no surprise when the same thing happened. This time it was a Greek goalkeeper called Nik. I genuinely don't know how old Nik was but the way he bent down to tie his boots suggested he was about 70. Either that, or he'd spent the majority of his goalkeeping career bending down and picking balls out of the net. I've got MND and don't move particularly well, but if you stood us together and asked us to touch our toes, you'd have been hard pressed to guess which one of us was a goalkeeper.

At the end of training, we finished off with a shooting session. Stan's famous words, 'Tell the Greek c**t to get his gloves on, we'll pepper a few past him and then he can f**k off back home,' will long live in the memory.

Nik (or Nik the Greek as he was affectionately called,) was unbelievable. There must have been about a hundred shots, but I'm sure he only let in four or five. Nik the Greek ended up missing only a handful of league games that season, as both he and the football club surprised the whole division. It was Burnley's first season at this level for some time and they only missed out on the play-offs by two points. So, irrespective of what you may or may not have thought about Stan, he had, yet again, done a great job.

There were, though, other questionable acts from Stan. One was during the team talk away at QPR. They had a young Peter Crouch playing for them, and Stan's advice was to 'Let him have the ball at all times. Look at the state of him. He's shite!' Actually, Stan, no, he wasn't shite. He was brilliant. In fact, he played over 40 games for England. Never judge a book by its cover, Stan.

My personal favourite of that season was Stan's treatment of Ian Cox (Coxy). Coxy was a great lad, one of the nicest you will ever meet in football. He was also a really good footballer, lightning quick, great in the air and good on the ground. We signed him from Bournemouth, and after he moved to Preston we became good mates and driving partners. He became guilty by association, getting terrible stick from both Sam and Stan. But it was all good-natured, and they really valued him as a player and as a person. This changed, for Stan, anyway, when Coxy was selected to represent Trinidad and Tobago. The manager was Ian Porterfield, another one who had history with Stan. Stan decided that Trinidad and Tobago was not good enough for Coxy's talents, and labelled the team a 'tin-pot outfit'. But Coxy went anyway, and Stan publicly slated them. When he got back from his little excursion, Stan ripped into him. He was clearly taking out his frustration with Ian Porterfield on Coxy. I'd just had my operation on my Achilles, yet both myself and Coxy were selected to go on the away trip to Portsmouth. I genuinely believe that I was asked to go there to support Coxy, who was really getting it in the neck. But there was more to come!

We got to the hotel, and there was Ian Wright waiting for us. Obviously it was great to see him and it was good of him to meet up with us. It took him about three seconds to detect the tension between the manager and Coxy. And then he came into his own. Stan always insisted on being called 'gaffer'. Even players who have long since retired call him gaffer. I never understood it myself. In any other industry, you call your boss by their first name. But not football! It's always gaffer. It's as though the managers believe that they're up there on their parapet looking down on the minions. What a joke!

Anyway, Wrighty was having none of it. It was always 'Stan'. Come to think of it, Andy Gray called him Stan as well. Maybe it's a southern black thing. Today though, he really stepped it up. Like I said, Coxy was the nicest person in the world, and would avoid conflict at all costs. So while we were having dinner Wrighty, who was on our table, started shouting over to Stan. In his strong Cockney accent, across the room, he bellowed, 'Stanley, Staaaanley! Coxy said, you're a w**ker!'

That was it for me, I was in hysterics as Coxy was pleading with Wrighty shut up. I was nearly wetting myself as I waited for Stan's reaction. But nothing! Not a word. He didn't even look up. But his face was getting redder and redder. So, Wrighty decided to crank it up a bit.

'Staaaanley! Coxy said, "Who are you calling a tin-pot outfit?"' Again, nothing. By now, Coxy was nearly under the table. I was absolutely pissing myself. Then he let loose, even louder this time with, 'STAAAANLEY! Coxy said, "You can shove your game up your arse. I didn't want to come here anyway!"' I was absolutely dying, and I've never seen anyone cringe as much in my life. Wrighty was like a little kid, his shoulders were going as he was giggling. It was brilliant. It was, honestly, one of the funniest things that I had ever seen. And the best thing about it was, Stan never said a word. He just allowed Wrighty to completely belittle him. Anybody else, he'd have been all over them. But Wrighty could do no wrong.

The highlight of that season for me other than the Wrighty episode was probably the event around the Christmas period. On Boxing Day, we played away at

Barnsley. It was a tight game, and in the last minute I went for a header in our box. Nik the Greek had shouted for it, but I decided to try to head it away anyway, just as I always would. The ball skimmed off my head and went out for a corner, from which Barnsley scored the winner. In the dressing room, Stan was apoplectic. He really launched into me, not for the first time. But I just sat there and stared at him. That was the occasion when the lads told me that I was smirking. Stan totally lost it. In the press room after the game, he was still fuming. He just started ranting, 'That's it! Christmas is cancelled! Everything is cancelled! Those players are having a laugh! I've stuck up for them in the past, but they're having a jolly! They've had too much turkey and too much plum duff and they have no desire. There will be no more days off!'

It was a Stan classic! I remember Radio Lancashire playing the clip to Eminem's 'Stan'. It was brilliant.

On the back of that defeat, Stan decided to put us in a hotel on New Year's Eve for the New Year's Day game at home against Wolves. Yes, we were playing at home and he decided to bring all the lads in from their homes and families and shove us in a hotel for a home game. Talk about losing the plot! I don't know what he expected us to do, but he had never done this before. Like I said, I think the pressure of managing in his home town was just too much. So we all arrived at the hotel in Burnley at around three o'clock. I don't even remember its name, but it was separated into two distinct parts. There was one part that was absolutely buzzing. There was going to be an all-night party and, unsurprisingly, the management staff were staying there.

And then there was our part… To his credit, there was a bar where we were staying, and we were allowed *one* drink.

After dinner, we all met in the bar. The management staff slummed it with us for about 10 minutes before shooting off to the party. They were all togged up and ready to revel. It was a complete piss-take! There we all were sat in the bar, which was now completely unmanned. Our section of the hotel was virtually closed. There was absolutely no staff around at all. I can't remember whose idea it was, but we decided to help ourselves to a drink. Now, if I'd been at home, I'd have had a couple of drinks and that would have been it. I'd been in professional football for 15 years and had never once gone out on New Year's Eve, and never once overdone it the evening before a game.

One drink became two, which became three… It ended up being a great night, and it never cost us a penny. Some of the lads abstained, but the rest saw the New Year in with champagne. I'll be honest, from my point of view, it was a complete act of defiance. I always hated it when I felt that I'd been dealt an injustice, and that was my grown-up way of dealing with it. That'd teach him!

The following morning some of the lads were a bit shaky. We went for breakfast, and you know when you're on your way to a hotel restaurant, you can smell the aromas. This time, there was nothing. Not a thing. As with the night before, there were no staff on duty. So we ended up rummaging through the cupboards, trying to find something to eat. It was ridiculous. And if the previous night was poor preparation for a game, this was hardly ideal. When we arrived at the ground I was a bit surprised to hear my name being read out in the starting eleven. I'm not sure whether I was happy about it or not. Amazingly, we started off the game really well, with Graham Brant scoring after about five minutes. But that was as good as it got and we faltered badly. We lost the game 2–1 and walked into another roasting.

The following game, a 0–0 draw against Gillingham, meant that we'd gone seven games without a win. Goals from Andy Payton and myself partly atoned for the debacle on Boxing Day as we beat Barnsley 2–1 in the return fixture. But I was starting to struggle again with my Achilles tendon, and a few weeks later my season was over.

Fortunately, life outside football was going from strength to strength. For some strange reason, Nadine had stuck to her promise, and on 16 June, a month after the season ended, we were married. Our reception was held in a hotel halfway between Preston and Burnley and, despite being hijacked by a number of Burnley fans, it was a great ending to a pretty awful season.

CHAPTER 18

WHAT A WASTE

The following season was a complete write-off for me. I hadn't trained since February and came back to pre-season a million miles from where I needed to be. It was mid September before I was finally firing on all cylinders. By this time, we had won seven out of eight league games, losing only to Man City. I did manage to get the odd substitute spot, but further injuries to my back and calf, which was becoming my new nemesis, meant that I didn't actually start a game, and only managed six substitute appearances that season. By contrast, Stan had fallen back in love with Westy, who missed only a handful.

Towards the back end of the season, Stan tried to pull off another masterstroke by signing Paul Gascoigne. We had been up and around the top six pretty much all season, and Stan had hoped for the same impact that Ian Wright had made a few years previously. Unfortunately, that wasn't the case. Gazza really struggled to make any impression, either in games or in training. He was surprisingly quiet; most of the lads were expecting a loud, bubbly sort of guy, but he was quite subdued. That season also saw the return of my former colleague, David Johnson. He again showed what a good player he was, but the 'little shit' who left Bury, as Jeppo used to call him, came back a big shit. He was loud, lairy, arrogant and not particularly likeable. As with other former teammates, I met up with him recently, and he was great. Perhaps some people just need to live up to their reputation.

Ultimately the season ended in disappointment. We were pipped for the last play-off spot on goal difference by Norwich, who won five and drew two of their last seven games, whereas we had lost our penultimate game to relegation-threatened Grimsby.

As usual, the day after the season ended, we all met up at the ground to find out which players would be released and which offered new contracts. It didn't come as a complete surprise to find out that I was one of those picking up my P45. I drove home in a complete daze, wondering what on earth I was going to do now. I knew that I had a few more years left in me, but I'd already begun planning for the future, and was over halfway through studying for that degree in sports science.

After a brief holiday, I spent the rest of the break training hard and sitting by the phone, waiting for a call that never came. As the start of pre-season got closer, I phoned my old mate Stan and asked if I could do pre-season with them. It was important that I kept up my fitness, in case I was contacted by another club. I had a great pre-season, and fitness-wise I was head and shoulders above everybody else. A few weeks in, I was asked to go and train with

Blackpool Football Club. My mate Paul absolutely hated that, (football logic means that fans usually hate the club which is geographically closest to them), but work is work and I'd already made the change from Blackburn Rovers to Burnley, so this wasn't a problem for me. I trained there for about a week and played in one pre-season game. At the end of the week, the manager, former Liverpool midfielder Steve McMahon, who was one of the strangest people I'd ever met, said that they wanted me to sign a contract with them.

I was to meet the chairman before the final pre-season game, a week before the season started. The idea was that I would sign a contract, get unveiled before the fans and then play the game. Sometimes, things just don't work out as planned. The contract that I was being offered paid me less than a third of what I was earning a Burnley. McMahon told me that it was the best offer that any of the new players were getting, and that I should think very seriously about signing. I'd gone in there with all my facts and figures sorted out. I had never needed an agent to tell me how much money I wanted, and I wasn't particularly bothered what anybody else was on; I just thought I knew my worth. But football at this level was changing. The collapse of ITV Digital meant that clubs outside the Premiership had less to spend than they'd budgeted for. This, though, became a great bargaining tool for the football clubs, and the phrase 'the collapse of ITV Digital' was being repeated up and down the country. Blackpool were no different; they told me what a great contract it was, and that with the collapse of ITV Digital I'd be lucky to get any more anywhere else. I took my chances and politely turned down their offer. Still, I agreed to playing in the game, and in keeping with the previous two years, promptly went on to strain my adductor muscle in the first half. Credit to Blackpool, they allowed me to see their physio and use their facilities to get fit. Once I was, I was waiting by the phone again.

Out of the blue, I got a call from Stan. The collapse of ITV Digital – here we go again – apparently meant that they couldn't sign their previous targets, and after losing the first four games of the season he asked me to sign a short-term contract. The money wasn't as good as I'd previously been on, but was considerably more than I'd been offered at Blackpool. I had proved my fitness, and was named on the bench for the next game. I started the next few games, including the game in my last week of the one-month contract. I'd actually done quite well, but in that particular game I was pretty average. Stan knee-jerked yet again, and took me off at half-time. It wasn't great timing, but I was reassured a couple of days later when my name scrolled across the bottom of the TV on Sky Sports News. Apparently, Burnley were going to offer me a contract to the end of the season. I'm not sure where that news came from because the next day, Stan pulled me in and said that he had to let me go. It was a crushing blow!

A few days later, however, I received a call from my old teammate Andy Preece, who was now manager of Bury. I was invited to play in the local derby at Rochdale, and had a stormer of a game. The following morning, he offered me a contract, or rather a non-contract, which basically gave me no rights whatsoever, but meant I could leave without notice. The money was terrible, and I thought back to the words of Steve McMahon at Blackpool. He'd offered me a two-year contract, but there was nothing I could do about it now, other than just play and hope for better.

Like a recurring bad dream, a few weeks in I pulled my hamstring. I was starting to get regular strains and pulls, which when I look back now was probably the result of coming back from injuries too soon, poor rehabilitation, and overtraining on poor pitches. I was beginning to get fed up of football. I was starting to think about my future, once again. As with Burnley a few weeks earlier, I got the call from Andy Preece to say they were letting me go. I had gone from playing in the Championship to being released by a club in the middle of the bottom tier. To be fair to Bury, I'd been injured for the last three weeks and they allowed me to get fit before releasing me, and paid me too.

After my release, it transpired that Andy Preece had been talking to Brian Flynn (Flynny). Flynny was a former Burnley player, and would often come down to watch training if he was between jobs. He was a really nice guy and I got on well with him. Apparently Flynny asked Andy Preece whether he thought I could still do a job. Flynny was now manager of Swansea and they were really struggling in the bottom division. They were in serious danger of going out of the league and were actually bottom of the division when Flynny took over. He phoned me up and explained the situation. He said it was his intention to completely change the squad and I would be a big part of the plans. Swansea had just suffered a sixth defeat in a row, and had lost 10 out of the last 12 games. After a brief upturn in results following Flynny's appointment, Swansea had hit rock bottom again. I spoke to Nadine. She said that she would support me, whatever my decision. I also spoke to close friends who advised me against it. They'd only ever been to Swansea to watch a football match, and the journey to the ground meant going past Port Talbot steelworks; not the most attractive of sites. In the end, I didn't believe that I had anything to lose, so drove down the day before a game, stayed overnight in a hotel, and met Flynny the following morning. We briefly discussed terms; it was the same as I'd been offered at Blackpool, but more than I'd got at Bury. He also promised me travel expenses and allowed me to train at Burnley during the week, only turning up for games. By the time I'd signed towards the end of January, Roberto Martinez had also signed. Experienced striker Kevin Nugent had been signed too, and was shortly followed by the now sadly departed Kieron Durkan, and youngsters Alan Tate and Leon Britton, who went on to become Swansea legends.

My Swansea debut ended in a 2–0 home win. It was shortly followed by a creditable 1–1 draw away to league leaders Rushden & Diamonds. Victories against Darlington and Macclesfield followed before an away trip to Bournemouth. It was decided that I should drive to the game from Preston, and although I was picked up with about 80 miles to go, when I got out of my car I felt like I'd been sleeping in a box for a week. We started the game really well, but after about 20 minutes, the journey finally took its toll on my hamstring, and that was me out of the game. It was shades of Bury all over again, and I waited for Flynny to have *that* chat with me. He did want to chat with me, but it was to reassure me that it didn't make any difference, but that he really needed me for the last ten games. I had five weeks to get fit, and I told him that I was more than confident I would be ready. Burnley allowed me to go and see their physio and, bang on cue with ten matches to go, I was declared fit.

We'd lost the game at Bournemouth 3–0 and my injury coincided with the run of one win in seven games, putting us right back in deep trouble. We lost the first game on my return, but a five-game unbeaten run after that meant that we'd given ourselves a real chance of survival. Two defeats followed before a hard-earned win against Rochdale in the penultimate game of the season. Another three points in the last game at home to Hull City would ensure survival, but anything less meant that we would be relying on other results to go our way.

A crowd of almost 10,000 packed the Vetch in what was undoubtedly the club's most important game. We took an early lead through a penalty before two quick goals from Hull saw us in the final relegation spot at that time. A second James Thomas penalty meant that we went in level at half-time. Had the score stayed as it was, we'd have been relegated, but early in the second half I managed to get on the end of Robbie Martinez's free kick and guide the ball into the net from close range. James Thomas sealed the game with his hat-trick goal to spark delirium from the Swansea fans.

Back in the dressing room, there was a carnival atmosphere. I found that really hard to take, and didn't join in with the wild celebrations. I totally understood it from the supporters' point of view, but we really hadn't achieved anything. Yes, we'd stayed up on the last game of the season, but for me that wasn't an achievement. I know it sounds crass, but that was the remit when I signed. Looking back, I am more than aware of the part that result played in the future success of the football club, but at the time it really was a case of 'isn't that what we get paid for?'

So I skipped the party, and drove home to Nadine, who was ready to give birth any day to my daughter Elizabeth.

On the way home, I got a call from Flynny saying that he wanted to meet me the following week to discuss a new contract. It didn't come as a surprise, but what did was when he offered me less money than I'd been getting as a non-contract player. I really don't want it to sound like it's all about money, because it isn't, but it was a bit of a shock. Apparently, the club were desperate when I'd signed in January, so had agreed to pay me a bit more. Now that they'd stayed up, they had more bargaining power. It seems crazy, but that was the reality. I'd hardly played football for the last 18 months, and was in no position to start shouting the odds. Plus, I loved my time at Swansea, I loved the city; the people were incredibly friendly and made me feel very welcome. This was in stark contrast to my experiences in North Wales, where I had people racially abusing me in the street, or even worse, shop owners abusing me.

I also fell in love with the club. The supporters were unbelievably passionate, and made it really difficult for the opposition. In truth, I loved being part of a team again with a dressing room that was full of down-to-earth people who knew how to have a good laugh and a good time. This, added to the fact that I was now 33, *and* I was being given the chance to play for a club that wanted to go forwards. So I signed the contract, with no regrets, then went back home.

A few days later, on Cup Final Day, Elizabeth Hope entered the world. As births go, it wasn't the best. The midwives were like lions with wildebeests. Nadine was black and blue, and didn't feel any better when she realised that the midwife had forgotten to take out the epidural needle. To be fair, I didn't feel a thing. I really didn't know what all the fuss was about! But all that pain, or rather me watching Nadine suffering all that pain, was worth it. Elizabeth is an absolutely wonderful child, and is growing up to be an amazing young woman. She has always been very sensible and conscientious, but when I was diagnosed with MND she really came into her own. She slipped straight into 'mother' mode, and was there to help me no matter what she was doing.

When she was doing her GCSEs, I was advised that Elizabeth could ask for special dispensation. This would allow her a certain number of marks on the assumption that her current plight would have affected her level of study. But she wasn't having any of it. Somehow, she managed to compartmentalise her life, studied tirelessly, and came out with amazing results.

Elizabeth has her mother's steely determination, although unfortunately, not her dress sense!

Elizabeth's entrance meant that I could finally have some sort of celebration. A fluctuating season had ended on a good note, and for one day only, it was time to let off some steam. Crazy nights out in Preston were becoming a bit of a rarity. Yes, I know that at 33 I only looked about

23, but *I* knew the truth, and hanging around in pubs and clubs that were full of 15- and 16-year-olds somehow didn't seem right. Getting blind drunk in the sanctity of a nice Italian restaurant, however, was more than acceptable, so that became my occasional release. Not exactly rock and roll!

CHAPTER 19

THE END IS NIGH

My last season in professional football started brightly. Buoyed by a number of new signings, the city of Swansea was full of optimism. New faces included Karl Connolly and Lee Trundle, who'd played under Flynny at Wrexham.

Lee Trundle could possibly be the most gifted footballer with whom I ever shared a dressing room. His technique was incredible; he had fast feet and was a lot quicker than people gave him credit for. He, along with another new signing, Andy Robinson, and Alan Tate and Leon Britton were unbelievable that season. But Trunds was the star of the show. Some of the goals he scored were world class, and in almost every game, he would perform some sort of party trick. *Soccer AM* used to do a feature called Showboating, but after a few weeks it just became the Lee Trundle section. There was one game where I literally stood and applauded. We were 2–1 up with about 10 minutes to go, so the game wasn't dead by any means. A long ball got played down to him. He had a defender marking him, and his only option seemed to be to hold the ball up and wait for support. But Trunds had other ideas! He got the ball, turned and flicked it up in one movement, and balanced the ball on his neck. Then he flicked it past a defender and ran towards goal. All this was on the halfway line, and he did it as though it was the most natural thing in the world. The defender wanted to kill him; Trunds had made an absolute mug of him. He used to do this in training every day, but to do it in a game was something else.

Trunds loved living in Swansea. He loved all the stardom and adulation that came from being arguably the best player in the team. He was loud, confident and flamboyant; nothing like me. But I loved being in his company. He was a genuinely nice person, and would do anything for anyone. It's no surprise that the likes of Trunds, Leon Britton and a couple of other lads from that team became ambassadors for Swansea City.

Injuries meant that I started the season playing as a central defender. Despite this obvious handicap, we beat my former club, Bury, 4–2 in the first game of the season, and followed that up with victories in the next two games. After ten games, we were flying high in first place with 22 points. The home fans were incredible, and their vociferous support would be crucial to any success that we might have. The flipside to that was when we went through a sticky patch, they really let others know. That didn't come as a complete surprise, but what did was to hear that one of the most vocal fans was the chairman, Huw Jenkins. Huw Jenkins will go down in Swansea history as the man who spearheaded the club's rise up to the Premiership. Under his stewardship, they built an identity and enjoyed unheralded success. He was a supporter of Swansea Football Club, but during the early period I felt that he forgot he was not just a fan, but the chairman. I also felt that his passion for the club sometimes clouded his judgement. That became glaringly obvious to me a few months later.

We lost Robbie Martinez and Lee Trundle through injury, which hit us hard. Our form became very sporadic, and further injuries to Kieron Durkan and Karl Connolly really stretched the squad. By the time we entered the last game of the year, we'd slipped down to seventh place, but a 3–2 win against Yeovil Town in front of a crowd of nearly 10,000 saw us end the year in fifth place. After beating Macclesfield the following week in the FA Cup second round, we were drawn at home to Preston North End. The week before, though, we had a league game at home against Cheltenham Town. The squad was further depleted when our left back pulled out the day before the game, and I was asked to deputise. About five minutes into the second half, I felt my calf go, yet again. We were really struggling for players, so being the brave soldier that I am, I played on. I instantly thought about the game against Preston but had to put it out of my head. After hobbling around for about half an hour, I was finally substituted. I knew as I came off that I was out of next week's game. I'd sacrificed myself for the good of the team, but I shouldn't have bothered. If I'd come off straightaway, I'd have had a chance of being fit, but now there was no chance.

We beat Preston in the third round of the Cup, but were still struggling in the league. That victory against Yeovil was the last before a run of six winless games. The fans showed their displeasure with their feet. We were in freefall and had dropped out of the top 10. Fewer than 5,000 fans watched us beat Leyton Orient in our next home game. It felt like the majority of that 5,000 vented their frustrations on the manager. Flynny's mood around the dressing room changed. He was always such a positive guy, but you could tell that he felt under pressure.

A second victory in succession brought the crowds back and over 8,000 fans watched us gain a home draw against current leaders, Doncaster. This clearly didn't appease the fans as a crowd of less than 6,000 saw us draw our second home game in a row, this time against Rochdale, who were struggling near the bottom of the division. The team walked off to a chorus of boos!

I returned for the next game, another draw, this time away to Southend. In our next game, away to Macclesfield, I was again asked to fill in at left back. It was a truly awful game on a truly awful pitch. We lost the game 2–1, and for the first time, to my knowledge anyway, the away support turned on Flynny. Real hard core football fans is my opinion of those who travel the length and breadth of the country to see their team play. These are diehard fans, who watch their team through thick and thin, and normally get behind them. But they'd had enough. They questioned the manager's tactics and team selections and were not happy that players were being played out of position.

The following morning, it became apparent that the chairman felt the same as those travelling fans. All the credit that Flynny had built up from the previous season had been used up. We'd gone from top of the league to clinging on to a top 10 place. Crowd attendances were falling, and the atmosphere was becoming toxic. At this point, I have to say that the supporters never, at any time, had a go at the players. They remained behind us, always willing us to win, but whenever we conceded a goal, the mood changed.

In a very short meeting the players were told that Brian Flynn had been sacked. Alan Curtis was installed as interim manager. Curt was a Swansea man through and through. He'd been at the club a long time, and had the respect of all the players. As with any club when a manager gets the sack, some of the lads will be disappointed, and those who have to work at getting a game will be delighted, but I generally think all the players were gutted to see Flynny go. But appointing Curt was a smart move. It got the players onside straightaway and lifted the mood. The King is dead, long live the King!

I was missing from Curt's first team, after straining my back during training the day before the game. A 4–2 win partly vindicated Huw Jenkins's decision, but if he thought sacking Flynny would bring the crowds back, he was very much mistaken. Fewer than 4,500 fans turned up to see that victory, and with little or no chance of making the play-offs, the Vetch Field never saw crowds anywhere near the 10,000 who attended during the heady days.

On the way into training on the following Monday I received a strange phone call from Karl Connolly.

'Have you been paid this month?' It was an unusual question and one that I didn't have the answer to.

'I assume so, why wouldn't I have been paid?'

'Just check your wages! Me and Durks (Kieron Durkan) haven't been paid, and there's a rumour that you haven't!'

I knew there was absolutely no reason why I wouldn't have been paid, but I checked anyway. Connors was right! My wages hadn't gone into the bank. When we got to the training ground, that was all people were talking about. Apparently, Huw Jenkins wasn't happy that Connors and Durks had spent a lot of time on the treatment table, and decided they hadn't deserved their wages. Basically, he had spat his dummy out at the downturn in results, and saw fit to start flexing his financial muscle. Now that was bad enough, but I had hardly missed a game through injury. Obviously, the first thing I did was go and speak to the chairman. He started questioning my devotion and loyalty to the club. I didn't have a clue what he was talking about. Then it suddenly started to become clear. A couple of weeks before I got injured, I had spoken to the manager about his plans for next season. I explained that I was 34, and as I was about to complete my degree I wanted to know so I could plan. I explained that I wasn't holding a gun to his head about a new contract; if they were going to offer me one, then great, but if not, then I would apply to go into teaching. He said he would speak to the chairman about it and that was it. I'd not given it too much thought.

Huw Jenkins (remember I said I thought he was more of a fan than a chairman), had sat on this for weeks. Apparently, my question showed a lack of loyalty. The fact that I was planning for my future really riled him, and he clearly took it personally. I went on a bit of a rant. How dare he question my loyalty and commitment to the club? I'd put my body on the line, knowing that I would miss what was possibly the biggest game of the season. I'd compromised my performances by playing out of position when the club was short, and I'd played in games when I wasn't fit. And then he had the nerve to question my commitment to the club.

'Who the hell do you think you are? What right have you got to stop my wages when you clearly know nothing about me?' I think he was taken aback a bit. 'Just because I don't wear boxers with the Welsh Dragon and don't kiss the badge doesn't mean I don't care about the club.' (That was a reference to one of the players who would do just that – although, to be fair, he did end up managing the club.) I followed up with, 'You can do what you like now, but there is no way I'm playing for this club again while you're the chairman!'

He looked to me, open-mouthed. 'You can't do that!'

'Watch me!' And I just got up and walked out.

The next day, he pulled me into his office, and told me that he had agreed a deal with Macclesfield. They'd wanted me to go on loan, and as I wasn't going to play for the club again, he'd told them I was going to go.

'I don't think so,' I said. 'Why would I want to go to Macclesfield, why do you think you can make me go to Macclesfield?'

He was basically pleading, saying that he'd agreed a deal, but I wasn't having any of it. Again, I walked out and got into my car to drive home. On the way back, I got a phone call from Peter Jackson, the Huddersfield Town manager. He'd heard I was available and wanted me to sign for them.

Huddersfield had been relegated the season before, but were flying high in third place. It would have been the perfect move, considerably closer to home and with a real chance of gaining promotion. Then I got another phone call, this time from Huw Jenkins. He had clearly decided that I was too much trouble, and said that he wanted to pay up the remainder of my contract. Of course, he initially tried to offload me with a pittance, but after a bit of toing and froing, we agreed on a deal, and that was me finished at Swansea City. I got a bit of gear together to drive over to Huddersfield to have talks with the manager. On the way I decided to ring my old mate, Stan. Burnley were having a shocker of a season, and were in real danger of being relegated. I told Stan that I was on my way to speak to Huddersfield, but that I was fit, and if he wanted to, I could come and help him out. He told me to go and speak to Huddersfield, see what they had to offer, and then give him a call. He gave me an idea of what Burnley could offer, and we left it at that.

I met up with Peter Jackson, and he really sold the club to me. I was all ready to sign when he showed me the terms of the contract. It was less than I had been on at Swansea, and less than half what I'd been offered by Stan at Burnley. I really wanted to sign for them, and the fact they were playing Swansea in their next game made it even more interesting. But there was no way I could have signed for that; I'd have been selling myself short. So we shook hands and said our goodbyes.

CHAPTER 20

COME BACK TO
WHAT YOU KNOW

I was straight on the phone to Stan, and after completing the relatively short journey from Huddersfield I arrived back at Turf Moor. Within minutes, I was a Burnley player for the third time. At training the next day, it was as though I'd never been away. Many of the same lads, with the same great atmosphere.

After missing the first couple of games I was on the bench for the next three. I started the next game, against Wimbledon, and victories in that game and the next one against Derby secured survival. I played pretty well in those two games, and showed that I was still fairly fit. The next game was away at Rotherham, and during the warm-up Sam pulled me to one side. The manager was surprised at how well I'd done (cheeky git), and had decided to offer me a contract for the following season. Happy days!

The final game of the season was at home to Sunderland. Despite losing 2–1, there was a party atmosphere at the end of the game. Stan stayed out on the pitch, and waved to all sides of the ground. He had tears in his eyes, and it seemed like they were giving him a send-off. After my conversation with Sam the previous week, I knew that couldn't be right. But it was! In the days leading up to that final game, the directors had held a meeting with Stan. Obviously I don't know what went on, but the upshot of it was, Stan would be leaving at the end of the season.

I automatically thought about myself, and where this would leave me. Brian Flynn was rumoured to have been in with a chance of the job, and he phoned me for what was a very cryptic call. He never came out and said that he had the job, but there was a smugness in his voice. I guess that smugness disappeared when the new manager of Burnley Football Club was announced: Steve Cotterill, not Brian Flynn had taken over. A few days later, I received a phone call from Steve Cotterill, and was politely told that I was being released. It didn't come as a complete shock, but it left me a little bit in no-man's land. I'd actually had enough of football by that stage, although I would definitely have signed had I been offered a new contract. I spoke to a few clubs about training with them in pre-season, and even went to Accrington Stanley and Carlisle. But my heart just wasn't in it, and after a couple of training sessions, I never went back. I'd hoped that being around a football club would have stoked whatever fire was left, but there was nothing. There and then, I knew that my football career was over. So 17 years, over 450 appearances, a few regrets, lots of happy memories, but ultimately, it was over! I had always said that I didn't want to play non-league; I was offered the chance at a number of clubs, but for me, that was it. The end of one chapter, the start of another!

It was a strange feeling! I can't say I was excited by the prospect. I'd never been in this situation before, and to be honest, I felt a bit lost. After the event at Swansea, I'd applied to go on the teaching course, but having never had to apply for anything in my life before I guess the application was pretty rubbish. I didn't get accepted, so had no idea what I was going to do. Then, a familiar phone number appeared; not Stan this time, but Sam Ellis. He was working at Leeds United as assistant to Kevin Blackwell. He told me that he had a project for me, something that could give me a real step on the ladder. As I said, I had always been into health and fitness, and I was always particular about my diet. While at Bury, we would often travel down on the day to places such as Portsmouth, Plymouth and the like. There'd be soup and sandwiches on the coach, but I would always take my own food; usually it was pasta with tuna. The lads used to go mad about the smell, but there was no way I was eating the shite that was being served up.

At Burnley, we were more likely to travel on the coach and have an overnight stop. We'd have our evening meal, usually chicken or fish and rice. But in the mornings, it was a free for all. Most of the team would be tucking into a full English breakfast; it was as though some of them had never eaten before. Then, around midday, it would be pre-match meal. Again, for many, it was carte blanche. I had my own routine; cereal and toast for breakfast, and beans on toast or pasta for pre-match. Stan could never understand why we played so poorly away from home and he asked whether it might have something to do with what we ate! I suggested it just might be, and that perhaps a full English wasn't the right fuel the boys should be taking in before a game.

'That pasta, is it good for you?'

'Er, yes, gaffer. It's good, slow release energy food.'

Years later, people were talking about Arsène Wenger changing the face of football with his nutrition and training. I'd been doing it for years. He also got lauded for his use of creatine, but again, I'd done studies on creatine and its effects years before this. Did I get any credit? No, not a bit!

Sam Ellis was obviously aware of my obsession with health and fitness and invited me to Leeds United. I spoke to him, Kevin Blackwell and the full-time fitness coach, Dean Riddle, who had worked with the England cricket team, among others. The project? To get Michael Ricketts (Ricko) fit! Michael Ricketts had played for Bolton, and while there, gained an England cap. He was then transferred to Middlesbrough for £3.5 million. After an unsuccessful season, he was transferred to Leeds United on a free transfer.

They explained that Ricko was a player with immense talent, but in their words, had no arsehole. They questioned his desire and his fitness. So I was tasked with working with him, one-on-one, after training. After one training session, I knew exactly what they meant. He really was talented, lightning quick, great technique, good with either foot, strong and good in the air. It was easy to see why he played for England. It was also easy to see why he only played once, and why he was released by Middlesbrough after they'd spent £3.5 million.

Ricko was 25 at the time, and I was a retired footballer, yet when we went into the gym he would be nearly passing out after a few reps. His pain threshold was so low it was embarrassing. I have to say that he was a really nice lad. Most lads in his situation would be slating all the players who were playing when he wasn't, and slating the management staff. But he wasn't like that at all. The only time he ever spoke about individual players was to tell me how good he thought they were. Yes, he questioned the coaching staff, but never really laid into them. I suppose that may have been because he thought I might go and tell them, but we developed a bit of a relationship where I felt he trusted me.

In terms of work rate, though, it was a different story. We would do core stability exercises, just basic things like the plank. I would be trying to get him to build up to holding it for one minute, something that should be pretty easy for a professional footballer, but he would pack it in after about 15 seconds, complaining about the pain. It was the same with sprints. Remember, this guy was lightning quick, yet I would beat him in all the sprints. In the end, I would have it in my mind how many sprints I'd want him to do, then say to him that we had five sprints left to do, but that if he beat me in the first three, he could go in. He would suddenly come to life for those three sprints, and blow me out of the water.

Eventually, he was made to train on his own. Again, he never complained, just got on with it in his own way. This completely wound up Kevin Blackwell, who made him train on his own away from the football club. Dean Riddle knew somebody at Edgbaston cricket ground, so I had to drive down to Birmingham to do sessions with him there. This suited Ricko down to the ground. He was from Birmingham and never moved up, so training was now on his doorstep. By now, he knew he was never going to be a regular in the first team, so training being 10 minutes away as opposed to 2 hours was a sort of victory for him.

I really believed that I could get him fit and firing, but after all, why should I have succeeded where others had failed so miserably? It later became apparent that was why Middlesbrough had let him go. He was eventually loaned out, but the same story kept coming back about his fitness and desire.

In 2002, when Michael Ricketts represented England, he had scored over 50 league goals. After that game, and some 10 clubs later, he retired, having scored fewer than 80 goals. I take absolutely no pleasure in the fact that other managers tried and failed with him. It was such a waste of talent, but ultimately you have to want to do it yourself, and he clearly didn't want it badly enough.

Fortunately, I was given another role at the football club: to work with the reserves and first team who were coming back from injury. That was considerably more successful, and I really believe that I had a good chance of staying there for many years. Unfortunately, for me anyway, Ken Bates then took over the football club, and in an effort to save money, he decided to restructure the staff. Or in other words, get rid of anyone who wasn't under contract. That was completely his right to do, by the way, and I have absolutely no complaints whatsoever. I do however find it amusing that in situations such as these, the first to go are always the ones on least money. To his credit, though (?), he did refuse to allow the management team to select Seth Johnson. Seth had been injured for large spells of his Leeds career, but during the pre-season when I was there, he worked his socks off and got himself really fit. Unfortunately, it transpired that if he played one more game, Leeds would have to pay Derby County (his former club) a sum of money that they couldn't afford. So that was it for Seth Johnson at Leeds. That was also it for me. I was relieved of my duties with immediate effect.

CHAPTER 21

BLACK SWAN

The day I was finally released by Burnley, I actually went into the job centre. It wasn't a pleasurable experience! I had no idea what I was going to do; I now had a sports science degree but no inkling what to do with it. The call from Sam Ellis meant that I didn't have to worry about it, but leaving Leeds meant that I was back in the same situation. I didn't fancy the job centre again, so I started scouring the local paper. I found an advert for work in a children's home. It was the last-chance saloon for children up to the age of 18, whose next stop would be a youth detention centre. I was offered the job, and couldn't wait to get my teeth into it. But it was a total let-down! The workers allowed the children to do what they wanted: anything for a quiet life. The pay was pretty shocking and I suppose they thought the effort really wasn't worth what they were getting. Both the children and the workers got a massive shock when I started working there, laying down the law and telling them how it should be run. After about two weeks, I was invited to do a manager's course, but given that the current manager was working about 80 hours a week and his stress levels were going through the roof, I decided it was not for me. So it was back to the local papers.

The day before I went on holiday, I found a job involving cardiac rehab. It sounded right up my street, helping cardiac patients back to fitness. While on holiday, I received a phone call offering me an interview.

I was interviewed by the chief executive and one of the fitness instructors. In what I thought was a strange interview technique, the chief exec told me that I was overqualified for the job, that there was no chance of progression, and that I would be bored very quickly. I told them that I would be the judge of that, and he offered me the job on the spot. He was, though, absolutely right. I was basically an overqualified timekeeper. The role involved leading circuit training sessions in a gym. The majority of the sessions were spent starting and stopping a stopwatch. It wasn't all bad, though. It was only part-time work and I finished at lunchtime every day, which enabled me to practise my new-found love, golf. I became quite good, very quickly, but working part-time as a gym instructor didn't really pay the bills. So I set up a gym at home and worked as a personal trainer.

Other events were going on in my private life that meant I really needed to focus on gaining more stable employment. There was a small matter of Nadine expecting our second child. She was due to give birth on Boxing Day 2005, and after the debacle of Elizabeth's birth, we decided that Patrick would be born at Chorley hospital.

Christmas Day and Boxing Day came and went without so much as a twinge (for me, anyway). But on New Year's Day, things started happening. I whisked Nadine off to Chorley, but there were some minor complications. This meant that we had to change our plans and go to Blackburn hospital (what is it about me and East Lancs?)

New Year's Day passed, but the following day the contractions started. So it was back again to Blackburn, where, after about an hour or so, we were sent home and told to come back once the contractions started in earnest. In truth, I think they just needed the beds. We were only home for about half an hour, when, right in the middle of *Coronation Street*, Nade began complaining of more severe pain. Apparently, the strong contractions really hurt. Obviously, these women have never experienced being kicked in the family jewels!

The journey to the hospital was, to say the least, dramatic. Traffic lights were just there to make the road look pretty, and the speed limit was just a guide. Worse than that, though; throughout the journey Nade was squeezing my hand as though her life depended on it. Now I know what you're thinking, but no, not once did I complain! Now, that's love!

When we arrived at the hospital, I practically abandoned the car and got Nade into maternity as soon as possible. This time round it was an altogether more enjoyable experience, and within a couple of hours, my little mate PJ entered the world. He was absolutely gorgeous, and Nade defied science by looking as though she'd just got ready for a night out. It was incredible, although I shouldn't have been surprised.

Elizabeth showed the first signs of her maternal qualities by immediately looking after Patrick. She became his protector, and is still like that to this day. They have got such different characters. They argue, like, well, brother and sister, but each of them knows that the other will be on hand if they were ever in trouble. They are now 16 and 14 years old, and it's still the best thing in the world watching them play together. Kids, who'd have them?

I met some real characters while working at the cardiac charity, but I wasn't being challenged. I was becoming bored, but bored as I was, I couldn't leave until I found another job, something I found very difficult. A few years in, Nadine suggested that I should go into teaching. Although it was something that I'd looked at previously, at this point in my life it was the last thing I wanted to do. I had my own kids; I had no desire to look after somebody else's. But she's very persistent, that wife of mine, and after months of gentle persuasion I applied again, this time to Liverpool Hope University to get on a teaching course. Always one to learn from my mistakes, this time I sought advice on how to complete an application form. A few weeks later, I was invited for an interview. I laboured the points about how I wanted to use health and sports to engage children, and it seemed to do the trick. I got a place on the course, knowing that the hard work was about to begin.

I combined working at the cardiac centre with my own personal training work and doing the course. To be honest, I hated studying theory; for me it was all about being in the classroom. In my very first tutorial I was told I needed to do the bare minimum in order to pass the course. It was music to my ears when he also said that what really matters is what goes on during the placement. I took the tutor's words a little bit too literally, and although I didn't fail the course, I had to resubmit all of that theory nonsense stuff. This time, I put a bit more effort into it and went from a fail to an A grade. That was pretty typical of me as throughout my whole school life, I only ever did what I thought I needed to do.

With the boring stuff out of the way, it was time to get my hands dirty. I can't stress enough how reluctant I was to do the course, but now I was on it I was going to give it a real go. And from day one I absolutely loved it. I didn't think that anything could match the feelings of being on a football pitch, but this was just the best thing that I'd ever done. The stark contrast of working with young people who were receptive to new ideas, who would sit and listen to your every word as opposed to working with an older generation who hated anything new: I felt completely revitalised. Amazingly, once the placements began, there was about an 80 per cent drop-off from people on the course. These were the people who blitzed through the theory, but couldn't handle the practical.

My first placement was in a Catholic school in Southport. The majority of children were well behaved and I passed with amazing, high marks. It was on my second placement where I realised that teaching was not all plain sailing. I'd gone from a Year 6 class to a mixed Year 1 and 2. The school was in a deprived area in Wigan; the children were a mix of travellers, children who were being cared for outside their immediate families, and those from low socio-economic status homes. There were so many issues, but they were incredibly resilient. But I realised that being a teacher was more than just about teaching the curriculum. To be honest, that placement was a bit of a struggle, but I was back on track on my last placement, at St Silas C of E in Blackburn. Although it was officially a Christian school, the demographic in Blackburn meant that many children were Muslims. Now that was an eye-opener! The children were absolutely incredible, very testing, but it was the best experience ever. Being in the thick of someone else's culture is definitely the best way to learn and appreciate things outside your own world.

Within a couple of weeks of starting my placement, I was offered a full-time post. I was asked to teach one of the Year 2 classes. Year 2 is a SATs year and I loved the pressure that brought. I have to say though that I was more than ably assisted by my teaching assistant (TA), Liz. I always felt that TAs were undervalued, but in my experience, a quality TA made life so much easier. Not just in lessening the workload, but also in helping to provide good quality teaching to the children. And I was certainly fortunate throughout the years, in having not only Liz, but also Anita, Shakira, Naz, Merinisha, and latterly, Ashleigh.

Clearly, I must have done something right as before too long I was being touted as a potential Senior Leader. I had totally transformed the PE setup, and was in the process of doing the same with maths. But the senior leadership post did not arrive. I was becoming impatient and decided to look elsewhere. I was open and honest with the head teacher, who then offered me the post. I accepted it, of course, but I was still determined to leave. It was around that time that I asked one of the teachers to record me doing my front flip. It was around that time that I broke my hand. It was around that time that my personal nightmare began.

Being told that I could possibly have motor neurone disease was, without doubt, the most frightening thing that I'd ever heard. I was about to start a teaching post in a new school, but all I could think about was the conversation with the consultant. I was still very fit, at this point. Cycling, running, weight-training, playing golf, anything and everything fitness-related. A couple of weeks before I visited the consultant, I had been on holiday with the family. I can fall asleep pretty much anywhere, and on this occasion it was lying face down on a concrete floor in our apartment. When I woke up, Patrick and Elizabeth were laughing. Apparently my shoulder was twitching throughout my little snooze. Obviously I didn't give it a second thought. It was a great holiday; we'd gone to an adventure park and I'd joined in with most of the activities; rock-climbing, abseiling and the like. My left hand still felt quite weak, but again, I'd already self-diagnosed, and it was nothing serious. A week or so after the holiday was my first visit to the consultant. It was on my second visit that I was told my possible diagnosis. Nadine and I both froze.

I still had to undergo the tests; this time the consultant stuck pins in my legs, neck and back. I remember looking at the screen – I don't know why because I couldn't understand anything anyway. While the tests were being performed, I convinced myself that everything on the screen meant that things were okay. There was absolutely no logic to it, whatsoever. Once the tests were complete, he told me that there was 'something going on' in my feet. That meant that there were only two areas affected, and for there to be a positive diagnosis (I hate the phrase 'positive diagnosis' as it suggests a good outcome), three areas needed to be affected. I was told I'd have to undergo tests every three months and that if the tests were clear for two years, then whatever I had was lying dormant. We left the hospital, and I convinced myself that he had messed up the test. He hadn't put the pins in my feet properly, or he hadn't read the screen correctly. Either way, he'd got it wrong.

There was a chance of another get-out. I'd been asked whether I'd previously suffered any issues with my back. That may have been the cause of the weakness in my hands. I had to go for an MRI scan, which would, in my mind, determine whether or not I had a terminal illness. By now, I had started my new post at Lowerhouse Junior School in Burnley. It was supposed to be a fresh start. I was on the senior leadership team, and in charge of PE and maths. But I started with this black cloud following me around. It was all I could think about. I tried to remain positive, convincing myself that if I had MND, I wouldn't be able to cycle 60 miles or train for hours in the gym, as I could. But I would have visions every few hours of what life was going to be like instead. I would get a feeling in my stomach, a bit like butterflies, every day. At home, we barely spoke about the possibility, but I remember telling my brother, and my neighbour. I was *reassured* by my brother telling me there was no way I could have MND, otherwise I would be dropping things and struggling to open the door, both things that I was currently experiencing. The neighbour went one better.

If I had MND, I would be dead within six months, just like a guy he knew.

My MRI scan had been arranged for some time in December. I was absolutely bricking it! I was at home, about to set off when I noticed a missed call on my phone. A message had been left saying that my appointment had been cancelled. I don't know whether I was more angry than relieved or the other way round. I eventually had the scan in January. Even though I knew what the answer would be, I asked the radiographer what they could see. Unsurprisingly, I was told that I'd have to wait for my results. My consultant had told me that, if the MRI results were clear, then there was a good chance that I had MND. It was three weeks before I got the results. Three weeks of praying for spinal damage because spinal damage was a better alternative to having MND.

That Wednesday evening when I was told I didn't have any spinal damage, I was crushed. In my head, I knew at that point what my diagnosis was going to be.

Nadine's mum was looking after Patrick and Elizabeth while we went to the hospital. When we arrived back at her house we just sat in the car and I broke down. We sat there for about five minutes, waiting for me to compose myself, and then went into the house. We painted a very pretty picture about how things were fine and then went home. Prior to my first visit to the hospital, I was never aware of my muscles twitching. But since that day, it was as though my arms started to torment me. They would twitch every night, getting progressively more obvious. That night, after my latest hospital visit, the twitching continued with unabated vigour. I was waking up in the middle of the night, crying. 'It's getting worse.' Nade tried to reassure me that it was my mind playing tricks, but I knew the truth. At this point, I had felt nothing untoward in my legs or feet. That was the only thing that kept me feeling positive.

I used to manage my son's Sunday football team. I had no problem taking training, or warm-ups. Then one Sunday, I felt my left foot cramp up. My heart sank! I didn't say anything to anyone, I just tried to keep it in and was almost succeeding in blanking it out. But the noises were getting louder and louder. MND was trying everything to let me know it was here.

The week that I started my new post, I went on a bike ride. It was nothing different from what I did every week, but the following morning I had a strange feeling in my back. I instantly thought that I'd trapped a nerve, and rested it for the next few days. The following Sunday, I played golf without any pain. But the following morning, I could barely walk. I arranged to see the chiropractor that same evening, and was assured it was nothing serious. She gave me a massage and said that if it wasn't better in a few days, to go back and see her. The pain had definitely eased but by the time I got back to my car, my back had started to ache again. I could barely sleep that night, and the following morning, again, I could barely move. The pain was excruciating. Getting in and out of the car was the worst. I had to try to hide my tears from the children when I was dropping them off at school.

I went to see the chiropractor who assured me that within three sessions, I would be fine. Five sessions later, I went to see my GP who told me to stop wasting my money. I was referred to a specialist, and given the strongest painkillers available. I was popping pills all day, just to get through. A few weeks later, a scan showed that I had a prolapsed disc, which was crushing a nerve. This was causing pain from the top of my hamstring all the way to the bottom of my calf. I was told that I would need an operation, but the waiting time was 18 months. Alternatively, I could opt for an epidural, which had a 50 per cent success rate compared to 80 per cent with the surgery. I was also told that with an epidural there was a good chance that the problem would return. I opted for the epidural, although even this had a waiting time of up to six months.

The issue with my back was the only thing that took my mind off the thought of having MND. I would lie down, alternating between a hot water bottle and an ice pack. The pain was so bad that I didn't even realise I was burning my skin. Anything was preferable to what I was experiencing.

During the less painful moments, my mind would flick back to my probable diagnosis. I would search the Internet, looking for forums about the symptoms that I was experiencing. A couple of these lifted my spirits, as apparently other people had experienced the same symptoms and were diagnosed with far less severe neurological diseases.

Christmas came and went, and a new term started. Three months had passed since my last consultation, and it was time for more pain treatment. The consultant had a terrible bedside manner. He was extremely dry and very matter-of-fact. Throughout this most vulnerable of times, he seemed completely devoid of emotion, and unaware of the magnitude of the situation. I fully appreciate that you need to have a certain level of detachment, but this was at the opposite end of the compassion scale. At the end of that final set of tests, the test that would determine whether or not I had MND, he simply said, 'We will send you a date to come and get your results.' And that was it. At least he didn't patronise me with 'try not to worry.'

At home, we decided to ban all talk of MND until we were sure. But I kept looking at the forums, trying to find some solace. I continued taking tablets to manage the pain in my back, which meant more burns. I wasn't aware at the time, but my performance levels at the new school were dropping. I had convinced myself that work was taking my mind off things, but in reality, work was making me more fatigued.

The day finally arrived! The day that people said would enable me to get a handle on things and get back to living my life. I had received a letter giving me a date for an appointment to discuss my test results. My head teacher told me that at least all the wondering would be over, and that I would know for sure. I kind of understood what she meant, although I wasn't sure whether knowing would mean that I felt any better.

We arrived at the hospital, Nadine and I, holding hands, but not saying a word to each other. We checked in at the reception and were kept waiting for about 45 minutes. We were then invited into the consultant's room. The conversation went like this. (Is it still a conversation if only one party is doing the talking?)

'Have a seat, Mr Johnrose. Your results show that you have got motor neurone disease! The MND nurses are waiting to discuss your next steps. Thank you.'

And that was it! Seriously, that was it. That was all he had to say. He told me that I had an incurable disease, a disease that could take my life within months. And that was how he broke the news! Jesus! Even now I think about it. I can't think of a way that he could have told me less sensitively. Yes, I know that however he broke the news wouldn't have changed the test results. But that – that was unbelievable!

He showed us out, and had closed the door before we'd reached the reception. The receptionist told us where we needed to go, and we were met by three members of the Preston MND team. I just broke down! Crying uncontrollably! What the hell had just happened? Nade put her arms round me, but I must have cried solid for about five minutes. We were then given a completely overwhelming level of MND paraphernalia; just the inside cover of the first booklet had a list of about 1,000 phone numbers. What on earth was I supposed to do with that? Talk about overkill! We got home, and I put all the MND stuff on a unit in our bedroom. Almost three years later, it's still there, untouched.

I had finally stopped crying by the time we got home. I'd suddenly become all pragmatic.

'Right then! We need to sort out my life assurance, my will, and find out what help and funding is available. What help will be available when I die?'

This pragmatism only lasted for a couple of days. As part of the services offered by the MND team, I was assigned to the physio, Amy Parkes. She, along with Wendy Bennett, kept me almost sane in those early days. In the first few sessions with Amy, we spoke about practical things, ways of ensuring that I could continue working for as long as possible. In truth, that was probably for ten minutes of a two-hour session. The rest of the time was a mixture of her assuring me that things would, one day, feel better, and her consoling me while I cried (again). She was amazing! She veered away from her role as physio to provide the individual care that I needed at that time. It wasn't prescriptive, but it was necessary. When she left the MND team, I was gutted. But we have kept in touch and she remains a very good friend.

Wendy would tell me that one day I would reach a level of acceptance. I insisted that there was absolutely no way that would happen. I told her that I knew the score, and that I would suffer a long, painful death. She attempted to reassure me that it may not be the case, but I wasn't having any of it. There was no way I wanted my family to watch me deteriorate, and I went home to research assisted suicide. I found the website – in Switzerland, Dignity in Dying. I explored the logistics, the cost, everything, and that was my plan. It's amazing what thoughts come into your head at certain times. My overriding thought was of not being able to wipe my own backside. For me, that would be the ultimate humiliation. I vowed that, when that time came, I would be booking my flight. This was something that I kept to myself, and only revealed 18 months later, the day I announced that I had MND.

I finally got to the stage where my thinking was very practical. Nadine and I decided to keep the news between the two of us because, apart from the disc issues, I was functioning relatively well. We wanted to protect the children, and didn't even tell family members. I think we told Nade's mum, but that was it. Other than that, Westy was the first person to know. Nade, quite rightly, decided that I should start to meet up with my old mates. We used to go out every Cup Final Day, spend the whole day in Manchester, never really taking much notice of the game but just having a laugh. Paul, Westy, Rob (Matthews), Nick and occasionally Chris would all be there.

Nade sent a message to Westy's wife, Sam, asking what he was doing over the next few weeks. Westy being Westy phoned me up straightaway. He knew that there was something wrong because of the tone of the message. And that's when I told him. At that point, it was the most difficult conversation that I'd ever had. Not because of what was happening to me, but because you are basically telling one of your best mates that you are about to die. Westy was brilliant! Westy's thinking is quite black and white. He didn't mess about, he just said, 'Okay, I'm going to sort out a night out. Who do you want to come?' In view of the fact that it wasn't yet public knowledge, we kept it to myself, Westy, Rob – and Paul. So I had to have the conversation with Paul. He was someone I'd known since we were 11 years old, and we've been through so much together. This was a conversation I was not going to enjoy. It was terrible! I was blubbing down the phone, he was blubbing down the phone. Both of us crying for the other one without a thought for ourselves.

Prior to the diagnosis, at home we used to joke about my hands being so pathetic. We used to high-five, but as I couldn't raise all of my fingers, we would 'high-three'. Those jokes stopped immediately! MND was already having an effect on our behaviours.

I applied for, and received a blue badge for parking. Patrick and Elizabeth were ecstatic. Their first thought was, 'Now we can park anywhere we want, Dad,' which was hilarious. They assumed the badge was because of my back injury, which made life easier for me and Nadine.

At work, I was running on about 60 per cent. I could normally be up until all hours and wake up as fresh as a daisy, but I was becoming more and more tired. However, I still told myself that going to work was the best thing for me. It had been five weeks since my diagnosis and I thought that I'd been handling things really quite well. Then one morning, I was on the way in, and a number of thoughts came rushing through my head. I was driving at about 70mph on the M65, when this thought appeared: 'If I veer off to the left now, all my problems will be solved.' I was 47 years old, and had never had a negative thought in my life, but there I was, contemplating ending it all.

The stark reality of what was actually happening had kicked in. Then I thought about Nade and the kids... Somehow I made it into work. Tears were streaming down my face! As I entered the building, the deputy head was there. Seeing what state I was in, she took me into the head teacher's office. 'The children will be coming in soon, we can't let them see you like this!' We sat and talked for a while, well, I blubbed (again). What a sight that must have been, because believe me, I am an ugly crier. She decided it would be best if I went home. There were two or three days left until the Easter break, so we agreed that I would come back after that. While I was off, she sent me a whole host of practice exam papers to mark. I like to think that it was because she wanted to keep me busy, but future events meant I questioned her motives. I received a number of phone calls from the head teacher during the break, but none from the woman who had seen me in such a vulnerable state.

During the Easter break, I was referred to a local hospice that provides support for people with various terminal illnesses, typically cancer and MND. I was starting to suffer from muscle pains and spasms, and they were offering complimentary massage. But this was the last place that I wanted to go.

From the very first second of knowing that MND was a possibility, it started to follow me everywhere. I would turn on the radio and it was there, I would browse the Internet, and somebody else had died from it. Driving around, I saw more and more people in wheelchairs, and obviously (in my mind, anyway) they were all suffering from MND. I used to listen to BBC Radio 5 Live (yes I know I'm an intellectual). They discussed the hard-hitting topics, real-life events, and I loved it. But now, my life had become too serious, so I even compromised my beliefs and found the antithesis of 5 Live. Don't judge me, but I started listening to talkSPORT. talkSPORT in my opinion is a radio version of the *News of the World*. But at that time it was what I needed, but I realised the gods were against me when I tuned in and they were discussing a charity football match that had taken place the day before, for a player who had been diagnosed with MND. As I said, it was following me everywhere.

The last thing I wanted from the hospice was a real-life fast-forward picture of what I was about to become, but I was reassured that would not be the case. All I would have to do was come in, get my massage and go home. Lunch was available if I wished to stay, but that was going to be my choice.

I arrived for my first session; all the staff were very nice, and I proceeded to have my massage. Being the social animal that I am, I thought it only right that I stay for lunch. What happened next was not what I needed. I sat down on a table with three other people, and one of the staff members came over to ask us what we wanted. For some reason, she decided that I was about three years old, and spoke to me as though I was stupid. She told me, 'It's such a lovely place here, we play games and have quizzes, you'll really love it.' She then went on to describe what was for lunch, ending it with 'We even have cake and custard. And if you like, we can mash your food up for you.'

Jesus Christ, I thought. Is this for real?

It got worse! On my table, the three others had all been diagnosed with cancer. The opening line on the table was, 'So, are you terminal then?'

'Yes, yeah. I've been given six months to live. What about you?'

'Less than twelve months, but I hate the chemo!'

I had to get out of there. I phoned Wendy, still at that time my MND nurse, and told her that I couldn't handle this. I needed to speak to somebody. Soon! She referred me to a neuropsychologist, who I visited every six weeks. He was absolutely brilliant; he assured me that I was handling it really well. Apparently some people are in complete denial. They refuse to wear any supportive equipment, refuse to speak to anybody about it, and decide to continue life as if they'd never been given a diagnosis. But I was different! I needed to talk about it, and that session was the best hour that I had in those six weeks.

At home, we never discussed it. Nade's coping mechanism seemed to be to throw herself into her work, while almost erasing the diagnosis from her mind. There were times when I'd be struggling to put on my shirt, or fasten my tie. I'm not the sort of person who likes to ask for help, but she would stand there, almost oblivious to my difficulties. It became obvious, to me anyway, that she was struggling. But there really is no right way to handle news like we'd had, and people deal with things in their own way.

On the complimentary massage front at the hospice, I pushed to the back of my mind everything that was going on around me. I even took part in the quizzes, although not perhaps in the way they'd have wished. On the board, there would be nine letters. You had to find as many words as you could within a certain time, but the real test was to find the nine-letter word. The people there would eulogise over finding three-letter words, but to be honest, I really wasn't in the mood, so I would just type the nine letters into Google and search 'find a nine-letter word'.

And that would be the end of the game!

At the end of one of the sessions, I bumped into one of the MND nurses. She suggested that I attend the group therapy sessions. People with MND along with their families would meet up once a month, talk about their experiences, and have tea and biscuits. It would be really beneficial for me, apparently. But yet again, this was not something I was ready for.

On about my fourth visit, a gentleman came in on a motorised wheelchair. I looked at him, and instantly knew that he had motor neurone disease. He had been diagnosed weeks after me, yet could barely walk. He was practically incoherent, needed a neck brace to hold his head up, and needed help feeding. I had to listen really carefully to understand what he was saying, but one thing he did say made me sit up and give myself a slap. Far from feeling sorry for himself, he just said, 'I treat this disease with the contempt it deserves.' Brilliant! Absolutely brilliant!

He also had an app on his phone which he would use whenever somebody asked him how he was. The answers ranged from 'pretty good' to 'f***ing shit'. Again, brilliant! He only attended about two more sessions, but I learned so much from him.

Cup Final Day was approaching, and I was now wearing hand supports. I knew that Rob would be wondering why, so I had the conversation with him while we were standing at the urinals in a pub. Well, there's not really a good place to break such news, is there? He didn't really say much, and we carried on with the day.

The counselling sessions were going well. My mood was still fluctuating, but I had become aware of when the downs were coming, and had been given strategies on how to cope. It got to the point where I knew when I was going to have a dip days before it came. I had been given DVDs to listen to, full of calming and relaxing sounds. It was a bit like meditation. I was also coping better at school, and though I wasn't quite my old self, I had certainly upped my game. As the end of the school year grew near, I was already planning for the following term. I had rediscovered my mojo!

Nadine and I had decided that we would use MND to our advantage, and in this instance, that meant accessing the national Motability Scheme.

I had been struggling to drive my car since the trampoline incident. My hands were becoming so weak that it took an eternity just to turn the ignition. So we ordered an all-singing, all-dancing car with a stop-start button function. With my old vigour restored, and a new car on the way, relatively speaking, things were going well. We had also booked a holiday, our first ever all-inclusive trip. Amid all the shit that was going on, this was a positive period.

Despite our upturn in mood, we still rarely discussed MND. We would go out for family meals, usually with Nadine's family, and they would watch me struggling to cut up my food. Never once did they ask a question. It couldn't have been more obvious that there was an issue, but everybody acted as though everything was perfectly normal. That was the great thing about being in school. The children would just ask, outright, why I was wearing hand splints. I used to say that I had a condition that meant my muscles were weak. Not really a lie, but not the total truth. Back at home, my own children had begun asking questions of their own. They couldn't understand why I was wearing splints on both hands when I had only broken my left hand. Again, I would say that although they were right, my right hand had also been damaged. It seemed to pacify them!

Meanwhile, Fran kept asking how I was. When would I find out what was going on? How come I didn't know by now? So many questions, and each time I told him they were still investigating. I hated lying to him, but we needed to shield the children. I have to admit, though, a part of me just wanted to tell them. I told myself that was because I wanted them to have more time to get used to the situation, but perhaps it was just to make myself feel better. I really don't know. Anyhow, we'd made a decision and we stuck to it.

That was it, school was over. My current situation meant that I had to give up my role as a football manager. Everyone assumed it was because of my back, and that was fine with me. The fewer questions, the better. Patrick was absolutely gutted; he loved it when we went to football together. He also loved me being his manager. But all that had to change! In just a few months, I'd already needed to make a number of adjustments to my life. I no longer cycled, there were no more sessions in the gym, golf was out, and now I was giving up a very important part of my family life. Added to this, our father and son PlayStation games had come to an end. These were the little things being affected that nobody told me about. The impact of having MND was reverberating around all aspects of family life (although I can't say that I miss being hammered by Patrick at FIFA. Why are kids so darn good at computer games?)

The first week of the holiday was incredible. We spent hours in the pool, which seemed to work wonders for my back. After a few days, I was even managing to have a kick-about with Patrick and a mate that he'd made on the trip. It was absolutely brilliant! I'm not sure whether it was a combination of the pool, the weather and the tablets, but I was getting virtually no pain. The stiffness in my legs had practically gone, and my arms, which had been causing me a few problems, had stopped aching. Towards the back of the holiday, though, things took a turn for the worse. It wasn't physical, however. Things were still okay on that front. But the churning that I had experienced in my stomach returned. It left me feeling listless, my mood darkened and I just wanted to go home. Our apartment was on the third floor, and on more than one occasion I actually contemplated jumping over the barrier. I had a prearranged appointment with the physio for the day we got back home, but until then, I just suffered. For three days, I was really struggling. Not wanting to get out of bed, but trying not to give anything away to Patrick and Elizabeth, or Nadine for that matter.

When we arrived back in England, I received a phone call from the hospital. About three months after my consultation, I'd been given an appointment for the epidural. It was to be in four days' time. That, and my upcoming physio appointment, lifted my mood for the moment.

The following morning I drove to see the physio. I still had an uneasy feeling in my stomach, but not quite as bad as it had been. I have no idea why, but after the appointment, by the time I got to my car, I was a wreck again. I just sat in my car, head in my hands, wailing. Cue another quick call to Wendy, who was fast becoming my go-to person. She arranged an urgent appointment with a neuropsychologist, and hey presto, things looked better again.

The day of the epidural arrived. Apart from those few days on holiday, I'd spent the last nine or ten months in pain. And I hadn't been able to tie my own laces, or wash my own feet (sorry, Nade). So I was really looking forward to my date with the needle. I arrived at hospital at around ten o'clock in the morning. I was due to go in at around noon, but there had been some emergency, so eventually I went in around 4pm. I was advised that it would be quite painful, but I knew it would be nothing compared to what I'd been experiencing. Or rather, I thought I knew.

The pain was incredible! My already high respect for women was elevated to new heights. This was not nice, at all. I grimaced throughout, played counting games in my head, anything just to will the time away. I apologised for the noises that I was making, but apparently that was nothing compared to the guy who had been in there before me. He had been screaming and swearing, threatening to sue them. Like I said, respect for all those women who go through childbirth with barely a whimper.

When it was all over, there was a slight pain in my back where the needle had been, but nothing else. In the morning, there was no pain at all. I even managed to wash my own feet. It was like some sort of miracle. Why hadn't I had this sooner? That afternoon, I went straight to the driving range and hit about 50 golf balls. It was great. So that was me, cured. All I had to worry about now was the fact that I still had MND.

Two weeks went by, and still no pain. I was back playing football in the garden with Patrick. It was like old times again. This particular day, we were taking free kicks. It was dinnertime, and we were being called in, but Patrick wanted me to have one more shot. So, I lined it up, an outside–

of-the-foot curler, but as I kicked my other leg gave way. I landed on my backside, and the pain came back, this time with a vengeance. I was back to square one. My mood changed, and once again, I was about to start a new term at school with this debilitating injury.

It had been six months since my diagnosis, and still, people were none the wiser. Still, people refused to ask questions. I found that difficult to understand, even though it meant that we didn't have to do any explaining. Things at school were becoming difficult, mainly down to my inability to use my hands properly. I was determined to continue working for as long as possible, so sought ways to combat my disability. I found a voice recognition program, called Dragon. This became a bit of a lifesaver, and was used to *write* my lesson plans. Marking was also becoming a problem, so again, we looked for solutions. We opted for bingo dabbers, and created the code for the different colours. For my comments in the children's books, I used a label maker in conjunction with Dragon. So, from a practical point of view, we were finding a way.

I was still getting no respite from the back pain, and spoke again to the consultant. There was nothing else for it; I had to go under the knife. But realistically, I didn't even know whether I'd still be alive in 18 months, so the thought of having to wait that long before an operation, well, it was not good. Fortunately, I had Westy as a mate. He made a call to the Professional Footballers' Association (PFA), told them about my diagnosis and the issues with my back. They immediately said that they would fund my operation, and I was booked in for November.

The operation was a complete success, but I was housebound for one month and unable to return to work for three months at least. That month of staring at four walls and watching crap daytime TV released all my demons. I sunk into yet another depression, and following yet another visit from Wendy Bennett was advised to take antidepressants. But that was a huge no-no for me; maybe because of the stigma, maybe it was just male pride, but I decided against it. Wallowing was a better alternative!

While I was off from work, I received a phone call from the head teacher. She had been offered and accepted another job, and was going to be leaving at Easter. I was genuinely pleased for her, but selfish me wondered what that would mean on a personal level. She had always been very sympathetic and understanding towards my illness. She read books and articles about MND, just to get a small insight into what my family and I had been going through. And I thought back to the way the deputy head, who would be the acting head, had handled the earlier situation. Time would tell whether my gut instinct was correct!

I returned back to work in February, a few weeks short of the Easter break that would mark a year since my diagnosis. There had been more questions from Patrick and Elizabeth, so Nadine and I decided that, during the Easter holidays, I would break the news to them. I could almost sense the relief, but was also completely dreading the situation. I thought back to my old friend from the hospice; he had told me that explaining his condition to his children was the worst moment of his life. And they were grown up!

I apologise for sounding like a scratched record (all you young people, google what a record is), but my mood was no longer fluctuating, it was on a downward spiral, getting darker and darker. I was finding it increasingly difficult to get out of bed in the mornings. Most mornings I would sit on the bed, just crying. Work really was my saviour, and by the time I got there, I always felt much better. But it was also becoming my enemy. By the time I got home, every evening, I was exhausted. That meant that the work that I should have been doing wasn't getting done properly. I felt like I was spinning plates: badly!

The churning feeling in my stomach was getting stronger every day. I just wanted to cry. I'd stopped answering phone calls from my nearest and dearest, which should have sent alarm bells ringing about my mental state. The twitching in my body, particularly in my arms and shoulders, seemed to be more prominent. It would keep me awake for hours, not because of the pain but because of what it meant. When I did eventually fall asleep, I'd be woken up by piercing cramps in my thighs and calves. So now, not only was it a massive struggle to get out of bed, I also had extreme fatigue to deal with. Like I said, I was spiralling. I had wanted to tell the children about my diagnosis for quite a while. There really is no right or wrong way to do it, but I just felt that the sooner they knew about it, the sooner they would come to terms with it. The flipside was, of course, that it would also mean that they would have to live with it for longer. Mentally, though, I was still wishing the days away to get to the Easter break, while simultaneously trying to hold back the time.

The Easter break was upon us. On Easter Sunday, we had Nadine's family round for dinner. My stomach was in knots, not the churning this time, but anxiety, knowing that the day was getting closer and closer. I'd be lost in thought, trying to decide how on earth to break this news to my beautiful children. What had they done to deserve this? It just felt so cruel. The next day, it was back to being a wreck again; crying like a baby, quivering, snivelling, and needing Nadine to make me get out of bed. What the hell had I become?

The next day, the same thing. It was almost becoming a routine. Go to bed, the twitching starts, lay awake for a couple of hours, fall asleep, the cramps start, lay awake for a couple of hours, fall asleep, wake with a churning stomach, cry uncontrollably, receive a pep talk from Nadine, and eventually get out of bed.

The following day was the big test. Nadine was back at work, so my crutch had disappeared. This day followed the same routine … right up to receive a pep talk from Nadine. No Nadine meant no pep talk. I stayed in 'cry uncontrollably' mode. And I cried, and cried, and cried. 'Five minutes and I'll get out of bed; just five more minutes; two more minutes and I'll get out of bed', and it went on, and on. I could hear Patrick and Elizabeth, downstairs. I had never previously stayed in bed for this length of time. 'I REALLY need to get out of bed, it's not fair on the kids.'

Eventually, I hauled myself up. I got dressed and practically dragged myself downstairs. The two of them were sitting down, watching a film, one of them on the floor, the other on a chair. I sat on the sofa, trying to keep it together, but when they asked the question, 'Are you okay, Dad?' that was it, the floodgates opened. Right there, in front of Patrick and Elizabeth, the two people who we'd tried to protect. I had completely and utterly gone. Those poor kids! There's no way they should have had to see that. They both just came up to me and hugged me, and comforted me. They were 12 and 14 years old, and they were telling me that everything was going to be all right. They were so brave. They really are the best children in the world!

It was now time for me to man up. I managed to pull myself together, and gather my thoughts. I took the deepest of deep breaths. (I'm trying not to cry right now, as I recall it.) *Jesus, what am I going to say to them?*

Another deep breath! My heart was beating faster than ever. Yet another deep breath. They were starting to become agitated. They knew this was not going to be good news. I thought again; they had done nothing to deserve this. I was now crying again, but this time it was controlled. Now they looked petrified, almost willing me to put them out of their misery. I couldn't do it, I just couldn't do it. I couldn't lie, so I chose to be economic with the truth. 'You know, I've been struggling for a while now. And you know you asked me why both my hands were strapped up when only one had been broken? Well, I'm not very well. My nerves are damaged, and it's affecting my muscles. At some point, that means I'm going to end up in a wheelchair.'

We were all crying by this point.

I had previously discussed with Nadine how to break the news to them. Nadine was insistent that I didn't tell them it was MND. She was worried about them doing pretty much what we'd done, typing it into Google and then reading all the horror stories. I understood that completely, but perhaps for my own benefit I wanted to tell them a lot of the gory details. I felt that I'd lived a lie for the last 12 months, as though it was some guilty secret. I hadn't asked for this, and had nothing to be ashamed of, but that's how it felt. It was as though I had something to hide. So, among the blubbing I managed to squeeze out the words, 'It also means that my life expectancy isn't what it should be.' I don't think Patrick took it in, but Elizabeth understood exactly what I meant and became hysterical. The three of us just sat there, comforting each other. It truly was, and still is the worst day of my life.

I've said before that they are the best children in the world, and the way that they responded just emphasised that. For the next few weeks, they were almost competing to see who could best look after me. They were quite incredible, always by my side, helping me with any and every little task. They say that children are resilient, but this was on a completely different level. I felt a huge sense of relief, although I still felt a little uneasy that they didn't know the full truth of what was going on. For the time being, though, I had to be content with that, and despite what was a truly horrific day, we enjoyed the rest of the Easter break as much as any other family.

CHAPTER 22

PEOPLE ARE PEOPLE

I have always been fascinated by people. I love the different characters. I love the way that different people react differently to the same situation.

You may have already guessed, but I have quite a high opinion of myself. I mainly appreciate what I'm good at, and recognise my faults, few though they are. I also know that I'm not perfect, and together with that, I can't expect others to be perfect either. So when I see behaviours that I don't agree with, although it may not be something that I would do, I realise that to those people that's their 'normal'. So it's not about right or wrong, it's about what is generally deemed to be acceptable.

I've always considered myself to be quite a liberal person, and one who could quite easily empathise with others. Having MND challenged all that. And it wasn't MND per se, it was more about having a disability. Having a disability opened me to a whole new world of people's perceptions and reactions. Very few things shock me, but a number of incidents have definitely left me questioning the day-to-day thinking of 'normal' people.

When I was with Ex-wife, her daily irrational behaviour led me to say this little phrase to myself, *you can't reason with the unreasonable.* The next few examples had me repeating this phrase to the people around me, by way of explanation.

Example One

Having MND has prevented me from doing a number of things, but until it is physically impossible, it will not stop me from drinking red wine (and copious amounts thereof). It did, though, prevent me from carrying heavy loads, so whenever I went shopping, I would take either Patrick or Elizabeth with me to help me out. On this occasion, it was Elizabeth, and as is customary on my weekly shopping trip, I'd wished to purchase a couple of bottles of claret. Elizabeth, who was 14 at the time, did what she always did, and began packing the shopping. When it came to the wine, she was asked if she had any ID.

'No, I'm only fourteen. Why do I need ID?'

'Because of the wine,' came the curt reply.

I intervened at this point, showed the almost unmissable handgrips to the cashier, explained that the wine was for me, and explained that I couldn't physically pack the shopping myself, hence the presence of my daughter.

'No, I'm sorry. I need to see her ID!'

'Didn't you hear me? The wine is for me. She's fourteen years old and hasn't got any ID, she's helping me pack my shopping!'

'Well, I'm afraid she looks under twenty-one, so I need to see her ID.'

I was now becoming a tad irritated. 'For the last time, the wine is for me. She is fourteen and does not have any ID. Which part of that are you struggling to understand? Look at my hands, can you see these grips? I can't pack the shopping myself.'

What she said next left me somewhat exasperated. 'Well, I'm sorry, but our under twenty-one policy states that, because I have asked her age, I now need to see her ID. So I'm afraid I can't sell you the wine.'

That was where the phrase 'you can't reason with the unreasonable' should have kicked in, but no. 'How have you got a job? I'm not dealing with this idiocy any more. Get me the manager, now!'

'I'm afraid he'll only tell you the same thing!'

'Are you deliberately being stupid? Get me the manager NOW!'

After a few minutes, the duty manager appeared. I launched into him (don't know why, it wasn't his fault), and explained how stupid the cashier had been. I then explained the situation, showed him my handgrips, and watched him squirm, apologetically. And then told him how I was going to report this incident to head office. I'd barely got my words out before he started bleating on about staff training and CPD, blah, blah, blah. Unsurprisingly, I was allowed to purchase the wine, but I kept my promise of speaking to head office. Hey presto, a sickly apology and a voucher to spend in the store arrived in my house within days.

The next day, I couldn't resist going back into the store with Elizabeth to buy some wine. We actually waited for our friend the cashier to come on to the till. Amazingly, there were no questions asked.

Example Two

I was out with Patrick this time. We had gone to Sports Direct in Preston to buy some trainers, I think it was. It was around the time that I'd started to feel sensations in my feet. My right foot in particular would occasionally drag on the floor. As we were walking down the steps, we were chatting about something, and as yet I hadn't learned that I needed to fully concentrate on each step in order to prevent what did happen. We were in the middle of a conversation when I did what looked like an attempt at a skydive, with no parachute. I hurtled down the full flight of stairs, in full view of about 30 people. I lay on the floor for a few seconds, just to see whether I was injured or not, or whether I could feel any pain. For those few seconds, everyone in the store just stood and stared at me lying there. Patrick rushed down to help me, and one store assistant, who hadn't seen but who had heard, came running to offer help. Together, the two of them helped me to my feet.

As I got my bearings, I could see people looking down, trying not to catch my eye. I wondered what they were thinking, and how they could see what had happened and not even think about helping. They watched an 11-year-old boy help his dad to his feet, and never once asked him if he was all right. As I've always said, we are not all the same. I am just grateful that I think differently to those people.

Example Three

I was expecting the delivery of an internal door. I had used this particular firm on many occasions, each time experiencing excellent service. This particular time, however, while out in the car with Patrick and Elizabeth, I received a phone call. The delivery guy had arrived at the house half an hour early. I explained that I was only five minutes away, and although he was, indeed, early, I would be back soon. He seemed a tad agitated, and asked whether I would like him to leave the door outside. I explained that this would mean me having to carry it in, but as I would be unable to do this, I politely asked him to hang around for a bit, again reminding him that he was early.

The drive at my house is round the back, but you can see the front of the house as you approach. When we arrived home we could see the van, and assumed that he was unaware of how to get round the back, something that happens on a regular basis. But no, he had in fact left the door outside, and was about to set off. Elizabeth bolted down the front steps, and asked him to take the door inside, as previously arranged. When she came back, she said that he'd been quite abrupt, and then driven away. I immediately called the office, demanding an explanation. They said that they would arrange for him to call me, if I wished.

About five minutes later, he was on the phone. I asked him what was the point of him asking me what I wanted him to do with the door, if he was just going to leave it anyway. His response was to question why I needed it carrying inside.

'Excuse me, pardon? You asked me whether I wanted the door leaving outside, and I said no, so you should have waited.'

He repeated his earlier response, 'Yes, but why can't you carry it inside yourself?'

'That's really not the point,' I said. 'Why ask – you might just as well have left in the first place.'

To be fair to him, he could sense this escalating, so offered to come round and have a face-to-face conversation. The discussion followed the same lines as before, only this time he thought he had more ammunition for his argument. Physically, I looked perfectly healthy, so now he could see absolutely no reason why I shouldn't have carried it in myself. I explained that, over the phone, as far as he was aware I could have been an 85-year-old man. I'd paid for the door to be taken inside, and that's what I'd expected. Then he said something like, 'There's clearly nothing wrong with you, you're just being lazy!'

Oh my lord, is this really happening? Is this what people have to deal with every day? I was now becoming a little annoyed.

'I don't have to tell you a thing about me, you little prick! For all you know, I could have an incurable illness that prevents me from carrying heavy loads. Just get out of my face!'

He decided to turn tail and go. I was beginning to realise that it really is impossible to understand what people are going through until you actually experience it yourself. I genuinely believe that most people are nice people, but, Jesus, they are incredibly judgemental and inconsiderate sometimes.

Example Four

This was the worst experience to date. I'd gone to the Bolton Wanderers Academy to watch my son Patrick play for Preston against the Under 13s team. Walking was beginning to become an issue for me, but fortunately the disabled parking bays were situated in full view of the pitch. I displayed my blue badge, and settled down to watch the match. There was then a tapping on the window; one of the two stewards on duty started waving his arms around, gesturing me to open my window (why do I always want to say 'wind down' my window?)

As I wound it down (sorry, couldn't help it), this guy started shouting about me having to move my car up. I told him that I was in a disabled parking bay, and asked why I needed to move up. 'To get more cars in. Now move up!' I was a bit taken aback, but explained again that I was in a disabled parking bay. 'Surely the whole point of being in a disabled spot is to get easier access in and out of the car,' I queried.

'Look! We need to get as many cars in as possible. This is what we do here, so move your car up!'

'Who do you think you're speaking to? I'm not moving my car anywhere.'

'Oh, we'll see about that. You don't even need the space, there's nothing wrong with you. You don't even have a wheelchair!'

I tried to remain calm. 'Look, you idiot! I'm not moving my car, so just get over it!' His reply to this was a classic.

'It's not a problem. As soon as you get out, I'll move another car in next to you and block you in.' Just like that! Brilliant!

I got out of the car, and went to speak to the other steward. I said that I'd had an issue with the first guy. 'Oh, I know. He told me all about it. What's your problem?'

'What's my problem? He asked me to move my car so that he could get another vehicle in a disabled bay.'

'Yes, so. What of it? That's what we do here!'

Again, this is where I should have said 'you can't reason with the reasonable' but again, no. 'I don't give a shit whether that's what you do here or not. They're called disabled bays for a reason. Why is that so difficult to understand?'

'Look, mate, I don't know what your problem is. What's the matter with you anyway? You look fine to me.'

By coincidence, earlier that day, former Bolton Wanderers player Stephen Darby announced that he had motor neurone disease. 'Not that it's any of your business, but I've got motor neurone disease, the same disease as one of your former players announced that he had earlier today.'

He sarcastically replied, 'Oh, what a shame,' and turned round to talk to his mate. His mate then slapped me on the stomach and said 'Just get over it!' Now, I was fuming, it was now that my old phrase kicked in.

I went back to the car and tweeted about my experience. The following morning, my phone was going mad. I tagged the football club into the tweet, and they panicked. Not good PR, apparently. I got the whole apology thing, but not from the people who mattered. The local paper covered the story, which again did not look good for the club. I then got a telephone call from their communications manager, who wanted to know how we could put it right. We agreed that the best way forward would be to carry out some sort of training for his staff. We arranged a time and date for this to take place, but the club cancelled. I, along with the MNDA, have since tried on numerous occasions to rearrange, but without success. It therefore came as no surprise that the next time I went to the Academy, a staff member had parked their minibus across two disabled spots. This would have saved them approximately 20 metres of walking. Incredible, but that's the sort of thing I now see every day. People, eh?

CHAPTER 23

HIGH AND DRY

After a traumatic Easter, it was back to the bread and butter of work. The change in hierarchy meant that I wasn't really looking forward to going back. The revelations and subsequent events of the last couple of weeks were beginning to take their toll, on Patrick in particular. We were both beginning to crash and burn, neither of us seemingly knowing how to find a way out. Going back to school didn't help Patrick, either. There was far too much going on in his head to concentrate. He was 12 years old at this point, not the easiest age at the best of times. But with the news of my illness still raw, looking back, there was only ever one way that it was going to go.

Patrick, my handsome little man, is like his mother. Whereas Elizabeth and I are pretty calm, they are a lot more up and down. The beauty of that, I suppose, is that you always know what they are thinking; whether they are in a good mood or not, whether they are pleased with something or not. With me or Elizabeth, well, I don't think we have ever got overexcited about anything: dead inside!

Within a few weeks of Patrick returning to school, we were getting phone calls. His behaviour, attitude and mood had dipped alarmingly. He was showing signs of aggression and displaying feelings of low self-worth. It was almost as though he felt that it was his role to make things better, but that it was out of his control. This was just the sort of thing that Nade had tried to protect him from. Speaking to him highlighted just how low he was feeling. Just as I had months before, he was having the darkest thoughts. He was a total wreck, and then I got dragged down to the same level. My head was all over the place and I really did not know who to turn to. I worried about what would happen when he went to school, so I called them and explained the situation. They were very sympathetic and said that they'd speak to him, and then call me to discuss.

I arrived at work with my head spinning. My poor little boy was having the same thoughts that I'd had, and I was now having those same thoughts again myself. Maybe I had been wrong about the acting head. Perhaps I'd misjudged her. I was about to find out.

I spoke to her and asked whether it was okay to keep my phone with me, as I was expecting a phone call from Patrick's school. And then went into graphic detail explaining the reasons why. I completely bared my soul to her with what was the most obvious of cries for help. Remember, this was the acting head, the one person at school who I should have been able to rely upon. This was her response: 'I know you are having a bit of a bad time of it, but if you can just get through these next eight weeks, you can have a rest over the summer.'

What she said didn't even register. I was far too worried about Patrick, and how he had got on at school.

Those next eight weeks were an absolute nightmare. Both Patrick and I continued to deteriorate, only being held together by Nadine and Elizabeth. My schoolwork was really suffering, but I continued to plough on. I began making mistakes at work, really elementary errors. I had gone from being 'head teacher material' to this shadow. I look back now, and it's obvious. I needed help! I was mentally shot at, depressed, and physically drained. Again, looking back, I should have taken time off work, and sought help. But more than that, the acting head should have insisted that's what I did. Instead, she threw me under the bus. She questioned my competency, and even got in HR to back up what she was saying. She started talking about 'disciplinary action' and even put a support plan in place. I was an experienced teacher, part of the senior leadership team, and yet she had me observing teachers who had been in the job for just two years in order to learn from them.

Every day, I felt like I was being watched. She would take samples of my work and criticise the life out of it. She questioned my judgement whenever I made assessments, and basically tore to bits everything I did. I was sinking further and further, and started to question my own ability to teach. Throughout all this, she never once asked me how I was. She never once asked me how Patrick was. And still, I tried to plod on. She started piling more and more work on me. At the time, I thought nothing of her behaviour, but looking back, it was as though she wanted to break me. I really feel that she wanted me to just pack it all in.

Two or three weeks before the end of term, she called me in for another meeting. And, without asking how I was, she suggested that I give up my leadership role. I said that I'd have to think about it; there would be implications regarding my pension, so I told her that I would seek professional advice and get back to her. She immediately started talking about disciplinary action and competency again. It's fair to say that did not help my mental state.

Around this time, Elizabeth's class had spent the week watching and discussing *The Theory of Everything*, the film that told the story of Stephen Hawking. She would come home and ask me questions about motor neurone disease. Initially I was sure that was her way of letting me know that she knew about it. But then she wouldn't say anything more, and that made me realise it was just a coincidence. Or so I thought… We recently discussed how she felt when I told her that I had MND. And that was when she revealed that she had known for quite some time. At the time when I should have been protecting her, she was doing all that she could to protect me. She carried this around for months, never letting on, just getting on with things as she always does. Remarkable!

I managed to get to the end of the year, but the acting head's behaviour continued in a similar vein. I was literally counting down the days to the summer break, and on the final day, she again called me for a meeting. We were supposed to hand over all the assessment data to the class's next teacher, but I'd got a virus on my memory drive, which wiped out pretty much everything that I'd built up over the last two years. She told me not to worry, but that I had a week to get it all redone and sent over!

I had the weekend off, and then called the union rep to discuss the idea of giving up my SLT role. As part of the conversation, she asked how things had been at school. I explained the events of the last two months and she was horrified. She made it absolutely clear that the acting head's behaviour was not acceptable, and furthermore, she had no right to expect me to produce the assessment data during my holidays. That was a relief, and at least I could enjoy the break without that black cloud hanging over me.

CHAPTER 24

UPRISING

The summer holidays were upon us. It always took me quite a while to 'come down' from working, so this year I decided to get my planning done early while I was still in the zone. School finished on Friday, but by Tuesday I was back in the building, planning the next term's literacy classes with a new teacher who was starting in September. As soon as I walked through the building, an uneasy feeling seeped through my body. I tried to ignore it, but it was going nowhere. I half-heartedly talked through the planning, but couldn't wait to get out. I had been mentally damaged by the place. The thought of returning filled me to the brim with anxiety.

I got home and tried to switch off. We had a holiday booked, and I looked to that to offer some sort of positive vibe. It worked, to a point, but I was still feeling pretty low. Patrick was a huge worry, and still Nade and I never discussed my condition.

By now I was desperate to talk about it. But I knew it was not going to happen, so once again, I sunk deeper and deeper. The holiday brought some respite, and last year's experience meant that I booked an appointment with the neuropsychologist for the day after we were due to return home. As expected, a few days before the end of the holiday, the churning was back. Once again, I suffered in silence.

My counselling session couldn't come soon enough, and yet again, it had the desired effect, albeit only for a few days this time. In no time at all, I was being drawn into this black abyss. I had finally told my family about my condition, each revelation being accompanied by floods of tears; mainly mine. It was difficult to gauge how they felt; I'm not sure whether, at that time, they realised the magnitude of what I was saying. Although more likely they did realise, and tried to play it down for my benefit. Either way, it wasn't something that was going to be a dinner party conversation, so I was left hanging, once again.

I was nearing breaking point! Please, somebody ask me how I am. Anything! Just have a conversation with me! There was so much that I needed to say. Suicidal thoughts were bouncing around my mind, and thoughts of flying to Switzerland. I really couldn't see a better way out. I thought back to one morning when I'd said to Nade that I didn't want to be here. She thought that I'd meant in the house. It soon became obvious what I meant!

Thoughts of going back to school, and how I would cope, flashed through my mind. That added to the anxiety, so I went to see my GP. He said there was no way I was in any state to go back to work, and signed me off for a month. That instantly relieved some of the tension. I called the acting head (who was now back to being deputy, as a new head had been installed), and asked for the phone number of the new head teacher. I said that I couldn't go into detail, but that I probably wouldn't be returning on the first week back. That was the last time she ever spoke to me! The new head, by contrast, was very sympathetic and understanding. 'Take as long as you need, and phone me if you ever want to talk about anything.' I really appreciated that, and like the previous head teacher, she has phoned me on a number of occasions to check on my well-being.

There was still no change on the home front. I needed an outlet, so spoke to Nade about writing a blog. She thought it was a great idea, until I mentioned wanting to make it public. From the second I was diagnosed, I'd wanted to do something to help others in the same situation. But I'd not been ready. By writing a blog, I could kill two birds. I knew that it would lift a huge weight from my shoulders, while also resonating with others. We were 18 months into the diagnosis (I say 'we' because it's definitely something that your family go through with you), but we still hadn't completely reached that level of acceptance that Wendy Bennett spoke about. So, for Nade, going public was a no-no. I started the blog in any case, but only showed it to Paul. He didn't know what to say!

After retiring from playing professional football, I was invited to do some radio commentary. I confided in both Scott Reid and Andy Bayes, knowing that they wouldn't tell anyone about my condition. Andy, though, went one further. If I ever wanted to go public with the news, he would do a radio interview. He told me that he would handle it sensitively, but there was no pressure. That invitation came back to me after my idea of the public blog was vetoed. Again, I asked Nadine what she thought, only this time she told me that if that's what I wanted to do, then I should do it. I texted Andy, and the date was arranged for me to go into BBC Radio Lancashire for what became the most pivotal point in my life since my diagnosis.

One Monday evening, in late August 2018, Andy Bayes conducted the interview. I mentioned earlier how I laid myself bare to the acting head, but that was nothing compared to this interview. Andy was brilliant, finding the right balance between sensitivity with his questioning and, basically, knowing when to shut up.

The interview was filmed, but I can honestly say that I was unaware of any camera. I spoke openly about my feelings about death and dying; my issues with depression and anxiety; about leaving my family behind; about not wanting to be a burden; about the implications for my work; about everything. And throughout that time, I never once wanted to cry. There was no churning, no anxiety. It was as though the old, frank, possibly slightly autistic Len had returned.

I walked out of the studio a completely different person. But there was still Nade to deal with. How would this affect her? How would it affect the dynamics of the house?

As soon as I walked in, she asked me how it went. 'It was fine!'

'When is it being aired?'

'On Wednesday, I think' – and that was it. Just then, I got an email from Andy; he'd sent the full recording of the interview. Just in passing I mentioned to Nade what it was, and then went out to pick up Elizabeth from netball. I felt liberated as I got into the car, but slightly disappointed that Nade hadn't made more of a meal of it. Nevertheless, I could sense that things were already beginning to change, for me, anyway.

When I got home, Nade was sitting there, waiting for me. She just looked towards me and said something like 'Wow!' She had listened to the entire interview, which was the last thing I thought she would want to do. She sounded genuinely proud of the fact that I'd been so candid. And she was suddenly open to talking about it. She started to look at MND forums, and talk to work colleagues about it. She even actively took part in organising charity events. This was a huge turnaround, for both of us. The situation became normalised, and from that point, we knew we just had to make the most of things.

After the interview with Andy Bayes, he'd said there might be some media interest. I completely dismissed that; that was not the reason why I had done it. Close family and friends knew about it, but it was still like I was carrying around a guilty secret. And I needed a way to try to get things back to some sort of normality. Even so, he insisted, it was bound to happen. And happen it did.

By Wednesday lunchtime, my phone was going mad. It became the lead story on the BBC Sports website, and I was suddenly being asked to do interviews by diverse media outlets. Most importantly, though, I received a phone call from the MND Association. I'd previously wanted nothing to do with the organisation, but now I was open to whatever they had to say. I spoke to a lady called Sue Muller, who said that, first and foremost, the welfare of my family was her main priority. We discussed how I was, and the things that we could do going forward. As part of that discussion, she mentioned a guy called Richard White. He was in charge of the events team at the Association, and wanted to give me a call. I was fine with that, so said I'd be happy to speak to him.

Richard called the following day. He just kept on thanking me for doing the interview (which felt a bit weird, to be honest). But he insisted it was so good to have someone 'in the public eye' bring the subject of MND to the fore. Apparently, over the years, there had been a number of well-known figures who had been diagnosed, but who'd not wanted to discuss it publicly. And while he agreed that it was completely their right, he did think that speaking up would help raise the awareness of the disease, where so little is known about it. My interview had provided a platform to raise awareness. I was finally ready to do what I'd wanted to do for the best part of a year and a half, and for the next few months we attended various awareness-raising functions.

I had finally reached *that* level of acceptance. MND was no longer in control of my life. Counselling had already taught me to try to focus on the things that I could do as opposed to the things that I could no longer achieve. But now my eyes were opened to so much more. There was a charity skydive, the London City fundraising swim in the Docklands (not bad for the world's worst swimmer) and a meeting with Princess Anne, to name but a few. But the most important thing was that this dreaded disease could now bring the family closer together.

If only it had been that simple…

CHAPTER 25

REALITY BITES

I was now thinking clearly again. No more thoughts of death and dying, no more depression and anxiety. Switzerland? Where? I had stopped thinking about myself, and finally realised the effects of suicide would have been irreparable. Work? After much discussion, I decided that life was too short, and consequently retired due to ill health. Anything that MND had to throw at me, I was ready for. I no longer worried about the twitches, in fact, they started to interest me. I became fascinated by the nuances of the disease. The involuntary curling of fingers, the muscle spasms, the refusal of some of my muscles to move when I wanted them to, the fact that I could wake up one morning and suddenly something else would have stopped working. I know that may seem strange, but I became genuinely interested. I even went to the neuroscience unit at Sheffield University to learn more about research into neurological diseases.

My mental state was as good as it had ever been. People even commented on my change of mood. While I felt completely fine, the actions and moods of those around me were way off where I was. I was doing all that I could to raise awareness and funds for research. I began working closely with the MND Association; I was up and running again. But I was beginning to find out just how many others my diagnosis had affected. Close friends, even very close friends didn't want to speak to me. I later found out that they either didn't know what to say or didn't know how they would react when they saw me. So they just didn't get in touch. It was the same with family members; too scared to ask me how I was.

The physical deterioration was beginning to manifest itself. Nade, Patrick and Elizabeth were living with this every day. The reality of having to care for somebody with MND had kicked in. Poor Patrick struggled the most. There were so many things that we used to do together which were now off limits. And at 13 years old, that was difficult to digest. We had some really tough times, but thankfully we are now over the worst.

Elizabeth was still in 'mother mode'. The maturity and empathy that she displayed belied her tender age. But MND had moved the goalposts. The family dynamics changed with every little progression of my disease. Nadine became the main breadwinner (every man's dream), but was also part-time carer and full-time housewife. The tasks that we used to share were now solely down to her. I can't imagine what that must have been like for her. Simple things, such as picking up a knife and fork, had become impossible for me. It was left to the three of them to feed me. More pressure! More responsibility!

Life became easier for me than for them. For Nadine especially, in my opinion, it became mentally exhausting, which in turn made it physically exhausting. Just getting through the day was and still is a task in itself. I had a number of falls; nothing too serious (unless you call a broken thumb or cracked ribs serious), but these added to the worry. I would spend most of the day at home on my own, but me being me would still try to do things that I really needed help in doing. Again, more reasons for Nade to worry.

I began conducting talks at schools and colleges, universities, places of industry. I saw and experienced things, day-to-day, that I believed people should know about. MND doesn't have the same exposure that other life-limiting conditions have, and I believed that was wrong. I was accused of being drunk (which I often am, but not in the middle of the day while out shopping with the children), I watched as people parked in disabled bays, just to save 10 metres of walking, and I was accused of 'not being disabled enough' to use a disabled toilet! I had people talk down to me as though I was stupid, or even better, pat me. Yes, that's just what I needed. Treating me like a baby would make all the difference.

It became my mission to change the way people think, so the more talks and interviews I did, the more exposure for MND. Other sportspeople revealed that they'd been diagnosed. Perhaps they'd found the bravery to do so following my revelation. Perhaps not! But it was vital that they did it, either way.

Meanwhile, MND continued to do what MND does; it progressed. Pushing buttons was becoming near-impossible, which meant getting in and out of the car was also near-impossible. Always one to look on the positive side, I brightened as it meant a new car was soon to be on the way. It also meant that I had to purchase various gadgets to attach to my house keys.

Washing myself started to become more and more difficult. Again, on the positive side, it meant that Nadine had to do it for me. I'm not sure that Nadine felt the same way, but that had been a secret dream of mine for quite some time. Shame about the circumstances, though.

Believe it or not, there are advantages to having MND. I've mentioned before how some people found it easier (for them) to keep their distance. Others, though, went above and beyond. The reaction from the 'football community' (I hate that phrase) was overwhelming. The support and goodwill that I received really made it so much easier to remain positive. But it was the reaction of people closer to home that tickled me the most.

Most families have a favourite child (don't ask), and ours was no different. Pete was always the golden child. Quite rightly, the rest of us stopped getting Easter eggs when we were about 15 years old, but Pete was still getting one, way into his forties. None of us had an issue with it, we just accepted it for what it was. Pete also seemed to get preferential treatment with Mum's special chicken.

Every Friday evening, Mum would make her special chicken, and some of the family members would hijack her house to enjoy the feast. I would occasionally go down, but wasn't allowed anywhere near the kitchen until Pete had had his fill. Once he'd taken all the best pieces, the rest of us were allowed to fight over the scraps. But all that changed after my big announcement. Suddenly, I was head of the queue, first in line to sample the newly cooked chicken. No longer did I have to wait until Saturday or Sunday for the leftovers. I was now in pole position.

Mum also treated me to a Caribbean cruise, although she insisted that we needed to book it quickly, just in case!

So there was the car, the blue badge, the cruise, the chicken, and the all-over hands-on from Nade. Talk about living the dream!

Day-to-day living continued to cause issues. Things that I had previously taken for granted, such as opening doors to get in and out of the house, were now impossible. I could no longer lift my legs over the bath to get into the shower, and walking up the stairs to go to bed was, quite frankly, taking my life in my hands.

One thing that having MND has taught me is to be adaptable, so we had to find different ways to cope with these little issues. Our house was like a building site for a few weeks, as we transformed the bathroom into a nonslip wet room. One of the biggest changes was the toilet. My fear of having to get someone to wipe my backside was alleviated when I discovered Closomat. Closomat are a company who specialise in wet and dry toilets. They supplied and fitted a lavatory which contained a wash and dry function. I can now sit on the toilet to my heart's content, and although it was initially quite strange having a jet of water up the backside, it has now become one of my daily pleasures. In fact, I now use it whether I need to or not, it's that good!

Another big change in the home was the installation of an automatic door. A simple press of a button and suddenly I had access to the great outdoors. We also needed to get an external lift fitted, to combat the steps outside the door. All of this came at a price. Fortunately, Westy started banging the drum again, and the PFA kindly funded the works.

Over the years, the PFA have come under criticism for the way that they've distributed funds, but I can honestly say that they've assisted me financially beyond belief, and in Simon Barker, Gordon Taylor and John Bramhall there are three people who have always been available at the other end of the phone whenever I've needed help and support.

Life for me, at the moment, is good. I am in tune with my diagnosis, and as my old friend suggested, I treat it with the contempt it deserves. I'm revelling in the challenge of defeating new obstacles. I'm not sure that, five years ago, the idea of using a computer program to help me write a book would have appealed. But it's just another of life's hurdles that we have to jump over. Likewise, using just my thumb to operate the TV and the fire is another mini victory. It is difficult to believe that, not so long ago, I was really getting screwed up over twitches, and now I'm just like, *bring it on*! The most difficult aspect is seeing those close to me struggling with my physical deterioration. I have gone on record as saying that too many people think about the endgame. But who knows when that is for any of us? It's easy for me to say because that's the way that I'm built, but why worry about something that we know is inevitable for all of us? Don't waste time feeling sorry or pitying me. Instead, look to the things we can do with whatever time we have left.

People have told me to live every day as though it's my last, but that's not really a rational thought, is it? I don't believe for one second that today will be my last, and for that reason, I'm not scared to plan ahead. What's the worst thing that can happen? I am, however, aware that this year may be my last. But not even that thought can prevent me from looking into the future, and crossing things off my to-do list.

As my condition deteriorates, the adjustments in our lives continue to increase. Scratching my head, blowing my nose or brushing my teeth are just a few of the things that have become part of Nade's daily routine. That, along with emptying and changing my urinary bag, I think makes me a somewhat more attractive proposition. Nade, though, draws the line at cutting my toenails. For that, it's a trip to the podiatrist. Strangely, she does seem to quite enjoy plucking out grey hairs from obscure places.

Time has moved on and I now have a PA (basically, a one-to-one carer, but PA makes me sound so much more important) who has become invaluable for my day-to-day routine. She gets me up in the mornings, showers and dresses me, and even cleans my ears. She seems genuinely fascinated by my regular full body spasms, and really doesn't seem to mind helping me to the toilet (that might be different if I didn't have the Closomat).

Then it's breakfast time. She makes the best poached eggs on toast, which is usually followed by a nice cup of tea. Having Zoë around has enabled me to get out of the house more, although watching me get in and out of the car is a sight to behold.

Inside the house, the motorised wheelchair is a real winner. And although I won't be winning any marathons any time soon, I can manage a few steps with my walking frame. Mealtimes are tricky as the family have to help me eat while trying to have their own meal. Do they let my food get cold, or sacrifice their own? Like I said, tricky!

On the personal front, my voice is starting to go. Similar to my arms and legs, I know what I want to say, but it's as though my throat won't allow it. The result is that I sometimes sound a bit slurred (another reason for people accusing me of being drunk). My throat also feels very tight, almost as if somebody is trying to strangle me. I must admit that this is not the most enjoyable of experiences. Fortunately, I am only aware of this at night-time. Perhaps the feeling is exacerbated when I'm lying down. Whatever the reason, I know that it's part of the deal. Remember, don't fret over things over which you have no control!

Another slightly unpleasant occurrence is the tendency to choke on certain foods. If only I could live on ice cream and red wine!

Each new day presents a new problem. And each new day, we have to find ways to combat them. Sometimes, the only way to do this is to accept that they're there, and then mentally push them to the background. As I approached three years since diagnosis, the parameters continued to change. The things that I now regarded as acceptable 'living conditions' are far removed from the early days. If I were able to live my life in my current state, I would be more than happy – probably the tenth time that I had this thought over the last few years. And I know it will change again. What will be the breaking point? I honestly don't know. But when it comes, I think I will be ready.

Today I spoke to Nadine about how our life isn't bad. It's difficult (more so for her than for me), but it's not bad. I don't feel ill, I'm not in excruciating pain, we still go out, we still socialise, I'm still sarcastic and extremely annoying: so many things have remained the same. It sounds so simple, but you really do have to focus on the things that you *can* still do. And for those things that you can't... Find Another Way!

CHAPTER 26

NOW . . . THEN

When I was young(er), I used to listen to the old people talking about the good old days. Things were always bigger and better, back then. Children had respect for their elders; crime did not exist; you could hear the lyrics in a song, and football was better and played by proper men.

I never wanted to become that person who would say, 'Things were so much better in my day!' so I'm having to choose my words very carefully. Undoubtedly, the game has changed. Not necessarily better, or worse, but certainly different.

When I first began watching football around the late 1970s, the game was overflowing with flamboyant players, real game-changers who would take opponents on, dribble, and get the crowd on their feet. Clearly, this is a metaphor, as most of the football supporters were standing anyway. But you know what I mean! But, from a personal point of view, it was brilliant. I couldn't wait for Saturday night's edition of *Match of the Day*, or *Kick-Off* on a Sunday afternoon. I always wanted to be like Kenny Dalglish (not so much now). And although I was a big Liverpool fan, I loved watching Spurs, with Glenn Hoddle and Mike Hazzard pulling the strings in midfield. I actually had heroes, for a short time anyway.

But it wasn't all good. Football hooliganism was rife, and football grounds were scary places, for me anyway. I knew people who were just nice, ordinary lads, some of whom I used to play football with way back when. But they would go to a football match and become some sort of uncontrollable beast. Fran would tell me stories of what they would get up to (I hasten to add, he was never involved). It was incredible, the effect that football had on them. In my experience, that is certainly one area where football has improved. Another is the acceptance of non-white players. In those days they were few and far between, and boy, didn't the fans let them know it. It certainly isn't perfect now, but it's like watching a different game.

Another massive change is the standard of football pitch, and stadia for that matter. The increase in revenue, mainly thanks to Sky TV, has enabled clubs to ensure their players play on surfaces that previously most of us would only experience by watching the FA Cup Final. The state of some of the pitches I have played on, well, it just wouldn't be allowed nowadays. I suppose that might be one of the reasons why the older generation of footballers tended to stay on their feet more. Diving has always existed, but not to the extent of the modern footballer. And knee sliding? What is all that about? I'd love to see some of today's footballers try to do a knee slide on Gigg Lane back in the 1990s. They'd have required surgery and probably been out of the game for six months.

The biggest change, and some people insist it's to the detriment of the game, is something I alluded to earlier. The money in football has absolutely rocketed. Again, thanks to Sky TV, one contract could see a player set up for life. I'm not saying that they don't deserve it. For a start, the modern footballer is the complete athlete. The hours they put in is incomparable to when I played.

Am I bitter or jealous? Not for one second. Because, despite all the riches, the lovely surfaces, the hero worship and so on, I genuinely believe that footballers in my era actually enjoyed themselves more; actually enjoyed being a footballer. The scrutiny that footballers are under today means they don't have much of a life outside of football. They can't misbehave, they can't even be seen with an alcoholic drink in their hand. Their diets are controlled to the *n*th degree. Jesus, some clubs don't even allow them to put tomato sauce on their meals. The game, in my opinion, has become sterile. No characters, no personalities to be seen or heard. Maybe it's a reflection of society, but some of these guys don't even seem to enjoy scoring a goal.

There used to be a time when footballers would have some sort of relationship with the supporters. But those days have well and truly gone. We used to have fans watching us train who would hang around afterwards for autographs. But now, you can't go near a training ground for all the barriers and security staff. Footballers no longer have anything in common with the fan in the street. I'm not saying that it's their fault, but I think the advent of social media has made footballers and football in general paranoid. I'm not saying that I want to get back to the days of spit-roasting, but surely there has to be a happy medium.

I went to watch a cricket match recently at Old Trafford. At the end of the match, all the Lancashire players stayed behind to sign autographs. Jos Buttler, a key member of the England cricket squad, was playing that night, and it seemed like second nature to him. The fans absolutely loved it. Nowadays, you're lucky if footballers stay behind to wave to their own fans after a game.

The way we play the game has also changed. I was talking to Westy a few days ago, and he described it as a chess match. Pass, pass, pass, wait for the gap, hope somebody comes out of position... Please, please, somebody just take somebody else on! This has been coming for quite a few years now. Back in the good old days, when some of us still had black-and-white TV, you could still tell the difference between certain teams. But now, everybody looks the same and plays the same way. It's a good job that they have names on the shirts instead of just numbers. It really is the only way that you can sometimes tell who's who.

So yes, football has improved in so many ways, and I'm not saying that things were better in my day, but I no longer sit restlessly on a Saturday evening waiting for *Match of the Day* to come on. And I certainly don't look forward to the two-hour post-match discussion about the game that I've just seen.

At least we have VAR...

CHAPTER 27

WHITE NOISE

I grew up in one of only three black families on the estate. The estate was made up of a number of maisonettes over two floors. I was four years old when we moved there and completely oblivious to race, colour and culture. As a family, we settled in very quickly and mixed, without issue, with the other families on the estate. At this point, I didn't see colour. I didn't feel that I stood out. Alex Haley's *Roots* changed all that. I was around seven years old when I watched this series, and it left an indelible imprint on me. Every Sunday evening we would gather together as a family to watch it. For the next hour or so, the house was in complete silence. I can only speak for myself, but it seemed as though we were all completely gripped, horrified and disgusted by the treatment the slaves were subjected to. I remember thinking, how is it possible that this could happen? I couldn't understand how so many of the slaves accepted this treatment as if it was an everyday, normal part of life.

Watching *Roots* didn't make me bitter, but it did make me aware. I'm not sure whether that's a good thing or a bad thing, but for the first time in my life, I sensed there was something different about me. Up until this point, that *difference* had never been pointed out, either in real life or on screen. Again, that was about to change. Cue the likes of Jim Davidson, and TV shows such as *Mind Your Language*, *Love Thy Neighbour* and characters such as Alf Garnett in *Till Death Us Do Part*. These programmes were aired on prime-time TV and billed as classic British comedies. Jim Davidson… Who the hell was Jim Davidson, anyway? With his character Chalkie and his mock Jamaican accent dressed up as humour and entertainment, he was an absolute sensation. Again, we used to sit and watch this trite nonsense, and as with *Roots*, it left me with a stomach-churning uneasiness. It goes without saying that I just didn't find it funny. But his popularity meant that his humour was filtering into my life. Children in school began to impersonate him, not necessarily directing it towards me, but just in general.

I have to admit that as a family we enjoyed *Love Thy Neighbour*. I always found it ironic, and the white family always seemed to get their comeuppance (yay, justice for the black people!) The same with Alf Garnett, although I was a little bit older by then. To me, it made a fool of the *racist white guy*, who himself was a foreigner to these shores. Sadly, the majority of people who enjoyed this show were too uneducated to understand the irony, and enjoyed the programme because of its racism – a bit of an own goal, really!

Although I still didn't see colour as an issue, I was becoming more aware of things such as apartheid (which stirred my love for South Africans at the time) and the Ku Klux Klan. I guess I was strangely political for one so young! Race and racism were becoming more prominent, I felt. I can vividly remember watching the Brixton riots, and couldn't help but realise that all the *perpetrators* were black youths. I was also becoming more aware of racism in football. The courage and bravery that the likes of Cyrille Regis, Laurie Cunningham, Brendon Batson, Viv Anderson and many others showed under intense provocation and ridicule were quite remarkable. Monkey chants! Actual monkey chants!

This behaviour went largely unpunished and was the sole reason that I never attended a football match at that time (that, and football hooliganism, which was also rife then. Pete and Fran used to go and watch Preston North End when the gates opened for the last 20 minutes, but I always politely declined the offer – I was basically too scared to go. So the first match I ever saw was the aforementioned game at Anfield. Talk about a baptism of fire.)

And who could forget Enoch Powell's 'Rivers of Blood' speech, where he vented fury at the number of immigrants being allowed into the country? That was in 1968, before I was born, but I was more than aware of it by the age of six or seven. Fifty years later and in the throes of Brexit, I'm not exactly sure how far we have progressed as a nation.

Back to football! My first encounter of racism on a football pitch was when I was about 13 or 14. I was representing my school team (St Thomas More, Preston) at a tournament in Stoke. We had a really decent team and we'd progressed to the semi-finals when we came up against a local team. About midway through the first half, one of their players called me a nigger! For the first (and possibly last) time in my life, I was absolutely speechless. It was also the last time that a racist comment from either a player or supporter had a negative effect on my performance. I went completely into my shell; the rest of the game totally passing me by. We lost, but I didn't care. Back in those days, losing a game would make me so upset that I would want to fight members of the opposition. But this time, nothing! Just numbness! I really wasn't sure how I would react the next time it happened, but fortunately by the time it did happen again, I had discovered John Barnes. I loved John Barnes. I loved the charismatic way that he played, the goals he scored. Left foot, right foot, headers! But what I loved most about him was his attitude towards racism and racists. I remember watching his video and marvelling at his silky skills, but the moment that really made me sit up and take notice was his reply when asked how he deals with racist comments. He said something along the lines of never allowing people with such ignorance and lack of intelligence to affect him in any way. To me, it was his way of saying that these people were too stupid to give credence to. That became my mantra from then on in, and was used on many occasions. One such occasion was when I was at Bury playing away at Crystal Palace. One of the Linighan brothers was playing for them, tall and wiry, but a decent centre half. I'd worked out that whenever we had a free kick, if you tried to take it quickly the nearest member of the opposition would stick out a leg to try to stop the ball. Now, in this period of football, if you were less than 10 yards away, you would get booked for stopping the ball, so I would deliberately kick it whenever I was close to a defender knowing that they would get booked. I must have done it half a dozen times over the course of that season, but Linighan was not impressed. He immediately called me a black bastard, and then went into some sort of apology meltdown. I genuinely think he was sorry, but one has to worry if that's the first thing that somebody thinks about in those situations.

I have experienced racism in all parts of my life. I worked in a predominantly Muslim school, where the Bangladeshi children would racially abuse the Pakistani children, the Pakistani children the same for Indian children and so on. But the one thing that many of them had in common was that they basically all racially abused the non-Asian children. These 'Christians' were all evil, oh, and they all drank wine (I only did this during the lunch break).

As my football career progressed, I was exposed to in-house racism. This was where the likes of Tony Finnigan, Mitchell Thomas and Ian Wright slated 'northern blacks' as though there was a particular way for black people to behave or sound. Listening to The Smiths meant that I did not match the ideal model. Surely I should be listening to Bob Marley or some other tedious shite. Not some 30-year-old white guy with daffodils stashed down the back of his trousers, wearing National Health glasses. Whenever they started on me, I just used to whistle, 'Stop me if you think you've heard this one before'.

Now I have a lot of time for Ian Wright. When he came to Burnley for a spell, he demonstrated how articulate, intelligent and modest he was. He was also extremely funny, and a fantastic footballer, even though he was coming towards the end of his career. But I hated his public persona. I always felt he had sold out, making himself out to be like an idiot for TV, or dumbing himself down to appeal to a certain audience. He completely changed my mind in that short time when we shared a dressing room together. I read his autobiography, and taking away all the things that went wrong in his life that 'weren't my fault', it was a pretty good read. I now found it interesting again, watching him on *Match of the Day*, claiming 'racism' at every given chance. Could it be that certain players are targeted because 'intelligent fans' think they are rubbish? Was it possible that the reason Raheem Sterling received 'dog's abuse' was down to his performances when wearing an England shirt? Oh no! That would be too simple! The national press had an agenda. It frustrates me that whenever a black person is abused, there is always an assumption that it is because of the colour of his skin. I always hated the phrase 'chip on his shoulder'. But the constant whining, malingering and proclamation of racism gives fuel to the people who use this phrase.

The advent of social media has meant that faceless people can say pretty much whatever they want. So, among others, black footballers are being targeted for missing penalties, perceived poor performances and other such heinous crimes. I say among others, because footballers of all colours and creeds are being attacked for the same reasons. But cracking down on racism is the new fad. It's almost as though this is the only form of prejudice that should be addressed. Yes, it's absolutely unacceptable, but is it any worse than homophobia, sexism, sectarianism? The list is almost endless. I hear cries urging the throwing out of the likes of Montenegro, Serbia, Bulgaria and other 'less-developed countries' from tournaments. When Danny Rose and Raheem Sterling were abused, there was outcry: 'These clubs shouldn't be allowed to play in UEFA tournaments'.

The country (England) went wild. But hang on, it was only a few weeks previous to this incident that Chelsea fans racially abused Raheem Sterling; that Spurs fans racially abused Pierre-Emerick Aubameyang. Strangely though, there were no calls to kick Spurs and Chelsea out of the Premier League. People forget that we have a racism problem in this country (both in society and in football), yet still we stand in our pulpit and preach to other countries. Until we get our own house in order, surely it would be prudent to refrain from such judgement.

More recently, there have been threats to walk off the pitch if England players are racially abused. Seriously? Get a grip! Are you really going to walk off the pitch because some uneducated idiot starts name-calling you? Think about those players I mentioned earlier, and the stick that they took. They would never have dreamed of walking off the pitch, they would never have shown these cowards that they could affect their performance, they would never have let these people win. Maybe society has changed; maybe people are not as mentally tough as they once were. I understand that people don't feel they should put up with anything, but by its ridiculously tribal nature, doesn't football encourage players to be abused, week in, week out? How do we assess what form of abuse goes beyond acceptable? Is it only racist abuse that we need to sanction? There is an awful amount of hypocrisy being demonstrated, but the crux of the matter is that we either stamp out all forms of abuse or none. Who is to say that the footballer who gets called a w**ker is less affected than the footballer who gets monkey chants aimed at him/her? It's all relative, right?

Football's equality and inclusion organisation Kick It Out recently got involved when Bernardo Silva tweeted a joke about his mate, Bernard Mendy. It was abhorrent, apparently, that Silva used a racist stereotype to insult somebody. This was a joke between two mates, and although they might have expected the reaction they got by sharing it publicly on Twitter, surely Kick It Out have better things to do with their time? Going back a few years, I remember Rio Ferdinand expressing his disgust that Kick It Out representatives refused to wear their Kick It Out T-shirts during a high-profile court case between his brother Anton and John Terry. Time has moved on since then, and perhaps if it happened now they would act differently, but surely this was the time for them to stand up as an organisation and let the whole world see them representing a black player, irrespective of the fact that it was against former England captain John Terry.

I have absolutely nothing against the organisation Kick It Out, but I can honestly say that I have no idea what difference they've made to the level of racism in this country. I go back to what I said earlier, are things better now than they were 10, 20, 30 years ago? I will leave that one with you!

CHAPTER 28

DEAR DIARY I

August 2019

It is almost exactly one year since I publicly announced I had MND. The last few weeks have been really tough. My son, Patrick, my handsome little man, is still trying to come to terms with the news, and the obvious changes to his dad. He is angry, very angry. He finds it very difficult to talk about it, but the stress of the anguish is manifesting itself in aggression.

Nadine, my beautiful wife, my lobster, is also struggling with the changes. The extra burden that's been placed on her has started to take its toll. Elizabeth, gorgeous, sensible Elizabeth is doing everything she can to hold it together. She has become my rock, at 16. But MND is starting to play its hand. My personal outlook remains positive but I'm starting to feel like I'm becoming a burden. The one thing that I didn't want when I was first diagnosed! I have always said that I'm not afraid of death or of dying. I sometimes wonder whether it would be better to slip away quietly now before things progress even more. When I was first diagnosed, it was a real consideration to go to Switzerland for assisted suicide. In August 2018, after my public revelation, the weight that was lifted allowed me to think more clearly. I recognised the impact that going to Switzerland would have had on my family, and while I would never criticise anyone for the decisions they make, it was something I didn't feel was right for me at the time. Fast forward 12 months, and it is something that I'm considering again. I haven't shared this information with anybody, but it's there in the background as an option. For me, talking has always been the best way to deal with situations. This becomes difficult when those around you find it difficult to talk. Perhaps in a day or two, I will feel differently, but the impact of having MND cannot be underestimated.

November 2019

One of the 'perks' of having MND is access to national charity, the Motability Scheme. The scheme entitles individuals with certain disability benefits to use part of said benefits to lease a car. In my particular case, I am entitled to a benefit called Personal Independent Payments, or PIP for short, because of the nature of my diagnosis, and the short-term prognosis. My consultant signed the form which explained that my life expectancy *could* be as short as six months. The powers that be (Department for Work and

Pensions), then issue a three-year certificate which enables you to choose your vehicle. At this point, I was still able to walk fairly freely, move my arms and hands, and generally function pretty well.

Obviously, MND is a progressive disease, and unsurprisingly, my functionality has gradually decreased. This meant that I had to change the initial car I bought to one with an adapted gearstick. The strength in my hands had deteriorated greatly, so I opted for keyless entry, automatic lights and automatic windscreen sensor. I also chose a car with a larger boot space, knowing that I would at some point need a wheelchair. Again, my symptoms continued to deteriorate and I'm now in the position where I can barely walk and so make use of a motorised wheelchair. The benefits of a motorised wheelchair compared to the manual, foldaway kind far outweigh the negatives. However, one advantage of the manual wheelchair over the motorised is that it can easily be stored in the boot of my car. Cue yet another phone call to Motability, this time stating the need for a wheelchair-accessible vehicle. It's now two and a half years since my certificate was issued for PIP. Some may say that this is a good thing. Despite the bleak initial prognosis, I am still fit and well (relatively). However, I was stunned into silence (okay, not silence, I don't think anything could ever keep me silent, although I suspect MND is going to have a bloody good go), when, having been told that I needed to produce my PIP certificate, I phoned up the DWP and was told that as I have less than 12 months left on the certificate, and because I have a short-term-prognosis terminal illness, I would have to wait four months before

I would be able to apply for another certificate. In other words, because I have managed to stay alive for so long (yay!) I am likely to be dead before the certificate expires, rendering it not practical for me to apply for a wheelchair-accessible vehicle. The gentleman who I spoke to from the DWP sounded almost gutted that I had managed to remain alive for so long. I think that this has messed up their systems, and they clearly couldn't cope. Now, if I had realised that from the start, I would have made life easier for them by not taking the drugs prescribed to keep me alive for a little bit longer. Think back to the earlier part of this book, where I stated that I live my life for myself. Here's another example of my selfishness. The thought hadn't even occurred to me how many problems it would cause for so many people, if I were to remain on this earth for longer than expected. Self-interest personified!

So, instead of being able to sit in my comfortable wheelchair and drive it into a newly adapted vehicle, I have to continue to be pushed in a very uncomfortable manual wheelchair, be tugged, pushed and pulled in order to get me out of said wheelchair and into the car. My level of independence suffers, because I have to rely on people to steer me. If I want to go shopping, I need to go with two people, one to push me and one to hold the shopping bag or push the trolley. This obviously limits my opportunities for going out shopping (I shouldn't be greedy; I can always go window shopping). I will have to continue to use hospital transport for my numerous appointments, as opposed to simply travelling with my carer. But no bother. I will probably be dead in a few months' time, in any case, and those important employees of the DWP will not have had to waste time pressing buttons to issue me with a new certificate.

Again, I couldn't help but think back to the good old days of Jim Bowen's *Bullseye*, where they would reveal the prize that you'd just lost at the end of the show, and say almost smugly, 'Here's what you could have won!'

CHAPTER 29

THE SAME DEEP WATER AS YOU

It's over two and a half years since my diagnosis. There's one train of thought that I have to lay to rest. Over the last few weeks, I have had countless people sympathising with my condition. I have also had countless people tell me that MND must be the worst illness that anybody could possibly have. Worse than dementia, worse than the various cancers, worse than liver failure, worse than locked-in syndrome, worse than Huntington's disease. I could go on, but you get the point. Firstly, it really isn't a competition. All things are relative, and I don't for one second think that people with Huntington's sit around all day saying, 'It could be worse, at least I haven't got MND'.

The rationale of these people who tell me MND is the worst thing is that my body is gradually failing me, but my mind still works perfectly well (or as well as it ever has). Apparently, it must be awful, knowing and being aware that these things are happening to me but there being nothing I can do about it. Hmmm! Interesting theory, don't you think? I actually like the fact that my mind is still active. I like the fact that I can still think for myself and make my own decisions about things. I like the fact that I can enjoy watching my children play, argue and then make up. I like the fact that I can understand people's emotions, whether they are happy or not so happy. I like the fact that I can enjoy watching things on the TV, enjoy going out for meals – enjoy being able to write a book, for goodness' sake. I like the fact that I can express an opinion on things or even think about expressing an opinion. I like the fact that, despite having restricted movement, I can still think more clearly than most people who are able-bodied (in my opinion, anyway). I like the fact that I can be disagreeable if I so wish. And I like the fact that I can tell people to stop wrapping me up in cotton wool, and that just because I have been diagnosed with a terminal illness it doesn't mean I have to stop enjoying myself. Or that I have a bad life. I don't! I have a very good life. I am very happy. I still have aspirations and dreams. I still look forward to getting up in the mornings. I am still the same person I always was. I actually believe that what goes on inside your mind is what defines you as a person. How you respond to situations, good or bad, is psychological, not physical. Being able to be emotional about things is not a physical trait. Take that away from me, and I am nothing. Take that away from anyone, for that matter. So please, please, please think before you speak. Would you rather see me able to do all the physical things that I was able to do prior to having MND, but not being able to enjoy what I was doing, or even know what I was doing? I know which I prefer. Sympathise, by all means. But pity? Not so much! And misguided pity? No, not for me, thank you.

CHAPTER 30

DEAR DIARY II

20 November 2019

I received an email from the Motor Neurone Disease Association asking whether I'd be interested in a new initiative that they are working on with Google. I'm all for change (as long as it's progressive), so couldn't wait to see what was on offer. It appears as though they are looking to develop software which will recognise your voice even when it becomes very unclear, as mine undoubtedly will. They included a video for me to peruse. In the video was a man with MND demonstrating the software. For the first time in over a year, I envisioned what my life will be like sometime in the future. I also got those strange sensations in my stomach that I used to get during the dark days following diagnosis. The main difference is, back then I couldn't control it and didn't know how to deal with it. I couldn't park those thoughts, and I was completely consumed by them. This time, however, I embraced the fact that, despite the debilitating nature of the disease, there are things out there to help you maintain your independence and to keep your life 'normalised'. The human brain is a very complex entity. Unlike before, I can put things into little boxes, discuss difficult situations and scenarios, and basically get on with my life. The dark days are over, and I genuinely believe that whatever MND throws at me, I'll be able to deal with it. If only there was some sort of guarantee that my family would be able to deal with it in the same way…

25 November 2019

Three falls in a week, I bet you think that's pretty clever, don't you, boy!

As a teacher, I used to tell the children that it makes it easier for them to learn if they experienced things first-hand. MND means that I am learning things through my experiences every day. This week, I have learned that falling on bathroom tiles is considerably more painful than falling on carpet. I have, however, also learned that it is considerably more difficult to get blood out of the carpet than it is to get blood off bathroom tiles. Such a conundrum! My third fall this week has taught me that, if my legs really don't want to move, then to listen to them and not try to force it.

31 December 2019

I woke up this morning and realised that my left thumb had decided not to work. New Year's Eve, and MND chose today to flex its muscles. It really doesn't give a shit, does it? It's amazing what you can't do without your thumb. I guess that's why we have them! So now, I need to find another way of using my thumb controller to turn over the TV and turn the fire on and off.

So what does one do in situations like this? Well, my answer today has been to turn to the red wine. Nothing, but nothing will stop me wanting a glass of red wine. I've even thought about having one ready on my deathbed. What a way to die!

On the pleasant subject of death, I'm considering having a pre-death party. I really don't want to miss out on all the platitudes at my funeral. I also don't want to miss out on the food and drink. Surely it makes more sense to be present at a gathering that's being held in your honour. So that's the plan! Obviously, getting the timing right might be a bit tricky. Don't really want to leave it too late; and too early, well I might not get the sympathy that I would at a wake. So, as I say, that's the master plan. Watch this space! I would love to say that I've given the idea the thumbs up, but that luxury has just been taken away from me. Never mind. There's always red wine!

17 January 2020

Local authorities quite often get a bad press. However, in my experience they have been very supportive. They managed to arrange and supply things such as grab rails, riser/recliner chairs and other similar practical items. They even provided a profiling bed.

My latest experience has been less positive. The profiling bed that they supplied was a single bed, and an extremely uncomfortable one at that. However, it had controls that I can't access due to the fact my hands are pretty rubbish. When I spoke to the local council, they said there was nothing they could do about it. Okay, thanks for that! And then I mentioned the fact that, with it being a single bed, I would obviously have to spend the rest of my days sleeping alone. Their response to that one was that, at some point, I would need help getting in and out of bed, and that if they provided a larger bed it might be difficult for the carer to reach me. I'm not exactly sure how big a bed they thought I wanted. It got better! They then said that if I were over a certain weight, they would be able to supply a bigger bed. Now, I'm not sure whether they were explaining why I can't have a double bed or whether they were encouraging me to put on weight! So for the last few months I have had to sleep on a chair.

As my condition has progressed, I have been advised that I need to use a ventilator at night to ensure that my oxygen and carbon dioxide levels are in balance. However, due to those rubbish hands again, it's impossible for me to move the ventilator mask, should I need to. The concern is that I may vomit, and subsequently choke on said vomit. For this reason, I've been told that I need somebody with me whenever I'm wearing the mask. So, foolishly I thought this might be an adequate reason to approach the local authority regarding getting a double bed. Incredibly, as I'm still under the required weight, I am not eligible. So my options are as follows; don't wear the ventilator mask and run the risk of dying in my sleep due to lack of oxygen, or wear the oxygen mask and risk the possibility of choking. Not the best choice in the world. I'm really not sure which of those to opt for!

There is a possibility that the PFA will fund a new bed. The point to all this: I am in the fortunate position where I may be able to get funding from another source. But clearly, that is not the case with everyone. The bed is likely to cost in excess of £3,500 which I'm sure not everybody has to hand. So what do those people do?

I have nothing against anybody with any weight issues. Seriously, I haven't! But the fact remains that, because I have remained relatively healthy in terms of my weight, my needs are seen to be less important than those with weight issues. I'm not saying that my needs are more important, but I'm pretty damn sure that they're at least *as* important.

Now I know why local authorities get a bad press!

7 February 2020

As I lay awake last night, I pondered the changes in my life. It had been a bad day in the Johnrose household. Not for me; my approach to life means that very little gets me feeling or thinking negatively. But sometimes, you just have one of those days. And it seemed that Nade, Patrick and Elizabeth all chose the same day for that. So, despite the saying 'never go to bed on an argument', that's pretty much what the whole family did. It's at times like these that my thoughts always go into overdrive. It's the one thing that gets me frustrated, and is possibly my worst trait. I don't really do moods. Life is too short to be angry or annoyed, but it seems that not everybody thinks like that.

My thoughts centred around my impending death. I was really relaxed and thinking clearly, and came to the conclusion that, when it happens, I will be ready for it. People talk about having 'a time to go', or of not being ready, but I don't buy into that. I don't particularly think that it's 'my time', but I am ready. If it were to happen tonight, then so be it. I don't think that I will ever complete my to-do list. I seem to add to it every day. I will never be satisfied with what I have achieved, there is always so much more to strive towards, so it will never be my time.

I also thought about the one thing that I really do miss. I have always said that I don't want what I can't have, but after spending the last year or so sleeping alone, not having Nadine next to me, it's one thing I do wish I could change. I miss her being next to me. I really, really do. I miss her smell, the feel of her skin, everything about just being next to her. It's the one thing that I crave. I love being married, and spending each night with the one you love is a big part of that. For that reason alone, I will always be unfulfilled.

18 February 2020

Today, the day that I had dreaded since my diagnosis, finally arrived. Closomat, the gadget that is elevated above all others, ceased to work. It had literally been my lifesaver, preventing the one thing that three years ago would have made me book my trip to Switzerland.

Having completed the deed, I pushed my elbow onto the flush-and-clean button. But there was only a flush, no clean. I pushed again, and again and again. But no joy! Shit! Now what was I going to do? I reluctantly called my trusty PA, Zoë.

'Erm, I've got a bit of a problem. The toilet flush isn't working. Can you please check to see whether the button is on?'

'Yep, it's on!'

'Great, now what?'

'There's nothing else for it. That's what I'm here for!' And with that, it was on with the rubber gloves. This was a totally new experience for me, and trying to make a joke out of it, I said, 'Are you sure you need your rubber gloves?' Zoe just smiled. 'Okay, up you get!' So, always one to do as I'm told, I got up and leaned forwards. And then it happened! My life went full circle and somebody actually wiped my backside for me. But there were no tears, no drama, just the feeling of relief at being clean. Obviously my mental state is somewhat better than it was a few years ago, and I dread to think what would have happened had this situation occurred then, but it didn't, and today it was absolutely fine. Perspective is a wonderful thing, and this is yet another example of the parameters moving.

This little episode has opened the doors to all kinds of experiences. I had concerns about going on holiday, but now, safe in the knowledge that I can handle being a baby again, the world is my oyster. Cruise, here I come!

23 February 2020

And so to my last update. The quality of my voice continues to deteriorate. Fortunately, I'm nearing the end (no, not that end, the end of my book). Dragon software is struggling to pick up my words, and people are repeatedly saying, 'Sorry, I can't hear you,' or, 'It's a really bad line, could you please say that again?'

I am consciously saying less and less at home (some may say that's a good thing), to try not to bring attention to it. I'm also trying to suppress the fact that I'm struggling to cough, thereby nearly choking on a regular basis. I think that the family are aware, they just don't want to say it out loud. I was on BBC Radio Lancashire a few days ago and was acutely aware that I was struggling to talk. For once, I let the other studio guest monopolise the conversation. On the drive back home, my thoughts centred around what happens when I really can no longer speak. I have already banked my voice, but the logistics of it? Well, I don't know. The idea that I have so much to say, but won't be able to get that message across, stirs up a very uneasy feeling.

Being physically bereft really isn't an issue for me, but not being able to communicate is a completely different issue. Perhaps that will be the straw ... or perhaps I'll just get on with it. It's been a while since I've given someone the silent treatment!

My fingers are now almost permanently curled – ideal for holding my mobile, but not much good for anything else. Unfortunately, my grip is so weak that I can't use curled hands to any real advantage...

This MND lark has taken me on a fluctuating path. I have gone on record as saying that I wouldn't invite it round for dinner (or tea, depending on your class!), but as the chances of getting it are just 1 in 300, I guess I am pretty special.

I'm not sure what the immediate future holds, but here's to red wine, egg custards and *The Crown*.

CHAPTER 31

BLASPHEMOUS RUMOURS

I was brought up a Catholic (not my choice, I was baptised when a defenceless baby), and although we were not regular churchgoers (does going every Christmas Eve to midnight Mass count as regular?), we were 'believers'. Fran and I even had a stint as altar boys. I'm not sure about Fran, but my lure was that a couple of mates of mine were altar boys and were given Easter eggs (remember, we were poor). As the weeks and months went by, I became really committed. So committed that I even accepted an invitation from the local priest to take me swimming to Blackpool swimming baths (just me and him, hmmm?)

I survived that experience, but as I got older, I started to question the teachings. There were things going on in my world and the world in general that made me feel uncomfortable with the idea that there was an all-conquering force who not only knew that these things were going to happen, but allowed them to. Furthermore, he/she/ it actually instigated the torture and death of the very beings whom he had chosen to put on this earth. And why? To cleanse them of the evils that he knew they would be born with. Hardly seems fair, does it?

My altar-boy years meant that I studied the Bible quite rigorously, but it all stopped making sense. The stories were, for me, a guide on how to live your life. But they were all so unbelievable. I remember asking a priest whether he thought that the story of Adam and Eve was true, and if so, how could it have happened. And why would God do such a mean thing. I just wanted him to say that it wasn't supposed to be taken literally, and that it was there to help us along our way. But no! In his eyes, it was all true. Every single word!

And the talking snake? Yes, again, all true!

For those of you who are not familiar with the Adam and Eve story, let me bring you up to speed. God created Adam and Eve, and placed them in the Garden of Eden. Depending on which text you read, God used one of Adam's ribs in order to make Eve. I'm not sure why he chose that method, but there you go. Another version is that Adam was made in God's image: make of that what you will. Anyway, God kindly put a few trees in the garden and said that they could take their pick of the fruits. Not the most balanced diet, I have to say. God being God, though, also put in the tree of knowledge of good and evil. I know that it sounds like a mouthful, but this tree does pretty much what it says on the tin. Now, I know what you're wondering... I don't know why he put it there either, but in any case he forbade Adam and Eve from eating anything off that tree. Now what you have to remember is that although Adam and Eve appeared as fully grown adults, they were new to the world, so essentially they were like children. And in my experience, if you tell young people not to do something, what is the first thing that they do? Inquisitive, you see!

Enter the talking serpent. Why God decided to conjure up a serpent is beyond me. Everybody knows that serpents are crafty, so at the very least, it was a huge schoolboy error. So, the serpent manages to sweet-talk Eve (Eve gets quite a lot of bad press, by the way. Come to think of it, the women in this book generally do), and she takes a bite out of one of the apples from the forbidden tree. Not content with doing things her own way, she persuades Adam to take a bite. She's probably thinking, 'If I'm going down, he's going down with me.'

Instead of thinking to himself, 'Why oh why did I put that tree there?' God loses his rag and banishes Adam and Eve from the Garden. So off they go, with their new-found knowledge of evil deeds, but not before realising that they were naked. Even though they were the only two people in the whole world, being naked caused them huge embarrassment.

So they did what anyone in the same situation would do, and covered themselves up with fig leaves.

Now, I can only speak for myself, but quite a lot of this seems a little bit far-fetched. Anyway, I digress…

And what of the serpent? Well, God is understandably fuming, so curses the serpent, a curse which means that the serpent and all future serpents (I'm not sure how it reproduced) will have to travel on its belly for all eternity. I suppose that's a bit like cursing humans to walk on their legs. Not exactly the worst punishment in the world!

Adam and Eve, now living out of the Garden and eating whatever they wanted to, had a couple of sons. The sons, Cain and Abel, had a massive fallout. Cain clearly had anger issues, and decided to settle the argument by murdering Abel. Well, there was no way God was going to let Cain get away with that, so he condemned him to, wait for it… A lifetime of wandering! So Cain wandered off to the land of Nod (yep, that's what it was called), built his own city (no mean feat) and fathered loads of children.

Meanwhile, Adam and Eve had more children who, as must have been customary, had 'relations', which enabled the growth of mankind.

Now I don't know about you, but I think listening to that serpent seems to have worked out quite well for everyone.

I firmly believe that one of my roles in life is to get people to ask questions of themselves, of the way that they think, and whether some of the things they say and do are logical. So my question to you is, do you think the story of Adam and Eve is true? If so, what are you basing it on? And if it isn't true, we have been lied to all of this time. And if they are lying about that, what else are 'they' lying about?

There were other such profound stories, of course. To name but two, Jonah and the whale, and Noah and his ark, where God took it upon himself to destroy all of mankind, save for Noah and his family (seems a bit mean). He then apparently promised never to send another flood. I don't want to sound flippant, but he went back on that one.

So let's assume that these tales are simply stories to guide us. Surely they are too ridiculous to be true. But are they more ridiculous than the virgin birth, the parting of the Red

Sea or the Ascension? What is it that makes us believe that certain parts of the Bible are just parables, yet insist that other parts are genuine? The idea of that is irrational in itself. Why produce a book where some of it is made up but other parts are true? And how do we decide?

My theory is that it's fear that forces many to believe. And it's that same fear that prevents people from asking the question. This has always been one of the things that I disliked about religion. The fear that it strikes into so many people. The fear that makes them think irrationally, or rather not think. The fear that means they don't question anything in the Bible (or whatever their religious literature is).

Years later, I asked another priest why good people fell ill. His reply, 'Because that is God's will!'

What? Are you seriously telling me that this wonderful entity has chosen for this to happen? Sorry, but that really is not a nice thing to do. I am pretty sure that, if I had that amount of power, I would be putting it to good use, instead of persecuting people and leaving their nearest and dearest to deal with the shit that's left behind.

My killer question was, 'How exactly did Jesus dying on the cross save mankind?' There really isn't an answer to that. He spoke about God sacrificing his own son, thereby forgiving us of sin. But why choose that method? And how much of a sacrifice was it, when a few days later, Jesus was up and running again? Jesus knew that this was his role in life, but for me, the one who made the biggest sacrifice was Judas. He was hung out to dry, when all he did was carry out God's will.

So what is the point of all this? I promise you that it's not to mock. Indoctrination means that we cannot help what we believe. People do some strange things in the name of religion, not all of them good. For some people, it's their reason to live; for others, it's their reason to take life. But the one thing that they have in common is their justification for the things that they do. So, I'm quite happy with my non-beliefs, thank you. But what I'm not happy with is people trying to force their views on me. I have said before that I am perfectly happy with the way I live my life. Again, for the most part, I'm a pretty decent person. I don't wish for riches beyond belief, I don't revel in other people's misfortunes, and I don't wish undue harm on people. I try to tell the truth (some might say a little bit too brutally, at times) and I can even cross off a couple of the Commandments. Yet still I have people stopping me in the street, trying to convert me. A few months ago, I was out shopping with my family, and because I politely refused the offer of a religious leaflet, a woman followed me down the street, insisting that I was wrong because I didn't believe.

But worse than that, and this is the point of it all, is people's insistence that I *need* to believe. That this belief will somehow make my life complete. Since being diagnosed, I have had people say that they are going to pray for me. Pray for what? I'm not going to get better; I'm going to get worse! No amount of praying is going to change that. I have also had people invite me to their Christian meetings, where I can cleanse my soul and get ready for heaven. Is that a joke? The very thought that I can live my life the way that I do, and be struck down with a terminal illness, but not be allowed into heaven because I am a non-believer is somewhat twisted. Better that I am a mass murderer, but go to church every Sunday?

I have even had Muslims claiming that Allah will look after me when I die. Scant consolation, really!

So, to reiterate, I have had a very good life. I feel privileged to have grown up in the way that I did. I feel privileged to have met most of the people I have. I feel privileged to have been afforded the experiences I've had. There have even been positives in having MND. I can now fully empathise with people who have had similar illnesses. You really can't have a proper understanding unless you're going through it yourself. And having MND has also strengthened my resolve. I feel (and that's all that really matters) that I am a better person for it. And throughout all this, I've never once needed God and/or religion. And if there is a God, and I don't make it through the pearly gates, then so be it.

So there it is! I don't wish to sound ungrateful. There are so many well-meaning people who genuinely try to make others' lives better. But please don't make it about religion, and please don't use it as an opportunity to preach. I actually take that as an insult.

And surely it's better to be a good person because it's the right thing to do than to be a good person because you are scared of the consequences of behaving differently.

And there endeth the gospel, according to Len Johnrose!

CHAPTER 32

ALL-TIME XI

I am often asked, 'Who is the best player you've ever played with?' So, I've decided to compile a best eleven. This is so tricky, and there is the danger that I might offend someone. But here goes…

1) *Goalkeeper*: Dean Kiely – what a keeper! He wasn't the tallest, but definitely the most agile that I have ever played with. He was brave, and had a real nasty streak about him. That, together with his slight cockiness, made him even better.

2) *Right back*: This one is easy, Dean West – one of the first ever wingbacks (he was originally signed as a winger before being converted to a full back). For 90 minutes, he would overlap the winger and still have the energy to get back and defend. And he can also tackle, which is something you don't see too much in the modern game.

3) *Left back*: Lee Briscoe – he made playing football look like a chore, but he also made it look so easy. Composed, great in the tackle, a good passer, and another one who wasn't afraid to go forward.

4) *Central defender 1*: This is where it starts to get tricky. I played with some great centre halves, but unfortunately there's only room for three. The first one is David May. I played with Dave as a youngster at Blackburn Rovers, and later on in our final seasons as professional footballers, and even as a 16-year-old he looked ready for the first team. He was exceptional in the air, a terrific passer and striker of the ball, and very composed. He was also a great organiser, and absolutely loved a tackle.

5) *Central defender 2*: Steve Davis – could have been a midfielder, he was that good on the ball. For that reason, I would play him in the middle of a three. Another one who was excellent in the air, and a real threat in the opposition box.

6) *Central defender 3*: I thought about Colin Hendry but I didn't really play with him enough to make a fair judgement. So it came down to Ian Cox and Paul Butler. Coxy was like a Rolls-Royce, smooth and lightning quick. He was also good in the air and very strong. He was another centre half who liked to play football from the back. Butts too was very quick and strong in the air, but he was also nasty. And on the basis that, given the two, I would probably just about prefer to play against Coxy, Paul Butler gets my final centre-half spot.

7) *Centre midfield*: Andy Gray. This guy had everything; pace, power, aggression, technique, the whole lot. An absolute dream to play with. He could probably play midfield on his own, he was that good. He definitely improved my game, and made playing my game so much easier.

8) *Centre midfield*: Nick Dawes. A much underrated player, but it speaks volumes that Bury would train on Tuesday and Thursday evenings just so that Nick could join while he was part-time. Technically, he was excellent, very rarely got injured, and would chip in with some great goals. His game complemented mine and I feel that I enjoyed my best form when playing alongside Nick.

9) Okay, I'm stuck. I have now realised that this is far too difficult. There is no Colin Hendry, Mitchell Thomas or Leon Britton in my team. And how can I fit in Scott Sellars, Jason Wilcox, Lee Trundle, Glen Little, David Johnson, Chris Lucketti, Gareth Taylor and Andy Payton? David Speedie is another who deserves to be in, as does Rob Matthews. Call me a bottler if you like, but the fact is that I have had the privilege of playing with some great footballers, most of whom were also great people.

So, I'm going to leave it there, with apologies to those who I've forgotten to mention. Thanks to you all.

ACKNOWLEDGEMENTS

Writing this book has been an incredible experience. It has afforded me the opportunity to lay down some of my inner-most thoughts and given me the freedom to be both explicit and expressive. From the start of the writing process to the finished article, there are several people whose help, advice and guidance were invaluable. But writing the book was so much more than that.

Years of experiences and influences helped to shape and develop me, and provided the foundation to allow those thoughts, along with my hopes and dreams to become the mainstay of what I am now. So effectively, the people that I am about to thank are the ones to blame for me being the way that I am.

There really is only one place to start, and that's with you, Mum. For many years, you lived a hellish life and never once complained, or criticised those who were to blame. Instead, your determination and strength drove you to seek a better life. You went without so much, to ensure that we, your children had everything that we needed. You bought me my first pair of football boots, when you could ill-afford it, and set me on the road to becoming a professional footballer. But more important than that, the strength and determination that I spoke about, along with your sense of morality and kindness, made me, me. You gave me the tools to deal with adversity, to put things in perspective, and always try to be a better person. Mum, I owe you everything!

And now on to my siblings. Where do I start? You each have your different qualities and personalities (I prefer to say 'personalities' than 'weaknesses', but really, it means the same thing), but what you all share is a sense of family values. Hilda, you are so like mum. Dealt a pretty crappy hand, at times, but your strength of character means that, instead of thinking about the things that you can't do, you focus on the things that you can. You are such an inspiration.

Pete, my father figure when we were young. You were my main inspiration and influence, and you really toughened me up, both physically and mentally. I'm not sure if that was the plan, but if so, it did the trick.

Fran, my best mate. You have never been just a brother, which is a good job, because despite the fact that you are older than me, I have always seen you as my younger brother. We have been inseparable at times, and there is so much of you in me, more than you probably realise.

Stevie J, what a man! Talk about laughing in the face of adversity. You epitomise family life (although you are a bit of soft touch), and really value the important things in life. People say that we are quite similar, but you are aloof, arrogant, have terrible taste in music and clothes…

Johnson, you have shown that there is a huge difference between being family and being related. We never met until

I was in my thirties, but from that very moment, you were a massive part of my family. It wasn't awkward or strange, it just felt so natural. And how can two people be so alike, and so sarcastic without having met? Yes, you are family, all right.

Gathering the information for this book meant me relying on and recalling those who have impacted on my life. Without you, and without the experiences that we shared together, there would be no book.

Lee Chester (Ches), my oldest friend and fellow urchin. For 45 years we have been in each other's lives, and barely a cross word. Paul Turley – only 38 years, but no less impact. And Dean West, a mere 25 years. But how you have made up for lost time! Real friends, real friendships. So much so that I think you might even have got a mention in the preceding pages.

And so, to the writing process.

My gorgeous wife, Nadine, and beautiful children, Elizabeth and Patrick. Excuse my French, but you have been through some shit during the last few years, and have shown how strong and resilient you are, how incredibly supportive you can be and how patient you all are. I thank you all for this, and I thank you for being at my beck and call whenever I needed miking up to my computer, or adjusting my glasses so that they fit just perfectly. Or moving my computer two degrees clockwise (some things just have to be correct, I'm afraid), or making sure that my drinks bottle is perfectly positioned towards my mouth. Or pushing my wheelchair in at the right angle or moving my headset forward 2mm and ensuring that it is at the absolute optimum tension for my delicate head. Or ensuring that the strap on my mobile is at the correct length so that it sits nicely in my hand. Or just disappearing and leaving me the hell alone, allowing me to ramble into my voice-activated software, but not before ensuring that the blinds are closed/open/tilted at the right angle... (I think I have just realised that I am perhaps a tad fussy).

Most of all, I thank you for being there for me every minute of every day. You are my heroes!

Writing a book was something that I had contemplated for a while, but to be totally honest, I never really thought I had anything sufficiently interesting to say. Then, in a puff of smoke, appeared two special people, Sue Muller and former GP, Clive Barker. You gave me the encouragement, the confidence and quite frankly, the kick up the backside that I needed. It was you who gave me the belief that some people might actually be interested in what I have to say. Time will tell whether you were correct or not, but either way, without the two of you the preceding pages would just be thoughts swirling around in that big, empty space of mine.

Using voice-activated software to write a book might seem pretty impressive, but in truth, my first draft was littered with errors. Then, in true Sue Muller and Clive Barker style, Dea Parkin and Nikki Brice of Fiction Feedback appeared. You offered your services as my editors and somehow managed to fashion something legible out of the garbled mess that I presented to you. You replied to my incessant emails, and never once complained after receiving amendment after amendment. I owe you so much, and if this book has a modicum of success, then it is down to you and all the aforementioned people, and for that I thank you all!

 Matador